MANAGING
THROUGH
the Entrepreneurial
FOG

MANAGING
THROUGH
the Entrepreneurial
FOG

AN INSPIRATIONAL
AND PRACTICAL GUIDE
FOR LEADING OTHERS

TIM KOPROWSKI SR.

iUniverse, Inc.
Bloomington

MANAGING THROUGH THE ENTREPRENEURIAL FOG
AN INSPIRATIONAL AND PRACTICAL
GUIDE FOR LEADING OTHERS

iUniverse books may be ordered through booksellers or by contacting:

iUniverse
1663 Liberty Drive
Bloomington, IN 47403
www.iuniverse.com
1-800-Authors (1-800-288-4677)

Because of the dynamic nature of the Internet, any web addresses or links contained in this book may have changed since publication and may no longer be valid. The views expressed in this work are solely those of the author and do not necessarily reflect the views of the publisher, and the publisher hereby disclaims any responsibility for them.

Any people depicted in stock imagery provided by Thinkstock are models, and such images are being used for illustrative purposes only.

Certain stock imagery © Thinkstock.

ISBN: 978-1-4759-8712-6 (sc)
ISBN: 978-1-4759-8711-9 (hc)
ISBN: 978-1-4759-8710-2 (e)

Library of Congress Control Number: 2013907264

Printed in the United States of America.

iUniverse rev. date: 05/30/2013

*If it hadn't been for the fog, I might not have taken the risk ...
and I would have missed the experience of a lifetime.*

—Tim Koprowski

CONTENTS

PREFACE

While writing this book, I shared its title with many who have started and operated their own businesses. The reaction was always the same: an immediate long-reaching smile, telling me the title explained it all. For those of you who have the same reaction, this book may be merely an affirmation that you have not been, or are not, alone. However, you might find the journey a bit unique—in fact, I can almost guarantee it.

When driving through the streets of Anytown, USA, one sees countless small retail businesses scattered throughout, each with its own story to tell, all open for business and ready to sell to anyone willing to walk through the door and buy products off the shelf. Right alongside those businesses, sometimes even subletting office space from them, are those that are less obvious, even invisible to eager retail customers— literally thousands of businesses not exposed to the general public. These are niche companies providing solutions to other businesses that create the demand for what they have to offer. Whether it's graphic-design work, housekeeping services, or software development, they too are open for business.

When starting and operating a software development company, my management skills were put through challenges I never could have anticipated. You will first read about the management principles that helped me maneuver through the entrepreneurial fog you are about to understand and experience.

It was exciting to go to work every morning. There was never a dull moment—frightening moments, maybe, but never dull. We founded a true start-up company that was going to take on very successful companies as its competition. In every sense of the word, we began with just enough to open our doors: little or no money, no paying clients, and limited foresight. Yet we had an abundance of faith in our product, laced with hope and dreams for the future.

In the later years, I would say, "It should be a crime for me to deposit my paycheck, because I am having way too much fun."

This book is about a group of people who experienced all of that and much more.

ACKNOWLEDGMENTS

Lentz Ferrell:	Without your genius, there would have been nothing to write about.
Steve Huson:	Your support so early in the game encouraged us to move forward.
Dave Maclachlan:	We should have built a statue in your honor. Thank you for believing.
Myron Krause:	You should have been on our payroll. You were an incredible client. Thanks for all your support.
Pat Noonan:	Thank you for teaching me how to be a better executive.
Sal Ramirez:	You started something that was unique and special. Thank you.
Cortie Noud:	You are exceptional. Your time with us was too short.
Our offspring:	Deanna and John, Geoffrey, Trevor, and Tim Jr. and Cindy. Thank you for standing by us through thick and thin.
Deanna and John:	Your unselfish love and compassion have made everything worthwhile.
Deanna:	My editor-in-chief. Your passion for teaching was so evident that I became your willing student.
Gordon Ringer:	I am both honored and humbled by your support for me over the years. You are a role model for all fathers-in-law. Thanks, Dad.
Randi:	Our time together was not long enough. I miss you.

INTRODUCTION

You are reading about a software company that had a very efficient solution for automating materials management (purchasing and inventory control). For the most part, other than the second chapter, this book is about the company, not the product. You will read about the process that took the main characters from working on a project at a rural hospital in Oregon to leaving their jobs and starting a company that would compete with established and well-funded enterprises. We worked many eighteen-hour (and more, when absolutely necessary) days while experiencing some lows and some extreme highs during the process.

In order to successfully transition from an administrator at a hospital to the president and CEO of a software company, I needed a strong basis for managing people, regardless of their profession. Early in my career, I developed a management philosophy I call "Play by the Rules." It has been my foundation for facing the challenges encountered during my years as an executive. This book guides managers from the beginning by defining the philosophy in detail. Numerous anecdotes are used to connect the world of academia with practical applications experienced in a management environment. By using an entrepreneurial venture as a backdrop, the subsequent chapters then become a case study on management. Boxes are presented throughout the text to provide examples of how the rules listed in "Play by the Rules" were used to manage the company.

As the title suggests, although we definitely had the entrepreneurial spirit when the software project was transformed into an idea for a business, we also found ourselves in an "entrepreneurial fog." When we decided to start a company, we truly had no idea what we were getting ourselves into. The following months brought a path full of potholes to be navigated without a compass; thinking about the minutia necessary to run a business would only take away from the overwhelming euphoria that got us there in the first place. Our software fit on a computer tape that cost $17, and we planned on selling it to our first customer for the bargain-basement price of $60,000. For the most part, we were ready to open shop. During the thirty-six months prior to us making our decision to press forward, we were developing the software while I was concurrently checking what was available on the market. There was no doubt we had a product that was outperforming what our soon-to-be competition was offering, so it definitely seemed as if success was on the horizon.

Unfortunately, in our euphoria, we failed to see the patch of fog that was obstructing our view of that horizon. These are just a few of the stumbling blocks we encountered in the beginning:

- Although marketing was discussed, we didn't really understand what it would take to make the business a success with such limited resources.
- No thought was given to establishing credit to make it easier to manage cash flow. We soon discovered that without any assets, credit for the business was either unavailable or unaffordable. Ultimately, our personal credit (to the tune of $20,000 per month) was the only way to make it happen.
- After we made our first sale, our clients would be operating our software around the clock; therefore, we would need to provide twenty-four-hour customer support. In the beginning, we had only one programmer who also worked full-time for a hospital. We truly had unrealistic expectations of him.
- One obstacle not given much consideration was that approval for capital purchases were budget items linked to the fiscal year, which in many cases could mean waiting between six to nine months for a client to get funds for making a purchase. Especially in the early years, staying in business during the wait periods would prove difficult.

- We were accustomed to having 100 percent coverage for medical benefits paid for by the hospital, and some of us could not afford to go without them. As a result, we had to offer equal benefits for all future employees. It was an escalating expense that stayed with us throughout our existence.

The *fog* can possibly be seen as a good thing. Knowing everything required to start and operate a business is not necessarily a prerequisite for success, and perhaps is not even desirable. Entrepreneurs (synonymous with "risk-takers") often make decisions based on ideas that have never been tried before—how to "build a better mousetrap." When an idea is conceived and the decision is made to turn it into an enterprise, one can thank the heavens all contingencies are *not* considered prior to making that decision. If most entrepreneurs knew what they were getting themselves into, they would say, "Forget it; it's not worth it." Our company had no documentation, no office, no marketing material, and nowhere near enough cash to stay operational for more than six months. What we did have was a true start-up company that one might say was based on the proverbial wing and a prayer.

At the time the project of developing the software began in December 1981, only 27 percent of the nation's seven-thousand-plus hospitals were using computers to operate their materials-management (MM) departments. At the hospital where I had just been hired, purchasing a software package was not an option. I was told the computer resources were limited to an IBM System/34 and virtually a one-man data-processing department (today known as information systems or information technology) that supported the entire hospital. It is important to note, I am *not* a computer programmer; instead, my strength is in understanding computer systems and being able to find ways to automate processes. The way I look at it, my mind doesn't get cluttered with having to know the minutia required for writing the code; I leave that to the programmer. Instead, I am free to be a dreamer, and the programmer simply makes my dreams a reality. When I was hired, I was told that if I outlined a plan for automating the department, perhaps an automated solution for MM could be developed. I had actually met Lentz Ferrell, who was the director of data processing, when my wife, Jan, and I were flown to Oregon for my job interview a month earlier. Lentz came across as an incredibly positive individual who truly enjoyed his job. He was, and still is, fearless and unaware of his own limitations. One might question the worthiness of that last attribute, but even if Lentz did not know how to do something in the beginning, he ultimately made it happen. Taking advantage of this quality would prove to be extremely beneficial in the very near future, and for years to come. With his strengths combined with my sincere desire to make my job as easy as possible, we had the key ingredients for starting a project, not a company ... or so I thought.

Later, when I presented to potential clients, my opening line was, "People have often asked me how I ever got into this business, and my answer is simple: 'You are looking at the laziest person you have ever set your eyes on. So I used the computer to assist me with reaching that status.'" Most chuckled at my answer or gave me a look that said, *Just a cute sales pitch.* Though few took the statement as genuine, it was indeed—and still is—my approach to everyday life. The irony of it all ... *I had to work very hard to achieve my desired state of laziness.*

The first item I purchased for laying out my designs for the software package was a set of coveralls to wear over my suit while working alongside my staff in the warehouse. I did not see how I could possibly communicate my needs and desires to Lentz unless I did everything my staff members did to accomplish their jobs. Although the majority of my staff was on the lower end of the hospital pay scale, their responsibilities were crucial for ensuring quality patient care, a fact I stressed to all I encountered. Working with them was a humbling process that gave me a true appreciation for just how big of a project I had committed to undertake.

The software definitely satisfies a niche market; how many hospital materials managers do you know? When people consider hospital administration as a career field, MM is usually looked on as the bottom rung of the ladder for getting experience. I refer to MM people as the Rodney Dangerfields of health care—they get no respect. Yet I found the field to be one that afforded many opportunities for improving an operation that was in dire need of it. When I started the new job, all processes were performed without the aid of a computer. It soon became apparent that automating the department from the very beginning was going to require much of Lentz's time, a fact I had little control over. Fortunately, Lentz shared my level of enthusiasm from the very moment I handed him my first outline for the new system. When it all began, the internet was not available, pdf files hadn't entered the market, Microsoft's PowerPoint was still on the drawing board, laptops did not exist, IBM's PC had not yet entered the market to push Tandy's TRS80 to the back of the bus, and when files could finally be transferred from one computer to another, it was at the speed of twelve kilobytes per second. For anyone taking on such an endeavor, no matter how big it might seem at the outset, it was important to remember to take it just one day at a time. When I look back, I can honestly say that in the beginning I had no idea just how big of an undertaking was in front of us. I knew it was going to be big, just not how much it would change my life and the lives of those around me. I cannot say that, if I had realized just how big the project was going to be, I would have taken it on. However, as it slowly evolved, it became quite apparent there was no turning back.

1. "PLAY BY THE RULES": A MANAGEMENT PHILOSOPHY

If you are a manager and don't want to be regarded as a great boss, you should not be a manager in the first place. Regardless of the profession, you have the opportunity to inspire those under your purview to the point where they feel privileged to have you as their leader. Much work may be necessary for you to get there, but in not aspiring to be the best manager possible, you do a disservice to the organization, to yourself, and most important, to those you agreed to lead.

MANAGEMENT: A PROFESSION ALL BY ITSELF

Whether I was an administrator at a hospital or the president of a software company, I always looked forward to going to work each day. It was exciting to be able to work with people from all walks of life. My job was to provide a work environment conducive to their happy and effective efforts toward accomplishing the goals of the company. Throughout the years, I had the opportunity to witness and become involved with many different types of managers from around the country. Some were very experienced and some were brand new to their field; many of them were very good, and some were not good at all. Some were well educated, good at their jobs, and easy to work with, while others were just educated idiots. Often the managers with a limited education were among the best, while others managed with the attitude "It's just a job." This type of attitude was referred to in the military as being on the ROAD (Retired while On Active Duty). Unfortunately, it's also found in the civilian sector.

Have you ever had a boss you despised, one who made you think,

If I ever find myself in a position of authority, unlike this boss, I will do everything possible to inspire my employees? I had such an experience early in my career, which gave me the motivation to learn all I could about being a good manager.

Managers are in a unique position. They are in control, some more so than others. Unfortunately, many managers—especially new ones—do not know where to begin, which oftentimes relates to a lack of self-confidence or simply not knowing what it means to be in control. These managers are in a tough position; they got the job all right, but they are in need of some direction. Having been there myself and then having the responsibility for leading other managers, I believe it doesn't hurt to have some rules to follow as one develops management skills.

Although I have been a manager for many years, I never imagined that I would ever find myself in a position where I would be writing about a management philosophy of my own. There are two reasons I even dare to share this philosophy:

1. My professor (Dr. Croy) for the final class of my graduate program at USC gave us the assignment to write our own management philosophy or expound on our thoughts about others'. I chose to write my own. After I submitted the paper, entitled "Play by the Rules: A Management Philosophy," he returned it to me with the question, "Would you consider coauthoring a book with me?" I never answered him because when I graduated two weeks later, I received orders from the air force reassigning me to a base in Florida. I found myself extremely busy at a new job and getting settled with my family in a new home. Dr. Croy has since retired, and I have always felt guilty about not responding to his request; I guess this is my way of trying to clear my conscience.

2. When our company began to show relative success, I was asked essentially the same question by three hospital administrators: "As a vendor, how are you able to successfully manage my materials manager without having any line or staff authority, and do so with such positive outcomes?"

Instead of giving them a detailed answer, I simply thanked them for their comments. Unfortunately, the answer is not a simple one. Instead, it requires a rather detailed explanation. I apologize in advance, as many pages in this chapter will read like a textbook. Nevertheless, the philosophy is included for review. Many personal anecdotes of my own experiences as a manager are included throughout the text; these were events that had significant impact on my management beliefs and practices that formed throughout the years.

A COMPLEX MANAGEMENT SCENARIO

At our company, we were doing more than just selling an expensive piece of software; we were selling a solution to a problem impacting the way materials managers ran their departments. It was an absolute rush to work with the majority of the managers—they recognized the need for change and were willing to do whatever it took to make the transition to the new system a success. The majority of our clients became showcase examples who took advantage of all of the features our software had to offer, and eventually we were able to proudly use them as references for future potential clients. Through their own successes with our system, our clients assured us that what we were doing was worth all of our efforts.

Unfortunately, some managers treated their purchase (years later, up to $1 million for software and hardware) as a solution they believed would require minimum effort on their part—as if it was a plug-and-play piece of software. That type of motivation usually surfaced after our system was installed and the new staff received training for the file build. We could ill afford to have any of them unhappy, especially from the get-go. Consider the dynamics of the situation: on one side, these new clients just went through a rather involved process to acquire an expensive piece of software they believed would make their jobs easier and more efficient. The sales presentation was convincing enough, the references were glowing, the site visits were impressive, and they were able to sell their bosses on the idea that they had made the right choice ... and then the reality set in that what they'd observed and admired was going to take a great deal of work, work they either did not want to do or were incapable of managing. For our part, we had just sold our system to someone showing signs of buyer's remorse, not because they believed they chose the wrong solution, but because they didn't expect to be so overwhelmed.

As soon as it became apparent there was going to be a problem, our entire staff at Health-Ware Management Company increased its efforts for supporting those clients. Similar to the 80/20 rule, we had a 90/10 phenomenon where 90 percent of our time was spent supporting 10 percent of the clients. The clients' lack of management skills usually became apparent during the first training session, with managers finding reasons why the process would not work for their institution. The reaction was similar to that of a deer caught in the headlights. Since I always conducted that initial day-and-a-half training class, I was the one who first observed negative behavior on the part of any members of the new staff. If it happened to be the manager who seemed troubled, I had to do my best to delicately manage the manager, a position I did not relish.

I can now hear the comments: "How arrogant can you be?" Perhaps a lot, but people need to put themselves in my position. I had a client who, by making just a few choice phone calls, could put an unjustified black mark on the reputation of our company. I knew I couldn't let us take the fall just because this individual was insecure or, worse, incompetent. We knew how to make the system work well and so did others; given the opportunity, it could greatly improve the efficiencies of *any* operation. I had enough confidence in myself as a manager to take on the challenge of influencing the client to make the new project at hand a positive experience for all. When I recognized the possibility for failure, I had no choice but to carefully interject my influence on the new MM staff. Yes, it was self-serving, but the truth was I also wanted this new client to be successful. Almost always, the manager was open to advice and would eagerly act upon it. Ultimately, we bonded with a working friendship to the point where we were able to discuss any concerns either of us encountered in the future. There were those few exceptions where some managers were incapable of ever being able to see the project to a successful completion; later on, you will meet some of them.

I have heard some say that all it takes to be a manager is good common sense. I admit, that doesn't hurt, but it is not the only attribute necessary. I contend there are many more management concepts one must grasp to be a successful boss. I managed many unenviable situations to positive outcomes because I strongly believed in a management philosophy I developed and call "Play by the Rules." Two other philosophies must be understood before this concept can be applied: "Theory X" and "Theory Y" by Douglas McGregor, and Abraham Maslow's hierarchy of needs. An understanding of these philosophies is necessary before the features of "Play by the Rules" can be discussed.

KEY ELEMENTS OF THEORY X AND THEORY Y

According to Theory X, employees are inherently lazy and will avoid work if possible.

1. Employees require close supervision with strict levels of control in place, and for effective management, a narrow span of control must be adhered to at each level. Consequently, management believes that employees will show little or no self-motivation unless they are compensated for doing so.

2. Managers influenced by Theory X believe in not taking responsibility and in blaming someone else if a job is not properly executed.

3. Managers also think most employees are only out for themselves and their sole interest in the job is to earn money. Managers tend to blame employees in most situations when things go wrong, without questioning the systems, policies, or lack of training that might be the real cause of failure.

Managers subscribing to Theory X take a rather pessimistic view of their employees and believe it is the manager's job to structure the work and energize the employee. As a result, managers tend to use an authoritarian style that is based on the threat of punishment.

In Theory Y, management has a greater belief in employees' abilities.

1. Managers influenced by this theory assume employees are ambitious, self-motivated, anxious to accept greater responsibility, and capable of exercising self-control, self-direction, autonomy, and empowerment.

2. Management believes that employees enjoy their work, and that given a chance, they have the desire to be creative at their workplace and become forward-thinking. There is a chance for greater productivity by giving employees the freedom to perform to the best of their abilities without being bogged down by rules.

Managers subscribing to Theory Y are accustomed to exerting little or no control over their employees.

Theories X and Y have been around for about fifty years and are often used when referring to an individual's management style. Few claim to be a pure X or Y manager because of the extremist views of either label. An individual labeled as a Theory X manager without any qualifiers would be thought of as an authoritarian who leads with strong-arm tactics, while an individual labeled as a Theory Y manager without any qualifiers would be thought of as weak with little control over his or her subordinates, providing an environment for anarchy.

THE MANAGEMENT SCALE

Rather than use the label Theory X or Y, I prefer to employ my own scale when considering a designation for managers:

Play by the Rules
Management Scale

Authoritarian Decisive	Anemic Slow to Decide	Anarchist Indecisive
X		Y
10.0	5.0	1.0

The explanation is simple and eliminates the ambiguity that comes from giving just X or Y as a label. A rating of 10.0 identifies a pure Theory X manager, and conversely a rating of 1.0 indicates a pure Theory Y manager. Few managers are found at either end of the spectrum, but moving on the scale in either direction clarifies one's managerial practices and beliefs. In addition, you can add a dimension beyond the strict definitions given to both theories by considering the rating of 10.0 to mean very decisive and 1.0 to mean indecisive. Sizing up a manager this way differs drastically from McGregor's theory because it actually puts a manager who might lean toward being an X type of manager in a positive light. The 10.0 area normally has a strong negative connotation; however, when moving the designation a bit to the right on the scale, the meaning changes the rating altogether. It can be quite helpful for a senior manager to know subordinate managers' ratings when assigning responsibilities for certain tasks or projects.

To better understand the implications of the Management Scale, consider the following explanations of different ratings for a manager:

Rating	Explanation
3.0	Is less likely to make major decisions or innovations to the job environment. Believes in the capabilities of employees, thus believes minimal managerial guidance

is necessary for the employees. This manager would avoid conflict if at all possible.

5.0   Finds it very difficult to make a decision. Have you ever met a manager who was well educated, had a pleasant personality, and seemed ideal for his or her position— yet when it came to making a decision, even with all of the facts, and having considered all of the pros and cons, it seemed to take forever? This type of manager is consistently on the fence, not wanting to take chances and not doing so until the very last minute. If conflict was about to occur, deciding who to side with would be an extremely difficult task for this type of manager.

7.0   Believes in the employees' abilities and can be relied upon to make tough decisions when necessary, and would be an innovative manager. This type of manager would not intentionally cause conflict, but would not walk away from one if it meant standing up for his or her beliefs and/or employee.

BROADENING THE SCOPE OF MANAGEMENT INSIGHT

Unfortunately, there are managers who use the tools of Theory X and Theory Y as the only basis for their management principles. This is a mistake; it is imperative for managers to understand their employees if they want to be leaders others can proudly follow. The idea of a hierarchy of needs was introduced by Abraham Maslow (1908-1970) in 1943, and his motivational theory is a fundamental philosophy that is taught in most business, management, and psychology curriculums in colleges and universities throughout the nation. The theory suggests that people are motivated by satisfying specific needs as depicted in a pyramid.

Maslow's Hierarchy of Needs

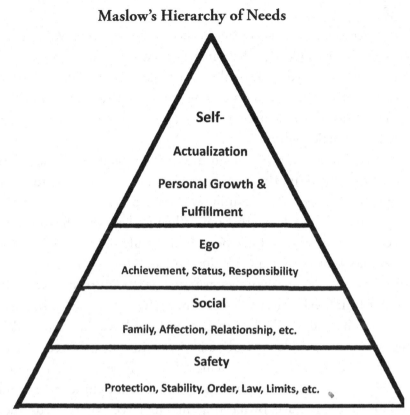

The theory suggests that all people start at the bottom of the pyramid and must satisfy a lower need before ascending to the next level. I'll describe each level in more detail and provide some examples of how managers can meet these needs—or not.

Basic

Basic needs are vital to survival, such as the need for water, air, food, and sleep. Maslow identified these needs as the prime and most instinctive needs in the hierarchy because all needs become secondary until these physiological needs are met. Fortunately, the vast majority of managers never need to worry about employees not having their basic needs met, especially since they are already employed.

Safety

Safety needs are most often related to job security, which ensures stability in an employee's life. A manager has a significant impact in this area, even in everyday life; making a simple comment like "I just don't understand you" can shake an employee's foundation and inject a level of insecurity. The employee needs to know that job security is good in order to function efficiently.

I remember working at an air-force hospital in the late 1970s when Pam Conklin, the best supervisor on my staff, came to me and announced she was "in a family way." When I congratulated her, she thanked me but looked rather sad. When I asked why, she told me she needed to leave the air force because she could only take six weeks of maternity leave. She and Gary (her husband) both wanted her to have as much possible time with their baby before she returned to work. They both felt six weeks wasn't enough time. After we discussed the matter further, she told me she had three months of leave time accumulated, but would not be able to get the additional time off approved. I told her I would rather lose her for three months than have the air force lose her forever, so I saw to it that she was able to take the entire three months off for maternity leave. By meeting this employee's safety needs, the air force was able to keep *two* outstanding individuals. Twenty years later, she and Gary both retired from the air force as chief master sergeants, the highest attainable rank for enlisted personnel.

Social

Social needs are usually associated with love and relationships and/or belonging to a group. There is not much a manager can do in this area other than ensure the workplace is a friendly environment for all—a more difficult task with larger organizations.

In the early '90s, I stumbled into a unique opportunity to enrich my employees' social needs by offering a benefit to them free of charge. My wife and I were visiting the Oregon coast and were at a coffee shop in the town of Rockaway Beach where we met a couple who owned eighteen rental homes/condos. Most of the units were fully furnished, with maid service and firewood provided. Many of the homes were right on the beach, and all of them had easy access. After looking at many of them, we signed a contract that was affordable enough that we were able to give all our employees a one-week stay per year, and if any units were available on weekends, our employees could stay rent-free. It was a benefit all of our employees were able to enjoy. One of our programmers went to the coast and took advantage of the offer at least once a month year-round.

Ego

Ego needs can be seen in the way all employees want to feel worthwhile, regardless of their position. As a result, when an employee grows within an organization, that individual seeks additional responsibility and status. Most managers can have an impact on an employee's ability to satisfy this level of need, especially in the area of promotions. Great care must be taken here, since promoting one employee over another can often create tension in the workforce. How this type of scenario is dealt with separates the good managers from the bad ones.

Years ago I was a patient at a multiphysician specialty clinic, and every time I had an appointment, I thought to myself that the attending nurse, Toni, was one of the most negative people I had ever met in a position responsible for dealing with the public. She seemed incredibly unhappy. A year later, my physician started his own practice and I opted to keep him as my doctor. When I went to my first appointment at the new clinic, I was surprised my doctor had chosen to bring Toni with him as his head nurse. Moreover, the real surprise was when Toni greeted me with a huge smile and acted as if I was a long-lost friend.

I couldn't let it go without saying something to her, so I asked, "Toni, what happened to you? I have never seen you so happy."

At first she was almost alarmed at my comment, and then she said, "You are right, Tim, I couldn't stand to work for that other doctor. I'm only sorry it was that obvious to you."

She elaborated about her dissatisfaction with the other physician, and it was only too apparent he was a 10.0 on the Management Scale and couldn't care less about his employees' personal well-being other than making sure they got their paychecks on time. From then on,

Toni always greeted me in the same friendly manner. Her ego needs had finally been satisfied.

From the beginning, as a manager, I did my best to get to know every member of my staff—I mean, *really* know them. When I went to work each morning, I made a point of greeting every employee individually, even if it was just to say hi. When people are having any sort of problem, it is normally difficult for them to hide it, if only through body language. It was those morning encounters that helped me "keep my finger on the pulse" of my staff. If any of my staff members didn't tell me about a problem but alerted me with a facial expression of some sort, I would take the time to ask if there was anything wrong. No matter how big the scope of responsibility, the more knowledge managers can gain about each employee, the better leaders they will be—and the more efficiently the employees' ego needs will be met.

After having had several different management positions over the years, I find it is easy to spot a good manager without even meeting the actual person in charge. Good management practices are exemplified through the actions of an organization's employees. As an example, it was rewarding to witness sound management practices coming from the top when I visited the emergency room of our local hospital in Newberg, Oregon. I arrived at two in the morning and was the only patient in the reception area. I was waiting to be seen by the triage nurse. When I chatted with Jo, the receptionist, I asked her how she liked working at the hospital. This young woman was very positive and had only good things to say about the hospital and her fellow workers. She really got my attention with the following comment: "I only work the midnight shift, and it is common for our hospital administrator to come to the ER this late at night, just to say hi and chat with me and the other employees, like you are doing right now. It amazes me how he takes the time to make me feel like we matter."

I don't know how good this administrator is at other parts of his job, but he understands the ego needs of those in his organization. For many patients, the first exposure to his hospital will be at the emergency room, and he cannot afford to have that first impression be a negative one. It only takes one disgruntled patient making his or her dissatisfaction known to many, especially in a small community, to reflect badly on an organization, so taking the time to scout for any potential problems only makes sense. This top executive was able to do so without making Jo feel threatened, and at the same time made her appreciate him as a person, rather than just as the chief executive of the hospital. Deliberately making the effort to spend time with one of the lowest-paid of his four-hundred-plus employees speaks volumes about the core of his management beliefs.

Self-Actualization

Self-actualization needs refer to the place in life where all people strive to find themselves—as it relates to employment, the ultimate job assignment.

People have asked me, "What if you have an employee whose ultimate goal is to have your job?" My answer: "Fantastic. In fact, I want all of my employees to have that same goal, because when they strive to have my position, they will need to be at their very best. By doing so, they make me look even better. My job is to make them comfortable with the fact that I am the one in charge and that someday, they may indeed be able to occupy my position."

"PLAY BY THE RULES" DEFINED

The two theories discussed above represent a good start for establishing one's management principles, but I believe they don't go far enough. As a result, I came up with "Play by the Rules" in order to offer a complete approach to management.

The main premise for this concept is that when managers are hired by an organization, they agree to support the rules of the organization and those of their senior manager. When an individual accepts a management position, of course he or she plans on being a good manager. Unfortunately, and despite the fact that it was determined they were capable when they were hired, not all managers prove to be necessarily suited for their positions.

"Play by the Rules" is a management philosophy based on the

TIM KOPROWSKI SR.

following twenty-three concepts that make it a functional tool everyone can subscribe to as a basis for the core foundation of their managerial principles. Not all are necessarily unique; however, the manner in which some are addressed may cause readers to rethink their understanding of them.

1. Use the Management Scale as a Guide

Senior management will use the scale for sizing up management staff, especially when assigning special projects to a manager. Self-evaluation lets you know where you fall on the scale and allows a better understanding of how you will be treated by others, especially senior management.

2. Know Your Employees Relevant to the Hierarchy of Needs

Being aware of an employee's status relevant to the pyramid will clarify the reasoning behind each individual's behavior. Managers should know as much as possible about each employee's family life, ensure that employees feel secure about their job, know what challenges and excites employees on the job, and know each employee's ultimate goal in life.

Over the years, I learned the importance of the need for understanding the hierarchy and how to effectively use it as a management tool. But before I started out as a manager, I had little training on how to properly manage people effectively. The following discussion allows one to experience what was thrust upon me from the very beginning of my days as a new manager.

I had just completed the air force's eleven-week course for hospital administration in Wichita Falls, Texas; packed up my family; and had driven to our first assignment, which was located twenty-five miles from Lake Superior in northern Michigan. It was December 29 and ten at night before we finally arrived at the base in the middle of a state forest. There was a minimum of four feet of snow everywhere, and we were greeted with a record-breaking temperature of 23 degrees below zero (later we understood why the locals claimed to have only two seasons, July and Winter). We checked into the visiting officers' quarters, which was a small hotel room we planned to occupy for at least two weeks while we waited for base housing to become available. None of that mattered, because I was about to assume my first managerial position. I was a new second lieutenant in the Medical Service Corps (hospital administrators) of the air force, and I was being assigned as the administrator in charge of finance.

The next morning I planned on meeting my new boss—but before I did so, my wife and I decided to take a tour of the base. While driving through base housing, a man who was passing us, going in the opposite direction, pointed to me and shouted something. Although I couldn't hear a word he was saying, it was obvious he was talking to me. After he passed by me, he made an immediate U-turn, and it was apparent he wanted me to stop. Not knowing if something was wrong with my car, I complied and pulled to the side of the road. He did the same, jumped out of his car, and ran over to me as I was stepping out of our car, and before I could say a word, he extended his hand to shake mine.

"Tim Koprowski ... Gary Neterer."

As we were shaking hands, I was stunned. I didn't know him—or anybody else on the base, for that matter. I asked, "How do you know me?"

"I am one of the administrators at the hospital, and we have been expecting you. We don't get many strangers up here during this time of the year. With your California license plates, a car rack full of luggage, and your wife and children in the car, I figured it was a safe bet on who you were. My family and I are leaving today for a three-week vacation, and we have been waiting for all of you to arrive before we left."

I didn't have much time to be confused, because he filled in the blanks as he spoke. Yet I distinctly remember my feeling of disbelief. Why would he be waiting for us just so he could welcome us to the base?

Fortunately, he answered each question as he spoke. He said, "Before I forget, here are the keys to our house. You and your family don't need to stay in the visiting officers' quarters while waiting for base housing. Our fridge is fully loaded, beds have fresh linens, and feel free to use the washer and dryer. Our home is your home."

As I tried to object, he walked back to his car and said, "Please, follow me so you can meet Eileen and the kids before we leave."

Disbelief does not adequately describe how we felt as we followed him. I remember saying to Jan, "He knows nothing about us, yet he is handing over the keys to his house. Is this some sort of a test?"

But it was not a test. Gary and Eileen were as genuine and nice a couple as one could hope to meet. After we spent time getting to know each other—while their seven kids played in the snow with our own three—we found ourselves waving good-bye from their doorstep as they drove away on vacation. For us, it was a surreal moment.

Even though Gary was never my boss, he had an immediate impact on how I felt about where I was relative to my *safety needs* and *social needs*. His kindness to me and my family was more than anyone could ever expect from a complete stranger. Furthermore, his welcoming me to the hospital's staff as one of his peers did wonders for my *ego needs*, a feeling that continued throughout our professional and personal relationship.

My next step was to meet with Major Larry Ciminelli, my new boss, who was the hospital administrator. He greeted me with open arms, invited me to his office for coffee, and asked about my wife and children, wanting to know if he could do anything to help with our transition to the base. He also invited our family over for dinner on New Year's Day, saying we didn't need to be spending the holiday alone. He then told me not to report for work until I was moved into base housing (almost everyone lived on base, since the closest city was twenty-five miles away) and not to consider coming to work until all of our curtain rods were hung. We spent less than a week at Gary and Eileen's home because our household goods arrived within a couple of days, and I was able to report to work just six days later.

At the beginning of my first day, Larry and I talked over a cup of coffee. He told me the finance department had received a marginal rating by the last inspector general and said that after reviewing my personnel records, he expected great things from me.

He took me to the finance department and introduced me to my staff. All of them were cordial and did their best to make me feel welcome. Larry went back to his office, I chatted a bit with my staff, and then I went into my office. I sat at my desk, looked around, and then I distinctly remember the rush of fear that moved through my body as I thought to myself, *What on earth did I just get myself into?* That feeling lasted for an entire ten seconds. My accountant knocked on my door and interrupted me to ask a question for which he needed my opinion. At that moment, I realized I was in control of the situation, and I was the only one who could screw things up. Believe it or not, I found that comforting. (It was seven years before I recalled the incident, after a college student asked me what it was like when I first became a manager.)

I was twenty-seven years old and had no training as a middle manager. Although I had the eleven-week indoctrination course for hospital administration, the main determining factor for giving me the position was my college education. It doesn't mean someone without the degree could not do the job, but a formal education is the attribute the majority of senior managers use for determining who they will hire to fill their open management positions—and it is a requirement in the military. When I was given my first management position, I admit it was both exhilarating and frightening at the same time. I had *no* experience in the field, yet I was given the responsibility for managing the hospital's finance department. It was sink or swim, and I could have failed, badly.

Looking back, I have come to the conclusion that for the most part, whether referring to civilian or military life, becoming a manager involves on-the-job training ... self-taught. After all, a manager is hired because he or she already meets all of the qualifications for the position; therefore training (even for newbies) is unnecessary. This whole concept of hiring managers based mainly on education is flawed and requires a better vetting process. The best process I experienced throughout my career was when I was brought in for my interview in The Dalles, Oregon. It was the only one where the management team spent fourteen hours looking me over, whereas all the others spent no more than two hours to do the same. It's a relatively expensive vetting process, but it definitely helps choose the better candidate.

3. Look the Part: Personal Appearance

This topic may seem like one that doesn't require elaboration, but it is an area often overlooked, especially for those promoted to a management position from within the organization. It is an important area not addressed very often when talking about the field of management. The belief that you need to "look the part" or "dress for the part" definitely applies here. It is easy to assume that in a professional organization, there is a dress code to adhere to, yet when it comes to filling a supervisory or management position, there are unwritten standards that do not apply to all employees. When applicants are interviewed for these positions, obviously they are going to wear their Sunday best, and chances are if a prospective manager does not, he or she will not get the job. If two applicants are interviewing for the same position and are equally qualified, it is only human nature for those conducting the interviews to choose the best-dressed and better-looking candidate. Maybe in the world of political correctness, this last statement is a bit unsavory, but reality dictates the outcome.

Perhaps the best way for presenting the case about dressing the part is when the supervisory position in an office where everyone, including the supervisor, wears the same uniform. Supervisors in such situations need to be more than presentable; they must be exemplary when presenting themselves to all those they encounter. They must be more than great at what they do; they must *look like the boss*. This idea may seem rather impossible, considering the fact the supervisor is wearing the same clothes as everyone else, but it's simpler than it may seem. The goal is to look better than one's subordinates. The task is easier for most men because there is nothing special required for their hair (nowadays many shave their heads), so the main focus is on ensuring their uniforms are impeccable. For female supervisors, the task is a bit more challenging, especially with regard to hair. There is never a good excuse for a female boss to ever report to work with unkempt hair. She must take the extra time to make sure it never happens. Feminists reading this next statement are going to be upset with me, but I need to say it anyway: "Do not let any of your female subordinates outdo you when it comes to your hair, uniform, or even your shoes. Always attempt to outclass them." Again, throwing political correctness out the window, females are under more scrutiny than their male counterparts when it comes to appearance. It is not fair, but it is true, and understanding this concept and doing something about it provides a better chance for acceptance by senior management and consideration for subsequent promotions. Let's face it, when you go to an interview, your credentials are already known to the interviewer, so the only reason for the one-on-one interview is to observe your behavior and see what you look like.

Managers not required to wear a uniform find it is easier to stand out from other employees. It usually costs more money to do so, but it is just one of the requirements for accepting a management position. Look at it this way: all managers should want to be ready for the time they might be required to go to the boardroom. The bottom line is, they should always look their best.

4. Play the Part: Personal Demeanor

I have met many managers over the years who are able to *look* the part but don't have a clue as to what it means to *play* the part. Yet there are managers who simply carry their position with a sense of dignity that conveys to others without saying a word, *I am one you can follow.* Some believe it is necessary to be stern and almost unapproachable when dealing with their employees; such behavior gives management a bad name. I define that type of behavior as the Ebenezer syndrome (forgive me, Charles Dickens), in which the manager does not care what others think about his or her behavior—after all, they know who the boss is. There are bosses who flaunt their position and have no problem doing so. That type of behavior can best be described by the following statement: "If you have to say who you is ... you ain't." Okay, it's terrible grammar, but there is no doubt about its meaning.

Fair, decisive, and caring bosses are able to lead with a distinction that far surpasses their peers. Very early in my career, I had the privilege of working for Air Force Colonel Gail T. Bulmer, who was the type of manager I aspired to emulate when I was fortunate enough to have others under my control. He is thirteen years my senior, and when I was his employee, I was way down the chain of command; yet based on the way he treated me, nobody would have ever known it. Perhaps the best way for me to demonstrate his demeanor is to share the last line in a letter of recommendation he wrote for me years later, when I no longer worked for him: "I would be only too proud to work beside him." That one line meant more to me than pages of accolades by others and is one I have proudly remembered for more than thirty years.

Keep in mind, a manager's actions give him much more credibility than beating his own chest for others to see.

5. Be an Effective Communicator

With all of the vetting normally performed on a managerial candidate, one would think that most managers would be able to communicate well. Unfortunately, being able to write well is not enough for a manager. The personal interviews give somewhat of an insight as to how well the applicants can express themselves, but public speaking is normally not a part of the interview process. So why bring it up? Middle managers must be able to adequately communicate with their staff, and when they are addressing their employees as a group, it is a form of public speaking.

Perhaps the most difficult part of communicating with others occurs when dealing with confrontation. A good manager must be able to express unpopular beliefs or policies such that the recipient of the news willingly accepts it. This scenario is even more difficult when speaking with someone not in the manager's line of authority (working for another department or organization). Those able to skillfully deal with this type of situation prove to be well-rounded managers.

When a manager is adept at speaking in front of a group and is knowledgeable about the topic of discussion, a form of leadership is exhibited that can be admired. At the same time, it instills pride among the staff members. With many employees within his or her scope of responsibility, the manager's need for effective public-speaking skills becomes even more imperative. I had the luxury of being slowly introduced to the need for the ability to speak before an audience. I found that I was more comfortable each time I was in front of an audience; the saying "Practice makes perfect" applies. As time progressed, I actually looked forward to the next event where I would be speaking before a group of people.

After my first time in front an audience, I realized I had to know my subject material well enough that I could be an expert who could easily field questions. It may seem like a foregone conclusion; however, I have been at a presentation when the speaker did not fully understand the subject matter and fumbled badly. Professional managers cannot afford such mistakes. In addition to being knowledgeable, the speaker must also be credible.

What separates good speakers from bad is that, when necessary, the good ones are able to say, "I don't know." Not having the correct answer for every question happens to the best of us. Admitting that fact demonstrates a human side of the speaker. Most people tend to forgive those willing to admit their own fallibility, provided it is an infrequent occurrence.

"Know your audience" may seem like another obvious point, but knowing the material and presenting it before the wrong crowd can be quite an uncomfortable event. I'll share a personal example later in the book.

One last point: to be an effective communicator, one must also be a good listener and willing to learn from others, regardless of whether or not you agree with the message. You do not need to like the messengers, either, in order to learn from them. Even managers who rate 10.0 on the Management Scale can offer words of wisdom at times.

Middle managers who want to climb the corporate ladder yet are unable to speak before others must find a way to master public-speaking skills. Otherwise, their climb will probably be a short one.

6. Embrace Change

Those managing successful businesses are almost always adept at enacting change inside and outside of their organizations. One of the most significant downfalls for struggling managers comes when they are unable to deal with change, whether it comes from their superiors or they need to implement some on their own. When a manager is at or below 5.0 on the Management Scale, there is a tendency to be less receptive to change and less decisive than counterparts who are at a higher level on the scale.

When initiating new concepts to a staff, having good communication skills is of paramount importance for attaining success. If employees trust their boss, they'll welcome and willingly implement new ideas. Those reluctant to adapt are so disposed because change involves risk. Risk can lead to failure, so it's easier to be safe and leave things as they are.

Managers who are not able to embrace change from their superiors will most likely find themselves either demoted or looking for a job elsewhere. When it comes to initiating modifications of their own, they must do so with conviction and support the change until it becomes a success or a failure. Failures will happen, but that doesn't mean you should avoid the implementation of change in the future. Instead, as the saying goes, "learn from your mistakes." When I was a middle manager, I introduced far more new ideas than my counterparts did, and the majority of those ideas were successful. I did make mistakes along the way, but I looked at them as life lessons that were beneficial in the long run.

To illustrate the need to roll with changes, I'll continue with the story of my first management experience. It had been ten months since my arrival at the air-force hospital in Michigan, and we were enjoying measurable success in the finance department. I got a call from Larry's secretary informing me of a staff meeting with him and the three other assistant administrators. I had come to admire and respect Larry as our boss and always found him to be very professional in his dealings with others. These meetings were usually amicable and informative. Larry asked us to give a status report on our respective departments.

When Jim, the administrator for materials management (MM), was making excuses for not meeting a deadline, Larry abruptly interrupted him by saying, "Jim, you're fired. Clean out your desk, and I want you out of materials management in the next hour. I'll find something for you to do until I can get you transferred to another base." (He could not actually fire Jim from the air force.)

Then, Larry pointed to me, causing a brief moment of anxiety—he might as well have been pointing a loaded gun at me. "Tim, I need you to move to materials management and clean up the mess Jim is leaving behind."

I immediately replied, "But Larry, I have no experience …"

He cut me off. "No buts about it, just run that department the same way you have managed finance and you'll do fine."

At the time of the incident, I didn't know enough about management, much less senior management, to realize that what Larry did at the time was wrong. Although we played squash-ball together six days a week, he never let on about his dissatisfaction with Jim; it wasn't until afterward that I discovered just how unhappy Larry was with Jim's performance. Larry was frustrated with the man's lack of professionalism and concerned that the department was not ready for the visit from the inspector general (IG) that was due within nine months, especially considering the previous marginal rating. The firing should have been a private moment between Larry and Jim. Having the three of us other administrators in the room at the time was just wrong. After the meeting, Jim could not look at any of us, and of course we were uncomfortable as well.

The outcome of the meeting reverberated throughout the hospital, causing many to wonder what could have been so bad that the hospital administrator would make such a drastic move. After all, my experience in hospital administration was limited to ten months, and only in the finance department, where I was responsible for a staff of three. The MM department actually encompassed two departments with a staff of twenty. At the time, I was clueless as to what was so bad there. I just knew I was about to find out soon, and very soon.

On paper, I was not the logical choice to replace Jim, not by a long shot. Jim was a thirty-two-year-old captain with a master's degree and six years of experience with MM, while I was a twenty-eight-year-old second lieutenant with only a bachelor's degree at the time, and *no* experience in MM. Gary and Bob, the two other assistant administrators, were both captains with advanced degrees and ten years in the field of hospital administration, so to outside observers, I did not seem like the logical choice for taking over a job that Larry considered as faltering—yet he relied on his gut instinct and chose me for the position.

I wish I had a picture of the faces of my new staff members when Larry introduced me as their new boss. The one word that came to mind is *disbelief.* (Some later revealed to me it was much harsher.) They were well aware of the fact that they had a black mark on them after the results of the past IG inspection. Their looks said it all: *How is this inexperienced newbie supposed to change things for the better?* (One might ask how I knew what those looks meant; it was because those same thoughts were going through my own mind.)

The job in finance was a good one for introducing me to hospital administration, but I can look back and see that my exposure to what it was like to be a manager was at best remedial training. What I was about to experience in MM was truly going to be a test of my ability to "learn as you go."

Surprised or not, the task before me was real and immediate. I had no time to prepare, and I truly had no idea what to do in the field of MM. I had nobody to turn to for advice; asking Larry would have indicated to him that he made the wrong choice when he appointed me to the position. As a result, I could think of only one source where I could seek help: my new staff. I immediately called an impromptu meeting.

I began the meeting by saying, "The looks on your faces say it all: 'What was Major C *thinking*?'" With that opening remark, they all laughed.

I continued, "Normally, when your boss leaves, you have six to nine months to mentally prepare for the change. If it's any comfort, I had as much notice about this change as you did. Bottom line: we're all in this together. It's no secret to any of you that I don't have any materials-management experience, but you should look at it in a positive light. I won't have any preconceived ideas of how things should be run. I am still accountable and will take responsibility for the department; as for your part, you just need to impress me that I could not ask for a better team to introduce me to the field of materials management."

I continued, "Major C told me to get the department ready for the next IG. I have one huge problem: *I* can't do it. But *we* can. I am going to need your help for making this transition a success." It was truly all I could say to them—anything else would have been fluff, and they would have seen right through me. Although I knew everyone in the department because I worked just down the hall from them when I worked in finance, I did not *really* know them. As a result, I made it my number-one task to get to know each and every member of the staff, as much as possible and as soon as possible.

7. Lead with Confidence

Unfortunately, just because people are taught how to lead does not mean they will be good leaders. It must come from within; it's as if there is something special in the DNA of a leader. The concepts for making one a better leader can be taught, but the *ability* to lead others cannot. Otherwise, all successful college graduates with a management degree would be outstanding leaders; in reality, nothing could be further from the truth. There are those in the field with advanced degrees who fully understand all of the concepts presented here but are unable to lead others. Yet there are those without any exposure to a college education who time and again prove to be most capable leaders.

Have you met people in a position of authority who exude confidence without arrogance, and are able to make decisions on the fly and do so with conviction? These leaders trust their gut, and as a result, they find many who are willing to follow. Successfully leading others requires the ability to tell others something they don't want to hear, and do it in such a way that they are compelled to say thank you afterward. This last distinction is difficult to pull off; it is one thing to understand the idea, but teaching someone how to accomplish it is almost impossible. After hearing all of the pros and cons of an issue, the intelligent leader will be decisive and choose the necessary course of action. Remember, when making a decision, even an unpopular one, never apologize for doing so. Just make sure it is conveyed in a professional manner.

To best demonstrate the need for leading with confidence, I will continue with the account about changing jobs at my first air-force assignment. When I was put in charge of the MM department, it was the best managerial experience I could have hoped to have at such a young age. I had the opportunity to cut my teeth on a department that was begging to be led. Jim knew MM inside and out … he just didn't know how to manage people. He wanted to be everyone's friend and wanted to be liked by all in every possible way. He was even on the employees' bowling team. Unfortunately, when it came to leading them, he was unable to separate being their friend from being their boss. Accordingly, he avoided situations requiring him to make tough decisions that not everyone would agree with, thereby losing the respect of those on his staff.

During the first two weeks at my new job, I was faced with a situation I can now reflect on and compare to that of an elementary school teacher trying to manage a small class of children unable to get along with each other. Each of my four supervisors (who were all older than me) constantly came into my office to complain about the other three, always about situations that had nothing to do with their work. This unhappiness from off-duty events was having a negative impact on the work environment. I was in my office with Randy Engen, one of the four, who was taking his turn to complain about the others, when I had finally heard enough and decided it was time to put a stop to all of the pettiness. I stood up abruptly, told Randy to stay seated, stuck my head out the door, and called for the other three supervisors to join us.

After they arrived, I told them, "Randy is not the reason I called you in. Rather, it was all of you who have prompted me to call this meeting."

Looking back, I must admit my next move was one of the riskiest decisions I ever made as a manager, then and throughout my career. It could have had a devastating outcome.

I said, "What I am about to tell you makes me sick to my stomach. None of you has permission to speak. It's my turn. My first impression of you as individuals is that you are quite capable at what you do on the job, but your personal relations are the worst I have ever encountered. Do you have any idea how many times each of you had come in here to complain about each other—not about job performance, but about what happens off duty? Too many. The problem is, your dissatisfaction with each other is affecting your work; you all tiptoe around each other and are unable to function as a team. I'm sorry, guys … the captain may have condoned this type of behavior, but I don't, and I have no desire to lose my job. You all know I have pull with the major, at least for now, and he said he will assist me with anything I consider necessary for improving the operation, including personnel changes. I can tell him I have a staff I can't work with and have all of you transferred, or you can leave your virtual weapons at the door and start all over. It's your choice."

With that said, the meeting was over. After they left my office, I didn't know if I had made the right move. I mean, saying "None of you has permission to speak"? What was I thinking? Was I *trying* to alienate them? Well, it didn't take long before I had an answer. During the next forty-five minutes, each of them, on separate occasions, stuck his head in my office and said, "Way to go, sir, they needed to hear that."

I was lucky. The meeting turned out to be just what they needed to hear, because each of them believed I called the meeting for the benefit of the other three. After the last supervisor took his turn, I realized I had stumbled on an irrefutable fact: all of them needed to know someone was in charge, with no apologies. That brief meeting was all it took for them to become a team. It was like I had waved a magic wand, because the environment changed from dealing with people acting like Cinderella's wicked sisters to working with Snow White's seven dwarfs, all whistling while they worked. The transformation was nothing less than miraculous. The attitude of the entire staff changed for the better. It was a good thing, too, because the workload quickly became chaotic. A major construction project for the hospital had just ended, and we had to move our offices and all of the supplies from the warehouse located in the basement to the main hospital. With weather already snowy and at subfreezing temperatures, the tasks at hand were, at best, challenging. It was that chaos that allowed me to find and exercise my leadership skills.

So what was the risk all about? When these guys left my office, they could have been saying, "Who does that young wet-behind-the-ears second lieutenant think he is, anyway, telling us we did not have permission to speak?" It definitely could have backfired on me. Instead, they understood what I was saying and considered my move a necessary one.

8. Be Consistent; Be Decisive

It is important that a staff can rely on its manager to be consistent. The one trait employees do not want to see in a boss is a tendency to shoot from the hip—not knowing how the boss will react to various situations is unsettling. Employees want to know their boss is level-headed and decisive enough to be the one they can turn to for direction. A manager will make mistakes, and that's okay. The main caveat is to acknowledge the mistake but never repeat the same one again. Otherwise, the staff will lack confidence and the willingness to seek the manager's counsel. A manager must be decisive and unafraid of taking a stand on issues. The better managers avoid making decisions with a black-and-white mentality and are able to weigh the pros and cons before making a decision. If all sides of an issue are not carefully considered beforehand, the consequences can be devastating. Such an example is provided in chapter 10 of this book.

Certainly my position at the air-force hospital in Michigan called on me to be consistent and decisive. Just two days after the meeting with my squabbling supervisors, two of them, Charlie Moss and Danny Kimball, came to me with a proposal. They suggested that the new warehouse floor should be painted before we moved into it, rather than living with bare and unprotected cement. It made sense to me—not only would it look better, it would also cut down on the amount of dirt and dust that would eventually be on the supplies we delivered to surgery and the patient rooms. At face value, it seemed like a reasonable request. However, there was one stipulation along with their request: they wanted to use the same marine paint used on the base supply warehouse.

Charlie said, "There is a new regulation stipulating that type of paint can only be used for floors that have already been painted, not for new floors."

"Why?"

Danny explained, "The base fire marshal says that when it is applied incorrectly, the paint chips easily and creates a potential fire hazard."

I replied, "If they are still repainting floors at base supply, that is about the dumbest regulation I have ever heard."

Charlie chimed in, "The guys at base supply have it down to a science and don't have any of those problems."

"Can we even buy the paint?"

Charlie quickly replied, "One of my friends at base supply will allow me to purchase it and said he would give me explicit instructions on how to apply the paint."

I asked, "Other than the new regulation, what's the problem?"

Danny said, "The base fire marshal will come to inspect our warehouse when it is ready to be occupied, and he will not be happy to see our floor painted."

"Well, you two have done your homework, and you have made a good case for pressing forward. Go ahead and order the paint. Make sure you bring the fire marshal to me when he shows up to inspect the floors."

Two days later, the paint was applied to the warehouse floor. Three days after that, a shipment of our new warehouse shelving arrived, all twenty-five tons of it. The shelving had been ordered prior to my taking over the department, and no plans had been made for its arrival.

Danny, who was my warehouse supervisor, came to me and said, "The semi truck with all of our new shelving has arrived. Where do you want the boxes of shelving to be off-loaded? We don't have any place to put them."

I thought I was on *Candid Camera*. "Come on, Danny, you must have some idea where we should put them." He was accustomed to getting permission for everything he did as a supervisor, and he needed to know he could make decisions and suggestions of his own and that I would support him.

He paused for a minute and then said, "The dining room, which is used for meetings, is the only place I can think of that has enough space for the shipment, but Lieutenant Robinson [the officer in charge of the food-services department] is out of town for two days, and Major

C is across base right now." Remember, this was twenty years before cell phones.

"Danny," I asked, "can we rearrange the tables and chairs to permit enough room for meetings and the shelving, and how long will it take for us to assemble the shelving before we can get it out of the dining room?"

"Yes," he replied, "we can rearrange the tables and chairs so there is enough space for meetings, and it should take at least three weeks before we can get it all assembled and placed in the new warehouse."

"Make it two weeks and you have a deal."

"You know, Lieutenant, I don't look forward to dealing with Lieutenant Robinson when he returns. He will not be pleased with this decision."

"You don't need to, Danny. Just turn him over to me when he returns." Three hours later, all of the shelving was occupying half the space of the hospital dining room.

Two days later, Danny came to me and said, "Lieutenant Robinson is on the phone, and he is not a happy camper."

I picked up the phone, and sure enough, he was angry. "What gives your people the right to take over my dining room without getting permission?"

Danny couldn't help himself—instead of hanging up the extension, he listened to the conversation.

"Robbi, Danny had *my* permission, and he did exactly what I told him to do. You were out of town, Major C was out of the facility, and I had a semi with twenty-five tons of shelving sitting at my loading dock, not to mention the bad weather that prohibited us from leaving it all outside. What would *you* have done? I made a command decision, and if you are unhappy with it, feel free to take it up with my boss. I am sorry about any inconvenience, but regardless of what you decide to do, you are stuck with the shelving until we get it assembled and placed in the warehouse. The dining room should be cleared out in two weeks."

Nothing ever came of the incident. I told Larry about my decision just hours after I made it, and he supported me without question.

One unexpected outcome from that event came back to me about an hour after the call with Robbi. Charlie told me, "Danny told everybody in the shop, 'You know, when the lieutenant says he's got your back, he *means* it. You should have heard him with Lieutenant Robinson.'"

I couldn't put a price tag on that type of positive PR being disseminated among the staff. Getting Danny on my side was a huge accomplishment.

With our warehouse floors newly painted and our new shelving assembled and in place, the base fire marshal showed up for an inspection of the facility. Danny escorted him to my office with a big smile on his face.

The captain asked me, "What made you think you could authorize your troops to paint this new floor? You know it is against a base regulation."

"I have a responsibility to the patients of our hospital to ensure that aseptic management is at the highest level in support of the Joint Commission for the Accreditation of Hospitals (JCAH). Therefore, I cannot afford to have the supplies stored on bare cement floors. We applied the paint according to the same specifications they use at base supply. If you need to, I can make an appointment for you to meet with the hospital commander."

He relented and said, "That won't be necessary." We passed the inspection.

It was another incident where I was able to gain the respect of my staff by simply backing up what I had promised. The ensuing months were exhilarating. We functioned as a team and were able to make improvements throughout the department that made us all proud.

During the following weeks, we had all become much more comfortable with each other and were able to joke around. Charlie and I were inspecting the new digs we were about to occupy when I noticed a sign hanging above my new office door with the word *Latrine*.

I laughed and then asked, "Charlie, do you know who put the sign there?"

"Danny put it there yesterday."

I felt like it was time for me to pull Danny's chain. I said, "Charlie, when we return to our offices, will you tell Danny I need to see him, and tell him you have never seen me so angry."

"He will ask me what it's about."

"Tell him I said it's a matter between him and me." Charlie agreed to give me a heads-up when Danny returned to the office. Thirty minutes later, Charlie stuck his head in and told me Danny was on his way back. When Danny came to my office I had to struggle, but I was able to put on a serious face when he knocked on my door. I waved him in, put my head in my hand, and acted as if I were reading something on my desk.

After he entered, I mumbled (without looking up), "Close the door and have a seat." He sat down, and I acted as if I was finishing what I was reading.

Then, without looking up, I said very slowly, "Danny, this is my way of getting even with you … for putting that *Latrine* sign above the door of my new office."

When I looked up, he was flushed, and then after I smiled, he stammered, "You mean you're not mad at me?"

I stood up, walked over to him, shook his hand, and reassured him. "Of course not, Danny, how could I be? I'm glad you had the guts to put that sign up there in the first place. By the way, turn around." The three other supervisors were looking at us through the window, laughing and pointing at Danny.

"You mean they were in on it?"

There wasn't a doubt in my mind this was *my* staff. We were a team, and we were going to do great things together.

The size of my new private office was obscene, in that it was half the size of the main office, which supported fifteen people. There were two doors: one leading directly into the warehouse and the other leading to the main office. We had a huge coffeepot that supported everyone in the shop (I think there is an air-force regulation mandating everyone must drink coffee). Space was tight, and a decision had to be made as to where the pot was going to be located. I was in a situation where I needed to connect with everyone in the office, so I came up with a rather unconventional method for making sure I saw more of them during the day: I told the staff that since I definitely had the space for it, I wanted to place the coffeepot in my office. I made the case that it would be central to both the main office and the warehouse, and I would have a chance to see them more often. In addition, I told them the only time they would not be able to enter my office was when my doors were closed. I said I would close them only if I needed to speak privately with someone. Otherwise, anyone could come into my office unannounced and get a cup of coffee. Even Larry thought the idea was a bit odd, but he told me to run my office any way I saw fit.

In the beginning, some staff members were a little uneasy, but as time passed, they found that I welcomed them and never made them feel uncomfortable when coming into my office. I didn't always carry on a conversation with them as they poured their coffee, but I did see and talk with them much more often than if the pot had been located somewhere else in the department. There were a few occasions when I observed someone obviously upset and was able get them to talk about the problem. I know in my heart that having the coffeepot in my office was the correct decision. But there was an occasion on which my staff's access to my office could have proven disastrous, and it involved the long-dreaded IG visit.

No matter how secretive the IG's team tried to be about dropping in unannounced at a base for inspection, there were always ways to pinpoint their arrival within a week's time. It was early September, and we were already three months overdue for an inspection, so we knew the IG's arrival was imminent. I told my staff just before the IG team arrived, "Folks, get me through this inspection with just a 'Satisfactory' rating, and I promise you a huge beer bust."

The team arrived on a Sunday evening and showed up at 8:00 a.m. sharp the following morning. My guys came to me first thing and told me the inspector for our department was Colonel Bus, the most senior administrator for MM in the air force. With my entire eleven months in the field and my lack of experience in the Medical Service Corps, I expected to be raked over the coals. There was nothing I could do about the situation, I just had to hope our efforts since I took over had been enough. He was going to be with us for an entire week, and our fate was definitely in his hands. When we met, he was polite but curt; he immediately asked me to take him on a tour of the hospital and the dental clinic to meet with all of the department heads. We went to my office two hours later, where he began to brief me on what to expect during the next four days.

Unfortunately, I did not close the doors to the office, and although most of the staff knew I was with the colonel and that we probably wanted our privacy, not everyone followed through on that assumption. The colonel and I were sitting across from each other while he was briefing me on what to expect during the ensuing days. At the same time, Kerry, one of the guys from the warehouse, decided he needed a cup of coffee and walked into my office with a mug in his hand. As he passed between us, he excused himself and proceeded to the coffeepot. I was shocked, but not as much as Colonel Bus, who stopped talking in the middle of a sentence. He watched Kerry's every move as he poured his coffee, added sugar and cream, walked between us again, excused himself, and returned to the warehouse.

After Kerry left the room, I asked the colonel, "Sir, do you want me to close the doors so we can have more privacy?"

He looked at me in total disbelief about what had just occurred. He stammered and said, "Well, uh, no."

"Colonel, I am sorry Kerry just walked in on us; I could have prevented the incident if I had just closed the doors to my office. When we moved into our new offices, it was shortly after my predecessor was abruptly relieved of his position, and I needed a way to frequently interact with everyone on my staff. There isn't really any space for the coffeepot in the main office, so I suggested it be placed in mine. I told them if I needed privacy, I would close my doors and they would need to wait for their coffee, but that it shouldn't happen too often. Out of courtesy, Kerry should never have walked in on us, but he has been known to push the limit. Though I wanted to, I didn't believe it would be wise to order him out of the office if I wanted to maintain credibility. Until now, there has never been a problem with our arrangement."

The colonel responded, "When we took our tour of the hospital, I thought you were too friendly with everyone, giving me the impression that you never spent any time in your own department. With this rather unorthodox way of getting to know your staff, I now realize you are just doing your best to know everyone you work with on a daily basis. It will be interesting to see if your method works in your favor when it comes to getting positive results."

Those first three days were grueling, mainly because I could not get a read on the colonel throughout the entire inspection. If he wasn't a poker player, he should have been; I never knew what he was thinking. Thursday was the last official day for his visit, and the colonel wanted to spend the last three hours of the afternoon with my supervisors without me. This last part was the most crucial part of the inspection, because it was extremely detailed. The colonel performed a review of the documentation that supported our operation.

I must admit, I was nervous as I waited for the colonel. There was a knock on my door about two hours later; it was my four supervisors, and when they walked in, they looked rather solemn.

Charlie spoke for them. "Lieutenant, you need to cancel the beer bust." My heart sank. He then continued with a huge smile, "Make it champagne. Sir, we came through with flying colors. The colonel said he was very impressed with everything he observed throughout the week."

Knowing we definitely passed the inspection caused high-fives to break out around the office. I asked, "Where is the colonel?"

Charlie said, "He left our office and went to the IG's conference room, where the inspectors are composing their reports and preparing for tomorrow morning's formal out-brief. The colonel said to tell you he would see you in the morning before the briefing."

Colonel Bus arrived first thing the next morning and asked, "Tim, can I use your phone?"

"Of course, sir."

As I was about to leave him alone, he told me, "No, Tim, I want you to stay here. Before I make the call, I want you to know I believe your unorthodox way of management has paid off. You have a great staff, and there isn't anything they wouldn't do for you. Congratulations."

With that said, he called Strategic Air Command (SAC) headquarters and wanted me to hear what he had to say. It was before speakerphones were allowed, so I was only hearing one side of the conversation. He called the SAC surgeon-general's office and spoke to the colonel in charge of operations. "Ken, this is Tom Bus, and I am here with Tim at your materials-management department at K.I. Sawyer."

He continued, "Ken, I consider his operation to be the best in your command, and I would not be surprised if it falls into the top ten of the air force."

It may have taken five days for the colonel to pay me a compliment, but with that type of endorsement, it was well worth the wait.

After the IG team gave us the out-briefing, they went back to their base in California, and as promised, we had our beer bust (including champagne) at the end of the day.

Larry joined us for the celebration and cornered me to say, "Tim, it's hard to believe these folks are the same ones you inherited just ten months ago."

I responded, "Larry, they *are* the same people. They just needed someone to see the best in them. I wouldn't trade any of them."

When Larry virtually thrust me into the middle of a poorly run department, I was doubtful as to whether or not he made the right decision. However, after it was made and I was forced to roll up my sleeves in the middle of an unenviable situation, I realized it was indeed the best thing that could have ever happened to my career. It was at that moment in time I knew I never wanted to follow a good act.

With a successful inspection for the entire hospital, Larry was rewarded with an assignment to a large medical center and left one month later. A month after his departure, I received orders from SAC headquarters to leave in ten days (just twenty-three months after our arrival in Michigan) for Shreveport, Louisiana. I was assigned to a regional medical center, where the major in charge had just been fired by headquarters. It was the beginning of an entirely new adventure.

The management experience I was able to acquire at a young age was invaluable. It provided the foundation I would need for even more challenging endeavors in the future.

9. Master the Interview

When one goes through the application process for a management position, normally the first step is to submit a résumé. If one is lucky enough, a telephone interview is the next step for the company to get to know the candidate as a person and to determine how well the candidate responds to the pressure of the interrogation. The last step of the application process is the personal interview that normally occurs at the place of employment. Without a doubt, this last portion of the process is the difficult part for most applicants. The key to a successful interview is to enter the room as if you were the only candidate for the job, which means you will have done all of your homework to know as much as possible about the new workplace before you show up for the interview. Make eye contact and speak with confidence but not arrogance; the people doing the interview must be comfortable enough with you to feel as if interviewing you is just a formality before they give you the job.

When a person is interviewing for a job and is currently unemployed, the dynamics of the situation are different than for those already employed. It is kind of like the saying, "Beggars can't be choosers." However for those who are already employed, it is important to remember that the interview is a two-way process in which the prospective employer is also being interviewed. Make sure you do as much research about your prospective new bosses as they do about you. It would be a shame to join a company that did not meet *your* standards.

An experience from a later phase of my management career illustrates this well. After being on the job for eighteen months at a hospital in Oregon, I was contacted by a headhunter for a position located in Brea, California, as a regional materials manager for American Medical International (AMI), the largest hospital chain in the United States at the time (two hundred hospitals). I was not seeking another job just then, but I never turned down an opportunity to look, especially since AMI would be paying the bill. In the middle of my interview with the regional vice president and his assistant, their secretary interrupted the interview to say that Rick Schlosser, the executive vice president from corporate headquarters in Beverly Hills, was on the phone and wanted to talk with them immediately. I was surprised when they put the call on the speakerphone and allowed me to hear what was being said. Rick wanted to know why the regional office was entertaining the idea of paying a finders' fee of $50,000 to hire me when it was against corporate policy to use a headhunter. He said he wanted to see me and verify that I was worth the money. My interview at the regional office was essentially terminated, and I drove to meet with Rick at corporate headquarters.

Rick's office was one of those corporate offices one expects to see at a very prosperous company; it was both tasteful and elegant. Rick was every bit the executive: cordial, professional, and down to business. After spending about twenty minutes with him, he invited his head VP to join us. It was then that the tough questions came out. They both asked me questions about my knowledge of the field of MM.

After another twenty minutes, Rick said, "Tim, what do you consider to be your major strength as a manager?"

"I am a positive thinker, and I am not afraid to make decisions. If I agree with the goals of the organization, I am able to lead a team of people from all walks of life to meet the stated objectives."

"What if you don't agree with the goals, Tim?" Rick asked.

"I look for clarification that would assist me with changing my mind, or I state my reasoning as to why I disagree. If I have any objections, I propose alternatives. I am a team player, but not a yes man for the sake of agreeing with my boss." I continued, "I also expect the same treatment from my own staff when they disagree with me."

"Okay, Tim, what do you consider to be your major weakness?"

I responded with a straight face, "Rocky Road ice cream."

They both laughed, and then Rick said, "I like that answer, Tim, but seriously, what is your major weakness?"

"I am intolerant with incompetence. Other than that, I don't have any more to share with you. I came here prepared and am ready to go to work. If you want to look for any other weaknesses I might have, I suggest you hire me."

I must have done a good job reading my audience. Rick told me he was not going to hire me for the position at the regional office; rather, he was going to get approval from his board of directors to create a new position for me to work with him at corporate headquarters. While I was waiting in Oregon to hear back from Rick, Mark (my boss) countered by matching Rick's offer—which amounted to a 26 percent pay increase. Jan and I decided to stay put and save our kids from being uprooted so soon after just getting settled. Besides, the pay increase would go much further in Oregon than it would in Southern California.

10. Motivate the Staff

First of all, it is important to realize that you cannot motivate a rock, so don't even try. That is not a statement from someone rated as a 10.0 on the Management Scale; it is fact. As with leadership, motivation must come from within. There are some people who just couldn't care less, and using all of the motivational dynamics in the world will not change that individual.

Keeping an employee on staff who is unable to meet your minimum standards is doing a disservice to everyone in the organization. This point is a tough pill to swallow because oftentimes, getting rid of an employee requires a great deal of work. My answer is, so what? Do the work necessary to make your organization operate the way you want it to. If you don't do it, then there are two individuals not doing their jobs.

The *rock* type of person is a rarity, and hopefully you will never need to deal with such an individual, but if you do and you don't have the luxury of removing that person (i.e. union contract and/or tenure), give him or her the least responsible job in your organization, because this individual is there just to collect a paycheck. To make such a statement goes against all of the teachings and experience I have had over the years. The only reason I can make it is because I did have such a rock on my staff. Trust me, it was painful.

For the most part, I have been fortunate to have many motivated people under my control, and it was an easy process when I needed to point some in a different direction. The truth of the matter is, most people want to do a good job and will do so when given the right direction. The most significant area in which a manager can make a difference to employees is satisfying their ego needs on a daily basis. It is a balancing act for the boss to ensure those needs are being satisfied for all employees, but it is a must in order to get the most out of everyone concerned. If it sounds like too much work, then being a manager is not for you.

11. Define Expectations

Articulating what you expect from employees and letting them know what they can expect from you as their boss is an important step for establishing a solid rapport. There should never be any guesswork on the part of the staff when it comes to knowing what is expected of them. Just as important, employees perform better if they know what they can expect from their boss, even if it has to do with recreation.

When I first took the position at the hospital in Oregon, I found myself working an incredible number of hours while designing the requirements for a new software system. During a department meeting, after about three months on the job, my staff commented on how I was such a workaholic that I did not even take time for lunch breaks.

I interrupted them by saying, "I am working these ungodly hours because of this huge project, and I need to ensure we stay on track. However, please understand, although I will always put in a full day's work, two years from now you won't be able to find me at the hospital between eleven and one because I will be at the racquet club."

They all laughed and chided me, saying, "Sure, Tim, but we don't believe you."

Twenty-two months later, I had ten times the number of employees on my staff, yet I joined the local racquet club and began meeting with my boss, the COO, at eleven thirty almost every morning. Two months later, I scheduled a one o'clock meeting for my entire staff. I was five minutes late (that was the last time I scheduled a meeting following a lunch hour), so I apologized, telling them my match ran late.

Mindy, a member of my staff, then said aloud, "You warned us, Tim, and we didn't believe you at the time."

I asked, "What do you mean, Mindy?"

"Two years ago, you predicted that in two years, you would take two hours for lunch. We didn't believe you, because you were working so many hours at the time."

The people on my staff never made me feel uncomfortable about my lengthy lunch breaks. Honesty and openness is definitely the best policy, regardless of the message.

12. Instill Teamwork

The saying "Two heads are better than one" is a good way to start this section. The ability to instill teamwork among employees separates the great managers from the good ones. It is important to realize the best resources for getting the job done are the people on your staff. Some managers have mistakenly considered it a weakness to seek advice or counsel from their employees; there are those who believe because they are the boss, they alone are responsible for making decisions. These people don't understand the distinction between being responsible and being accountable. When employees are given the freedom to make their own decisions, they are also *responsible* for them. However, the manager is always *accountable* for the actions of the staff. I am not splitting hairs with this distinction—it emphasizes the need for the boss to know the capabilities of staff members before he or she delegates decision-making responsibilities to them. At the same time, it is important to stress that mistakes will be made, and the way managers react to them defines how skillful they are when it comes to managing people. Those who stay at a 5.0 on the Management Scale may keep the number of mistakes at a minimum, but they will also be reluctant to make very many decisions.

Management is somewhat like marriage in that the manager and staff must learn how to trust each other in order to make it a successful union. Managers have the advantage simply because of the nature of the relationship. Yet contrary to what many may think, the majority of the work lies with the manager to make the alliance work. Outstanding managers are able to delicately lead others to the point where they want to be a part of the team and will gladly follow their boss's direction.

If you are about to be a new manager and have a group of employees on your staff, your first actions as a leader will be under scrutiny by both your boss *and* your new staff. As you get to know your employees, you will identify key players who will be crucial to your success. With their input, you can begin the team-building process. Of course, if the staff is already accustomed to working as a team, your job will be easier as you assume the leadership role. If you are about to follow a good act (I always avoided such a situation) and all have a high regard for your predecessor, your job can actually be more difficult than if it was the other way around. Even if you find areas that require significant improvement, avoid making a big deal about it and simply introduce your solution for making the necessary changes. Avoid putting down the previous boss.

Regardless of how others feel about your predecessor, your most important job is to bond with your new staff members and have them function as a team. How you manage your staff will be your defining moment as a manager and should be one of the most exciting times of your career.

13. Be a Team Player for the Organization

This concept is not just an extension of "Instill Teamwork," because it emphasizes teamwork from a completely different perspective. The sayings "think outside of the box" and "push the envelope" are commonly used when referring to innovative ideas and accomplishments. These same expressions apply to management when you want to improve the overall performance of the organization. There are some who are able to manage their area of responsibility and do it well. Yet when it comes to assisting senior management with tasks beyond their assigned duties, they tend to shy away from being a reliable go-to person. Oftentimes this type of manager is not an effective communicator, unable to embrace change, or is an effective leader with limitations. Many find themselves unable to work out of their comfort zone and prefer to simply be a reliable manager in their own area of expertise.

The role of top management is to not only ensure stability with the present course of action but to look beyond the current environment and plan for the future. The pool of managers is often looked to as a source for creativity, and many times middle managers will be asked to offer new ideas. Those able to step up to the plate when called upon for furthering the efforts of the organization will find their credibility with upper management is enhanced. Furthermore, when opportunities become available in the future, their chances for advancement are also improved.

14. Respect Others' Time

The saying "Time is money" and its relevance to the way people manage others cannot be overemphasized. Have you ever been summoned by the boss to a meeting and made sure you arrived on time, only to find yourself waiting ten minutes for the boss to show up? No matter what type of excuse is levied (other than a family emergency), that type of management practice is inexcusable. For example, if just six people are waiting ten minutes for their boss, one hour of productivity is lost. There are managers who think nothing of such tardiness and consider it a necessary evil that goes with the territory—a rationalization that exudes arrogance and a lack of respect for those waiting for the meeting to start. Since payroll accounts for 75 percent of the operating budget in most businesses, the need for sound time management is an area all managers need to focus on.

I have always been fascinated (I am being kind) by health-care professionals who seem to think their time is more valuable than that of their patients. There are some who even threaten to charge a patient for being fifteen minutes late for an appointment, yet they think nothing of having you wait fifteen minutes, thirty minutes, or even more and do not reduce their fee when *they* are late. Their reasoning is usually that the previous patient took longer than expected. Perhaps if they scheduled their patients based on the severity of the patient's reason for the appointment rather than just allocating thirty minutes for each appointment, the flow might be better than expected. A medical appointment is a two-way street when it relates to time and should be treated accordingly by both the medical-care practitioner and the patient.

15. Be Careful When Promoting from Within the Organization

Employees within an organization are often promoted from the workforce to become first-line supervisors. However, promoting an employee to a middle or senior manager is a major event usually impacting more than the person getting the promotion. When a person in the military becomes a commissioned officer from the enlisted ranks, the practice is for the newly promoted officer to be transferred immediately to another military installation, avoiding the predicament where the officer instantly outranks all of the NCOs who were senior to the individual prior to the promotion.

On rare occasions, people are promoted to middle and senior management positions within an organization, a move that can present difficulties up and down the chain of command. It's a double-edged sword, with those promoted always welcoming the change yet finding themselves dealing with an entirely new dynamic, as those who were their peers are peers no longer. It is important to understand that if the now-subordinate has a problem with the promotion, it is that person's problem. Unlike the military, most organizations don't have the luxury of transferring the new manager to another facility. Therefore, it is important to repeat this next point for the new manager: you must understand, when asking an employee to do something, it is *not* just a question, no matter how nicely it is posed to them. The work environment doesn't really change for the employees; instead, the one needing to change is the new manager. The first time the new boss speaks, it will be with authority, an adjustment that might feel a bit different. Nonetheless, it is a feeling that must become a natural one.

Another situation presenting a challenge to an organization is associated with promoting an individual to a first-line supervisory position. Oftentimes it seems like a logical choice simply because of the individual's time in the particular field of expertise. Also, hiring from within is much more affordable than hiring from outside of the organization. As mentioned earlier, the ability to lead is not something that can be taught, so being extremely good in one's area of expertise does not necessarily guarantee the individual will be able to lead others. Most often, the promotion does not involve a change of environment (maybe not even a private office) and the new supervisor works in the same exact place as before the promotion. Yet the new boss will have the responsibility for ensuring the staff performs up to established standards. Perhaps the most difficult part of the promotion for the new first-line supervisor is that many of the new subordinates are personal friends. There is no way to sugarcoat the situation, because it is indeed very trying for the new boss. As mentioned earlier, it doesn't need to be, depending on how well the newbie accepts the responsibility that comes with the position. Once again, employees must understand, when the boss asks them to do something, it is *not* just a question, no matter how nicely it is posed to them. Although I am being repetitive, it is an area in which the new supervisor and subordinates have the most difficulty when dealing with the new dynamics thrust upon them. If the new supervisor and the employee on the receiving end fully understand the new relationship, and it is presented in a palatable manner, there should be little difficulty.

16. Be Proactive When Dealing with Disputes

When a manager is a strong and decisive leader, disputes among employees should be a rare occurrence, because they will not want to disappoint their boss. Interdepartmental disputes are more common, especially when one of the departments is providing service to others. The best way to avoid disputes is to establish ground rules for the staff from the beginning, before the first dispute. When one employee is verbally attacked by another, it is never constructive to counterattack, as that rarely ends well. Instead, adhere to these guidelines when someone levels a verbal attack:

a. Never bring yourself down to their level.
b. Kill 'em with kindness.
c. Walk away from the situation.
d. If necessary, bring it to the attention of your boss, the one who's paid to be the SOB.

When employees are given these simple directions before any conflicts arise, they will have a tendency to think hard before they start anything. Questions will be asked in a less confrontational manner, and the manager's advice should be sought with such matters.

17. Be Sensitive to Friendships

A manager should be friendly, personable, and approachable—a statement that seems only too obvious. Yet there are people in management positions who are almost the complete opposite. How is that possible? Either the recruitment of these individuals was flawed, or the individual possesses unique qualities required by the organization—such as a financial wizard who is very capable when it comes to dealing with money, yet has no people skills. Sometimes senior management decides to take the good with the bad, especially when there is a capable first-line supervisor able and willing to be a buffer between the top guy and the rest of the staff.

Managers are not expected to be friends with their employees. In fact, many discourage the idea in order to avoid uncomfortable situations where the manager must give an undesirable directive to an employee who happens to also be a personal friend. Such an occurrence does not need to be uncomfortable, provided the manager is a strong leader and knows how to walk the tightrope of being a friend *and* the boss. I found it difficult to *not* be friends with many of my staff members, but I had no difficulty telling them to do something when it was simply a job that had to be done. There are a few points for the manager to remember that help when such relationships exist:

a. Never apologize for giving a directive to an employee.

b. Employees must understand when the boss asks them to do something it is not just a question, no matter how nicely it is posed to them.

c. Don't be so serious with your employees that they don't know how to act around you. Be able to give a directive without it coming across as "Do it or else!" There are many times I have had to make requests that were not well received, regardless of how I told them. Nevertheless, these were tasks that had to be done. Before I continue, I need to say, "I never tell anyone to shut up, ever." However, I have been known to use the following statement to get the point across: "You know, when I find myself in situations like this, I find it best to just 'shut up and color.' Nobody else is going to get the job done." This brash statement leaves little to the imagination, and when employees hear it, they realize there is no need to complain, because the job is necessary and the directive is nonnegotiable.

d. The first and only person who should ever hear of your dissatisfaction is the employee who is the subject of your disfavor. Telling others can only cause dissension, and it can never go well if the person in question discovers others know about it. Keeping the dissatisfaction just between the two of you is the only answer.

18. Avoid Using Committees

On occasion, senior management will assign a committee to foster development of a project. The best advice about creating committees is, *don't do it*. The intent of forming committees is usually acquiring interdepartmental input, and it usually involves several middle managers. Unless the committee has assigned one individual as the project manager who has managerial control, the committee is almost doomed to fail. It is a fact that the type of business with the highest rate of failure is partnerships. Two or more individuals who have equal control over an organization find it extremely difficult to make some of the important decisions necessary for success. It is much easier when the decisions are made by one individual.

One great example of a committee that failed badly is the congressional supercommittee assigned to cut government spending in the fall of 2011. Each of the six members had a personal agenda that fell in line with party affiliation. Nobody was put in charge to weigh the pros and cons and make a decision, thereby putting all of them in deadlock even before they began meeting. Of course, they ended in failure. Using a committee for making major decisions should be a last-resort alternative. Instead, for all important decisions, a project manager should be authorized to make them and seal the deal.

19. Focus on Time and Motion

Successful managers realize that each motion required for performing tasks related to the job translates to money spent on payroll. There is a challenge for all managers to change from being effective (doing the right things) to being efficient (doing the right things *right*.)

Don't be afraid to challenge the status quo and look for ways to improve. Just because a job has always been done a certain way in the past doesn't mean that's the correct way to do it. Only by questioning the time and motion associated with every action is one able to efficiently manage resources. You will find that the remainder of this book is a case study on how this type of attention to detail can revolutionize job performance.

20. Control the Bottom Line … of the Organization

This is another one of those concepts that seems only too obvious; however, many look at their responsibility as managing just those resources assigned directly to them and staying within their own budgets. With successful managers, there is more to it. They focus on the bottom line of the entire organization with the same level of scrutiny as they do their own department or division. Doing so emphasizes the manager's loyalty to the overall well-being of the establishment and confirms him or her as a team player. Imagine someone who not only reduces current expenses but reduces the next proposed budget as well—senior management will always take note. By the way, I am not referring to the type of budget decreases we see with the US Congress, where they only reduce the amount of increases for the future. Only those using someone else's money would see such a move as a reduction.

21. Maintain Focus on Your Home Life

Most managers are married, and I am not breaking any news when I say it is a difficult balancing act to be a good manager, spouse, and parent. Of course, I don't have any magic answers regarding this topic.

I do know it takes work on everyone's part. I have met too many managers who were extremely dedicated to their jobs but were unable to successfully keep their families together. The importance for one's social needs to be satisfied cannot be overemphasized, especially when addressing family life. It is almost impossible to be productive at work when there are problems at home. It is imperative that the focus is on satisfying both environments.

In the case of Health-Ware Management Company, my wife was also one of my business partners. After our clients were told Jan and I were married, it didn't take long before someone would ask us, "How do you two stay married when you are apart from each other so often?" It was actually an easy question to answer.

Jan and I had been married for more than twenty-two years when we became empty-nesters and Health-Ware began showing signs of real success. After four years, I found myself on the road almost 70 percent of the time, and Jan was on the road for 50 percent of the time—yet we were not traveling together. My travels were related mostly to sales presentations and conducting the two-day training sessions for showing new clients how to build their new databases. For the most part, I was home on weekends. Jan, on the other hand, would leave on a Saturday to train our new clients for the online conversions and not return until the following Sunday. As a result, we were not seeing much of each other. After about three months of these crazy travel schedules, we found ourselves at home together on a Sunday morning. I jokingly mentioned that, since we hardly saw each other, we might as well be divorced.

She smiled and said, "I know what you mean, this has become rather crazy."

I told her I had an idea that might be able to put a spark in our lives.

She said, "I'm all ears."

I responded, "We are really racking up frequent-flyer miles and have more than we can possibly use, so why don't we make use of them for hotels and rental cars and meet somewhere on weekends during our travels? It would be virtually free of cost since our airfare is paid for by the company. You travel on Saturday to get acclimated to the different time zones, so choose a city in the same time zone, and instead of leaving on Saturday, meet me there Friday night. We can tour the area or just crash for the weekend, and then go to our next destinations on Sunday evening."

Jan agreed to give it a try. Over the years, we met in Chicago, New Orleans, Boston, Las Vegas, Los Angeles, and Washington, DC, along with many other cities; our times on the road were special, and it must have been what it would feel like to have an affair. It was just that we were having it with each other.

22. Be Committed to the Organization

When managers endorse their paychecks for deposit, they must, in good conscience, accept the goals and guidelines established by senior management and agree to demonstrate support for the organization responsible for paying them. If it ever reaches the point where you can no longer play by the rules of the organization, there is one of two choices to be made:

1. Do everything possible to change the rules to where they become acceptable.

2. Leave the organization.

This last point causes many to pause, yet it should not be a problem for quality managers. The idea that managers would just get up and leave because they disagree with rules established by those up the management chain seems rather drastic. Yet why does any manager stay with an organization when ego or self-actualization needs are not being met? His social needs are probably being negatively impacted as well.

When I was hired by Jim, the VP of finance, for my job in The Dalles, Oregon, it didn't take long for me to realize I did not agree with any of his management practices. I loved everything associated with our move to Oregon except for the fact that I had to work for this man. Off the job, he was pleasant enough, but on the job, he was definitely a pure 10.0 manager, to the point where I could not relate. Throughout my years as a manager, I have come to the conclusion that "Between me and my boss there is one designated winner, and I ain't it." That revelation gave me clarity regarding my position with any organization from that point forward.

After only six months on the job, I found myself looking elsewhere for employment. I applied for a position in the San Francisco Bay area and had done well enough during my personal interview with the chief operating officer (COO) that he took it upon himself to call *my* COO in The Dalles for a reference check—something he'd agreed not to do, since I was using an executive recruiter that did due diligence for him. After that call, my COO, Mark, asked me to visit with him in his office. Imagine my surprise when he told me about the reference call, and said he was shocked to discover I was looking elsewhere after only six months on the job. Of course, he asked why.

I told him I liked the job and my staff, but I found the working conditions under Jim unsustainable. I knew I was not going to change his ways, so I had to move on. Mark told me he did not want me to leave, and he ultimately promoted me by giving me responsibility for three other departments. Because of the new position, I no longer reported to Jim. It was a good thing Mark was not offended by my move; instead, he offered me the new position. I never could have taken the new job to go work with someone who went back on his word by calling for a reference check. I dodged a bullet.

23. Above All, Have Fun

More than anything else, managing a staff of people toward common goals should be exciting and fun. The best way to make that happen is to use sound management principles that can be applied to everyday life on the job. "Play by the Rules" was the cornerstone for the way I managed people, and I definitely had a great time while doing so.

APPLYING THE PHILOSOPHY TO SMALL BUSINESSES

In the beginning, I was under the impression that putting a management philosophy into practice could only be done in larger organizations where managers oversaw many employees. It wasn't until I was given the opportunity to manage a small organization that I realized the need for sound management skills is one of the most important keys for ensuring success. Without skilled management, a small business is like a ship without a rudder.

The smaller the business, the greater the effort required to make it a successful venture. When you begin to read the chapters about our entrepreneurial experience, you will watch a very small enterprise evolve into one that successfully competed with companies that were literally a hundred times bigger relative to money and people. We could not have done so had we not believed in the concepts of "Play by the Rules."

SELF-ACTUALIZING

For years, I saw myself working in the field of hospital administration and retiring as a hospital administrator. I certainly never saw myself leaving hospitals and becoming an entrepreneur who would eventually run a software company. Yet after I made the transition, I realized I had found the job of a lifetime. The experiences I had with our employees and our clients were exhilarating. I have the best of memories about the vast majority of people I met and worked with over the years. I found myself in an enviable position where I had the best job I could have ever hoped to attain. I can honestly say that my self-actualization needs were satisfied.

THE BOTTOM LINE

Like employees, managers come from all walks of life. The main departure between the two is that managers can have a significant impact on the psyche and overall well-being of their employees, with the impact going mostly in one direction. This one fact illustrates the need for managers to have a sound, consistent means of guiding themselves when it comes to leading others. When using "Play by the Rules" as the foundation for managing people, many may discover that it can offer them the consistency necessary for leading others in a fair and decisive manner.

2. BEFORE THE ENTREPRENEURIAL EXPERIENCE

This book now leaves a rather academic approach to the world of management and offers a means for observing how the rules were applied when actually running a business. You will read about how we got started with our product in the first place—long before the entrepreneurial plunge—and how it became something that far exceeded our expectations and dreams.

When one accepts the idea that management is a profession all by itself and embraces "Play by the Rules" as a basis for leading people, then it is easy to understand how a manager can successfully transition from one field to another. It is this premise that allowed me to confidently leave my position as an executive in the field of hospital administration and move to that of the president of a small software development firm. The decision to do so gave me, and ultimately others, the courage to leave a sure thing relevant to job security, risk everything on the proverbial wing and a prayer, and start a new business. You will experience the apprehensions, the highs, the lows, and what it took to recover from those lows—making it all worthwhile for those of us who were willing to take a risk.

We were blinking dollar signs. If we could have bottled the energy emanating in the room where we conducted our first board meeting, our nation's dependency on foreign oil would have been obliterated. The seven of us had decided to take the plunge and introduce our software to the open market. We had a winner, we knew it, yet we were terrified of the unknown. All of us were good at our jobs, full of enthusiasm, and fearless. That said, many thought we should have had our heads examined. Yet nobody was going to convince us to change our minds, as there was a thick fogbank clouding the horizon. The long, slow, nearly four-year crescendo had finally reached its climactic peak.

There had been countless hours devoted to a project that started out with no thought about having an impact on anyone or anything beyond the walls of the hospital where it was developed. Even with the extremely high level of excitement around the table, we never imagined we would later become involved with such prestigious institutions as Ohio State University Medical Center, Washington Hospital Center, and the Mayo Clinic.

What was all the fuss about and how did it get to this point? It was December 1981 when I was hired by the chief financial officer (CFO) as the director of materials management (MM) at the Mid-Columbia Medical Center in The Dalles, Oregon. I was thirty-two years old and had previously been a member of the US Air Force Medical Service Corps (hospital administrators). In eight years, we'd had five assignments at five different locations, and my wife had been afflicted with a medical condition that precluded us from moving at the drop of a hat. When a job opportunity became available in rural Oregon, the idea of moving to a small town appealed to both of us. The interview process, which happened three weeks before I reported for work, was very professional.

The top three candidates were flown in with their spouses. While I was being interviewed by the hospital executives and meeting individually with selected hospital department directors, my wife, Jan, was given a personal tour of the local area by the wife of the personnel director.

Although the process was most impressive and exhilarating for the two of us, I was the second candidate to be flown in, and I believed the next guy was their preferred choice. It is common that the preferred candidate is the last one to be interviewed, and oftentimes the job is offered at that time. You can imagine how surprised I was when I was offered the job two days later.

THE MATERIALS-MANAGEMENT ENVIRONMENT

In the early '70s, hospitals around the nation were changing their approach to the way they managed supplies, beginning with renaming the purchasing department "materials management." The intent was to transform the position to what non-health-care companies had been doing for years: centralizing control over logistics management within their organizations, which included purchasing. In the hospital industry, it was the for-profit hospital chains that first realized the need for the change. In the beginning, nonprofit hospitals implemented the name change but did little else to go along with the altered nomenclature. The departments incurred no modifications to the procedures, scope of operation, or management. The director of purchasing simply became the director of materials management, in name only.

When the folks in The Dalles realized they needed to improve the MM department, they looked for an experienced candidate who had a graduate degree. At the time, such a prerequisite for a materials-management position was almost unheard of. When I attained my initial training and experience in hospital administration in the air force, I had been introduced to health-care materials management. I was accustomed to having a computerized materials-management information system (MMIS) to support the department. Unfortunately, my new department had no such support.

During my interview, I asked Jim, my soon-to-be boss, about a computerized system, to which he replied, "We don't have the $50,000 to $100,000 to purchase the hardware and software, but if you get the job, maybe you and Lentz in information systems can come up with something on the [IBM] System/34. Then you two can knock yourselves out."

Later in the day, I met Lentz Ferrell, the director of information systems (IS), who at the time was twenty-eight years old and had been in his position for two years. The hospital executives obviously recognized he was talented enough and that he had the potential to take on the job, despite his youth. During our thirty minutes together, I found him to be one of the most positive individuals I had ever met. I was able to appreciate his can-do attitude just by talking with him. It was evident he loved his job. My first impression was, *I can work with this guy.* It was a thought I would later act upon over and over again.

When Jim first told me the only way I would get an automated system for MM was if Lentz and I were to develop it on our own, I was a bit concerned the task might never be accomplished. It wasn't until I met Lentz that I realized maybe we *could* do it ourselves. If the hospital executives really wanted purchasing to be converted to an MM department, the only way it could truly happen was if an automated system became part of the solution. I had never designed a system before, but the prospect of doing so didn't deter me. If Lentz was only half as good as I thought he was, and I was able to present him with a plausible blueprint for a new system, I might be pleasantly surprised by the outcome.

LET'S DO IT

On the second day at my new job, I met with Lentz. After we exchanged greetings, I approached him about developing an automated MMIS. We agreed to work together, and the ball was in my court because I was told to provide him with an outline of what I wanted the system to look like.

I went back to my department and asked the buyer to purchase me a set of coveralls. When she asked why I needed them, I replied, "It is important I find out exactly what everybody does when they work in the warehouse. I need to submit a credible design to Lentz for an automated system, and I want to protect my clothes while doing so."

When I gave Lentz my first four-page design layout a week later, he stated, "I am used to getting a request scribbled on a torn piece of paper. This type of detail means you are serious. I'll look it over and get back to you if I have any questions."

Lentz obviously meant what he said, because the next day he asked me over to his office. I arrived five minutes later, and he presented me with a working model of my first design on the computer. With that quick turnaround, he virtually opened the floodgates for ideas that would come his way in the very near future.

He then surprised me with, "I will get a couple of terminals in your department so your people can play with it and begin to add data."

Lentz was a gold mine with his abilities and, just as important, his willingness to work with me. I knew that together, we might be able to really change things for the better, and ultimately have a positive impact on everyone working in the hospital.

My first weeks on the job were extremely busy. While beginning to work with Lentz on an automated system, I had major issues to contend with that had nothing to do with a computer system. My new department was a mess—it didn't just look bad, the organization for moving supplies itself was in dire need of being retrofitted. For example, when stock items were placed in the warehouse, they were actually placed in more than one place, as they were put on different shelves and segregated for different departments. That one feature by itself made it more difficult to manage the inventory. Imagine having to go to four different locations to determine how much to order of each item.

The hospital was in the middle of a major construction project when I started my new job. The majority of the ancillary service areas were being renovated. The finance offices, the dining room, and Lentz's offices (when I met him, he was working out of a trailer) were all under construction. A new office was about to be constructed for MM, so our desks would no longer be in the warehouse. When I saw the blueprints for MM, I saw that it was just going to be a single office for purchasing and myself. I immediately drafted a modification to the plans so that both the purchasing agent and I could have private offices. Next, I met with Phil, the construction boss, to show him my proposed modifications.

When I introduced myself as the new manager in charge of MM, he said, "You have been here for only one day? You have no idea how lucky you are. If you would have waited until three days from now, you would have been too late. You aren't wasting any time, are you?" The construction began three days later and included my modifications.

My rationale for aggressively pushing my agenda was that I knew the only way a computerized system would be of any use was if I rallied the troops, so to speak, to reorganize the manual system before attempting to use any type of automation. In actuality, the two tasks were being done at the same time; fortunately, I was the only one in the department burdened with the design of the computer system, at least in the beginning.

While looking at the blueprints for my office, I noticed the construction budget had allotted money for new equipment for the warehouse, but there weren't any plans for using the money. I went to my boss with a plan for new shelving to replace the worn-out and broken-down wooden shelving with $50,000 of stainless-steel shelving. Three weeks later, we began taking our stock off of the shelves, tearing down the old wooden shelving, installing the new shelving, and then reorganizing the inventory so that there was only one location for any item in stock. This change would have a significant impact on the way my staff provided service to all of the hospital departments. Meanwhile, I had to convince the nursing staff that they would be getting better service, not less, as a result of the changes. In the beginning, it was a sales pitch not well received by many.

SETTING THE STAGE

Rules Applied:

5. *Be an Effective Communicator*   6. *Embrace Change*
7. *Lead with Confidence*   8. *Be Consistent; Be Decisive*

Although I was a new manager, I had a good idea of what I wanted to accomplish, and until somebody told me otherwise, I was anxious to give the department a complete makeover. In addition, nobody on my staff really had any idea of how a true MM department was supposed to operate and what it should look like. I decided to take charge and lead them in the best possible way.

The basic concepts of materials management I was introduced to by the air force were based on sound logistics. The automated system had a good foundation as well, although it was based on keypunch cards for data entry. However, because of the centralized control inherent in multiple-site organizations like the air force, implementation of new ideas was slow to come to fruition, if it ever did. In fact, when I submitted what I considered a simple request—I wanted a report for specified items that showed corresponding usage for a given period and the respective departments they were issued to—I was told to expect to see one of my ideas possibly become a reality within two years.

One can only imagine how elated I was when I submitted that same request to Lentz and he had it operational the very next day. I realized I was just plain lucky to have him as a willing partner with this project; he never wanted to tell me he couldn't do something, and throughout all of our years together, he never did. To be honest, I felt like a kid who had just been given the key to the candy store. It became all too evident that Lentz's willingness to work with me was instrumental if I was going to accomplish both my short- and long-term goals. Of course, I had no idea what those long-term goals would later become.

FINE-TUNING THE DEPARTMENT

How *did* such a project—developed at a small 125-bed hospital operating at 50 percent capacity and located in rural America—become the foundation for an enterprise that would have a far-reaching influence on some of the largest medical institutions in the country? Well, it didn't happen overnight. Rather, it happened one day at a time.

Perhaps the most important task from the beginning was to give my new staff a sense of security. Their boss of sixteen years had just been fired, and their new boss was instituting changes at a very fast pace. I didn't have the luxury of hiring a new team already up to speed on how to properly manage an inventory, nor did I feel it necessary. I wanted to keep the staff I inherited; I just had to convince them to buy into the changes and accept them in a positive light.

I noticed hospital personnel were cordial to my staff in public areas like the cafeteria, but weren't treating them with much respect when interacting with them when they came to the warehouse. When hospital employees needed supplies immediately, the MM department was set up more like a self-service store, where hospital personnel could just walk into the warehouse, look for supplies, take them, and leave. The problem with that policy was that many of those coming to get supplies did not take the time to account for taking the supplies off of the shelves—a fact readily admitted later by those taking the supplies. Nevertheless, when nurses and other hospital staff members came looking for an item only to find it was out of stock, they would verbally abuse my staff. This was a practice that had obviously been in place for a long time and was accepted as the norm. And it was one of the first policies I put a stop to in order to get a handle on our inventory. To me, it was obvious my staff did not deserve much of the criticism aimed at them, and I knew it was important that I did all I could to remedy the situation.

SUPPORTING THE STAFF

I had to transform the mood of the staff to a positive one that would be felt beyond the walls of our department. Unfortunately, my staff was gun-shy when it came to dealing with people outside of MM. When I first took the job, they could not say anything good about the nursing staff, and it was obvious that was a two-way street. By others, especially nurses, the MM staff was looked upon as incompetent. I was told it was a common occurrence to hear one of the nurses or department heads yelling at one of the MM employees. My first encounter with such an incident occurred after only two weeks on the job, when I received a call from Mindy who worked in the warehouse. She was calling from surgery, where she had just delivered the wrong item. It was rather obvious Mindy was stressed when she called to ask if we had the correct item on the shelf. While speaking with me, I could hear an OR nurse in the background saying, "I can't believe your incompetence." I asked Mindy for the name of the nurse and then told Mindy to return to the warehouse, saying I would see to it the correct item made it to the OR.

I quickly grabbed the item and literally ran up the stairs to deliver it, passing Mindy in the stairwell on my way. She asked if I wanted her to deliver it for me. I thanked her for the offer but declined; I was on a mission to meet with Kathy in the OR, the nurse who had just been so rude to Mindy. The only time I had been to the OR since I took the job was when I had been introduced to the director of the OR during my interview for the job. When I arrived at the OR (OR and Surgery are synonymous when referring to the surgery department), I announced that I needed to speak with Kathy. The clerk saw the item in my hand and said she would see to it that Kathy received the item. I thanked her, but I told her I needed to deliver it to Kathy myself. The clerk was obviously uncomfortable but said she would find Kathy for me. My wait was short, and Kathy came out of her work area to meet with me.

I greeted her with, "Hi, Kathy, my name is Tim, and I am the new director of materials management. I am not in the habit of personally delivering supplies, but I felt compelled to do so after hearing you yell at Mindy the way you did."

When Kathy first came out to see me, she looked rather indignant, but after I spoke, her comportment changed when she realized just how serious I was. She was unsure as to how she should deal with this new department head who was so direct with her.

I continued, "Kathy, I just inherited my staff, and I am working hard to improve how we provide service to all employees. There is no incompetence in my department—rather a lack of training and education for rendering quality service, which was part of the reason my predecessor was fired. I need you to understand the situation and give my staff what one might call a probationary period. When you or anyone else in the OR find a problem that is totally unacceptable, call me directly. I will research your complaint, and you will promptly receive a response. I need your help and the help of all OR personnel to treat my staff with respect. It is the only way I can get my staff to give you the service you require and deserve."

Afterward, I returned to MM and requested an impromptu staff meeting. I told everyone of the incident and said I wanted to know of any such occurrences in the future so I could immediately address the situation.

I shared, "You will make mistakes, but none of you deserves to ever be treated with such disrespect. The next time any of you are treated in that manner by another hospital employee, I have two prescriptions for dealing with such an individual. First, *kill them with kindness*. Second, *never bring yourselves down to their level*. Just remember, I am the one who is paid to be a son-of-a-bitch. We are no longer going to be the Rodney Dangerfield of the hospital." They needed to know that not only was I their new boss, I was their advocate, and I was going to change the way others treated them. The staff seemed both surprised and relieved, and such incidents quickly dissipated as I completed my public-relations campaign throughout the hospital.

RESOLVING A DISPUTE WITH SURGERY

Rules Applied:

5. Be an Effective Communicator

I had to respond immediately to Kathy's treatment of Mindy. It was necessary to let her know that although she had a right to expect good service from our department, she did not have the right to treat my employee in such a manner.

I bypassed her supervisor so Kathy did not receive my complaint secondhand and was able to see me up close and personal. I did not intend to further alienate her; rather, I wanted her to understand that although it would be a slow process, service from MM would improve. Fortunately, service from the staff did improve, as well as the relationships between people in the two departments.

TRUST ME

The department makeover was a massive undertaking. It is difficult to explain just how much of an impact the transformation was having on the entire staff. However, maybe recapping a certain incident that occurred after I'd been on the job for only six weeks will give you some idea. I was working in the warehouse with the entire staff (including those working in central supply), rearranging the stock locations for all items in the inventory. I had just asked Karen Christiansen, a twenty-year-old woman who worked in purchasing, to move some boxes of syringes from one area to another, and she just lost it.

She abruptly threw a box of syringes on the floor and yelled, "Damn it!"

I was maybe fifteen feet from her and realized all eyes were on me, waiting for my reaction. I glanced at her with a raised eyebrow that was begging for her to elaborate.

She complied. "You are making so many changes, and you have hardly been here long enough to find your own desk! Yet you are having us renumber, recategorize, and relocate every item in the entire warehouse! You have us moving items from here to there and ..." She pointed to the others. "We just don't understand why! We seemed to be doing fine before you came. For the first three weeks, you gave us the third degree asking us what and how we did our jobs. We thought you just wanted us to teach you how to run our department. Instead, you are changing the way we do *everything*."

It was obvious Karen had been thinking about what to say to me for some time. With all eyes on me, I knew I wasn't giving an answer just to Karen, so I didn't feel it was appropriate to ask her to go into my office to discuss the matter further. Instead, I had to give an answer immediately to this young woman I had known for less than two months. I knew I had to calm her down and carefully choose my words while doing so. I wanted to take her from her current state of mind that gave her the courage to challenge her new boss in front of the rest of the staff, to a point where she understood me better and did not see me as the enemy. I didn't consider her a rebellious employee; rather, she was young and just didn't understand the scope of the project. Though I had spent a great deal of time trying to explain what was in store for her and the rest of the staff, not completely explaining everything to them was an intentional move on my part. Sometimes, hearing someone talk about what's coming down the road in detail can frighten and overwhelm those involved more than if they were just given the project one step at a time.

I calmly asked the question, "Karen, is there something you do extremely well when you are not at work, enough that perhaps you would consider yourself as maybe a cut above the rest, or even an expert?" Now she was truly puzzled. She had no idea where I was heading with this question. I continued, "You know, like photography, or maybe you are extremely good at something in the kitchen?" My intent was to put her in her own comfort zone, where she would feel more in control by talking about something she could elaborate on when questioned about it.

Suddenly she looked relaxed, and she smiled with confidence when she replied, "Yes, I am good at baking." Karen's demeanor changed completely. *(What syringes?)*

I inquired further, "If I gave you a recipe for an apple pie I really like, would you try it?"

She replied, "Yes, probably." (A response showing *her* in control.)

I then asked, "Do you have a basic crust you normally use for all of your pies?"

Without hesitation, she replied, "Yes."

I then asked, "Would you use the crust I suggested, or would you use your own?"

With a twinkle in her eye, she proclaimed, "I would probably use my own."

After I asked why, she replied, "There are certain things I do my own way because you know, I consider the kitchen to be my domain, and this happens to be one of the basics I would use."

Karen could not have played into my hands any better if she'd read a script I had written for her. I looked at her confident smile and replied, "Karen, I understand completely." I then raised my arms, as if to embrace the warehouse, and with great enthusiasm I replied, "Karen, welcome to my kitchen."

I then looked at all of my staff and stated, "I need you to trust me, and regardless of how new I am to this hospital, you need to understand that I have done this before. So, with your help, I would like to use *my* crust for completing this project."

From that moment on, Karen and the rest of the staff seemed to *get it*. They treated me with greater respect and understanding. I felt even more confident they would indeed see the project through to a successful finish. I admit, however, I had no idea what that statement meant at the time, as I couldn't possibly foresee the immensity of the project. Those one-day-at-a-time intervals lasted for more than three years.

ESTABLISHING LEADERSHIP

Rules Applied:

2. Know Your Employees Relevant to the Hierarchy of Needs
6. Embrace Change   *7. Lead with Confidence*

It was important that Karen did not feel as if she was being attacked. Putting her at ease with the question about baking allowed her ego needs to be satisfied during a difficult discussion. It was important that I take charge and, in a subtle way, let all in the room know that change was not a bad thing. This one incident was pivotal in the endeavor of getting all onboard with me as we began to change our work environment.

It was obvious the staff was still in need of direction, education, and self-confidence to keep up with the new pace. Unfortunately, there wasn't any choice—they had to step up to the plate or quit the game. An important part of my job was to work with them so they learned everything necessary to confidently and proudly perform their tasks on a daily basis. The economy for this small community of eleven thousand was very depressed; the two biggest sources of income were virtually dead. The logging industry was busy fighting with activists over a spotted owl that virtually brought that industry to a screeching halt, and the two aluminum plants, both located on the Columbia River within twenty-five miles of each other, were also dying. The plant right there within the town limits shut down shortly after our arrival, and the other plant was constantly undergoing layoffs. Vacant jobs in the local area were almost nonexistent. I couldn't have my staff afraid for their jobs because of a new hotshot young executive trying to make a name for himself. The only way I could hope for even the slightest kind of personal success was if I made my employees my number-one priority. I took the lead with the intent of making *them* the heroes; they followed my lead and became vital employees in very short order. Within seven months, I was responsible for over a third of the four-hundred-plus hospital employees, and I could never have managed had it not been for the support of my original staff.

LEADING THROUGH TEAMWORK

Rules Applied:

5. Be an Effective Communicator   *6. Embrace Change*
7. Lead with Confidence   *10. Motivate the Staff*
11. Define Expectations   *12. Instill Teamwork*

The staff was counting on me to know what I was doing. They were willing to follow, provided their leader was someone they believed they could trust. With all of the changes I was introducing to the entire hospital staff, it was as if I was living in a fishbowl. All eyes were on every move I made.

Getting my staff to work as a team was imperative if I wanted to see any measurable progress. I could not do it alone.

---

3. NEVER TOO LATE TO LEARN

Almost every day at my new job at Mid-Columbia Medical Center was a learning experience. During the beginning months, I was immersed in my project and didn't allow myself many distractions—yet I found myself to be deeply involved with organized chaos. Being the new manager on the scene who was ultimately responsible for acquiring all supplies and services for the hospital, I was constantly being bombarded by sales reps who visited the hospital on a monthly basis. Since the vast majority of supplies were purchased according to consortium contracts, I didn't see the need to spend much time with these frequent visitors. Instead, I promoted Karen (yes, the same one who threw the syringes) to be my new purchasing agent and let her be my buffer with the sales reps. I discouraged lengthy meetings with the reps unless there were problems requiring resolution. This policy was new to my staff and was confusing to them, since my predecessor spent many hours with the reps and often took business lunches with them.

My focus was on the time and motion associated with all tasks, both automated and manual. I stressed the importance of requiring visitors to schedule appointments in advance and told the staff not to see anyone who didn't have the courtesy to call ahead. At first, it was difficult for the staff to fully grasp the importance of this, but as time wore on and their responsibilities grew, it became only too obvious that there was little time for such interruptions. I did meet with each of the reps on his or her first prescheduled courtesy visit to welcome me to the area. For most of them, it was only at that one visit that we spent any real time together. However, after the third month, some of the reps would go out of their way to say hi and comment on the significant progress they observed being made in the department, giving me a virtual pat on the back.

I didn't give the overtures by the sales reps much credence and thought it was just as a way to patronize me. Still, as time progressed, some of them working for the larger vendors took a significant interest in our progress when visiting the hospital. They did their best to get my attention by asking me to make time for a cup of coffee. In the beginning, I was so busy, I politely declined their invitations. Also, my perspective on vendor-client relationships was rather distorted. I always considered their interest in meeting me only as a means to better their standing, so I would ultimately increase their level of sales to the hospital.

A TASTE OF HUMBLE PIE

Even though I was quite busy with the systems-development aspect of my job, I was encouraged to attend health-care seminars as part of my continuing education. Unfortunately, I remember the first meeting only too well. It was hosted by the Northwest Materials Management Group in Seattle in March 1982. I was one of the newest members of the group, yet I took it upon myself to volunteer my opinion with the audience of 150 of my peers, where I knew nobody.

With the thoughts about sales reps on my mind, and without giving the people at this meeting a chance to get to know me, I decided to float an idea to the crowd. I was recognized by the meeting chairperson and asked to give my name and the name of the hospital where I worked.

I stood up and said, "My name is Tim, and I am from Mid-Columbia Medical Center in The Dalles, Oregon. Since prices for the vast majority of supplies we order for our hospitals are already negotiated, why do we find ourselves letting the sales reps take us out to lunch? It seems like a waste of time when we have so much on our plate already."

It was like I had stepped on sacred ground without an invitation, daring to suggest such an idea. To the audience, I came across with an unintentional flare of arrogance, and the emotional reaction to my suggestion was rather alarming to me (as well as educational). From a political standpoint, it showed me just how naïve I was at the time.

The audience was obviously upset with me. I overheard one member say, "How could anyone from a small rural hospital possibly have anything to say that would be of value to most of us?" Many in the room represented hospitals that were up to five times larger than ours in The Dalles.

I will never forget watching Gerry Gardner, the director of materials management (MM) at St. Charles Medical Center in Bend, Oregon— just two and a half hours south of The Dalles—when he stood up and responded to my statement with guarded disdain: "I'm not sure I consider it a *complete* waste of our time, as I have had some positive outcomes resulting from some of those free lunches."

It was obvious he did not need an introduction to the crowd, and I could tell he was regarded with respect by everyone in the room. To be honest, I immediately liked him, even though he didn't agree with me.

Well, it was obvious I wasn't going to be part of the in-crowd with *this* group anytime soon. As Gerry was talking, I heard, "Small hospitals don't have the same needs as larger ones, and where does he get the nerve?" (One word: *stupidity*.)

WHERE ENTHUSIASM GOT THE BEST OF ME

Rule Applied:

5. Be an Effective Communicator

I may have effectively communicated my thoughts, but not only did I not know my audience, none of them knew me. It was a lesson I only needed to be taught once. Even if I was right, I was wrong; I embarrassed myself, and it only took a minute to do so.

Today, I still believe the size of our hospital didn't preclude me from contributing to the group, but those associated with the larger institutions had an air about them that said otherwise. I was, and still am, that "box-kicking and label-licking materials manager" (a phrase gleaned from the air force) who believes, for the most part, that all medical institutions, regardless of size, require the same supply discipline for managing their inventories. The larger ones just order more of the same than do those in smaller institutions. Of course, I oversimplify that relationship, as medical centers that are teaching facilities and/or involved with medical research have requirements that are greater than those of the typical acute-care hospital. However, after more than twenty years in the field of MM, I can point to many examples that support my premise that the size of the hospital does not change the procedures necessary for managing supplies. The one area that does require more expertise is that of managing people, simply because the larger organizations require more employees to support their operation.

Years later, I discovered that the majority of health-care organizations, regardless of size, maintain about the same number of stock items (between 1,200 and 1,600) in the warehouse. Fortunately, I did not share my thoughts about the size of hospitals with the audience at the time. I can only imagine the kind of reaction I would have gotten. Though I was politely welcomed at the local watering hole (the hotel cocktail lounge) later that evening, I was, to say the least, uncomfortable. One might say I was a masochist to enter such a gathering after what had just happened earlier, but I wanted to take advantage of the opportunity to meet other materials managers. No doubt, I was enthusiastic about what I was doing with my own operation, but I wanted to see if I could glean any ideas that might assist me along the way. Furthermore, I wanted to learn from others about the type of automated MM systems they were using. I found those at the smaller hospitals (anywhere from twenty-five beds to the size of my own at 125 beds) had little interest, since they believed they could never afford a system even if they wanted one. When I shared what I was doing at Mid-Columbia, the consensus was that it seemed like a lot of work that might not be worth the effort.

I remember Bev Coryell of Good Samaritan Hospital, located in Corvallis, Oregon, asking, "Don't you think you are stretching yourself too thin, and you might be ignoring some more important duties associated with your job?"

Others chimed in by echoing the same sentiments, so I responded, "I am passionate about making it so everyone on my staff is able to get the job done with utmost efficiency. After I am finished with this project, I hope when my boss first enters my office, he sees the soles of my shoes on my desk, indicating I have everything under control."

Someone immediately asked, "How is your staff going to feel about seeing your feet on the desk?"

I quipped, "I will have to let you know after it happens, because I need to go back and work my butt off to make it happen." With that remark they all laughed and wished me luck.

AN UNEXPECTED EDUCATION

This segment might lead one to think I was the head of the PR firm for the American Hospital Supply (AHS) Corporation (which was later acquired by Baxter Travenol Corporation in 1985 and then sold again). My reason for such an elaborate recount of this experience is to illustrate the significant impact that one relatively small event had on my life for years to come.

Most sales reps called on our hospital on a monthly basis. However, Chris Tew from AHS was at our hospital every two weeks. I always let Karen deal with sales reps when it came to discussing pricing and service levels. Chris came to me and we never talked about increasing business with AHS; rather, we discussed issues concerning the health-care industry in a macro sense. As a result, it ended up that I looked forward to his visits and was able to broaden my own perspective and attitude toward sales reps.

After ten months on the job, it was obvious we were on the right track for automating the department. Lentz and I developed a purchasing module that was being fed from the pick-lists coming from the warehouse, and our service level to the departments was at an all-time high. Cooperation by the hospital department heads was better than I could have imagined possible at such an early date. My staff had gained a great deal of respect from other hospital employees, which was reflected by the reduction in the overall number of complaints rendered toward the department.

Meanwhile, during one of his visits to our hospital, Chris mentioned, "Your staff seems to have a new sense of pride. It shows in the way they do their work, and above all it's obvious they are much happier." Then he asked, "Tim, do you think you could take five days off work to attend a seminar conducted by my company at its national headquarters in Chicago? I can assure you, it is not a means for selling anything to your hospital. Rather, it is an informational seminar for acquainting you with all AHS has to offer its clients. I think you would enjoy the trip."

Chris convinced me to take him up on the offer. I first thought the trip might just be a cursory look at the AHS operation and that the remainder of the visit would end up as a boondoggle. I found the event to be anything but; it was *much* more. It was an all-expense-paid trip for about fifty of their clients, where upon arrival we had virtually every minute planned out for us, from start to finish. For lack of a better description, it was an event similar to those that many in the health-care industry pay thousands of dollars for to satisfy their continuing-education requirements. Each presentation was topnotch, and if nothing else inspiring for all in attendance, or at least thought-provoking. All presenters were well trained in public speaking and able to handle the audience with ease. In addition, the presidents of their four divisions were all in attendance. At the time, I was thirty-three years old and surprised by the apparent youth of the AHS executives. All but one of the executives was under the age of forty, and all sported huge smiles signifying their satisfaction with their individual successes. They were energetic, happy, and engaging; each of them made a conscious effort to spend time with every one of the invited guests. Like a fine watermark on expensive stationery, the AHS brand of professionalism was always in the background of every discussion. It was obvious they were well qualified for their positions at American, and if they weren't natural salespeople, they were eventually groomed to fill the bill. They exhibited confidence but not arrogance. They were able to make those they encountered comfortable in their presence.

The guests represented a cross-section of hospitals from around the country, from small-sized institutions to very large ones. I represented the smallest hospital in the group. Our hosts wanted all of us to leave with a newfound respect for their company that subliminally would lead to a sounder business relationship between them and us. I never felt any pressure or like I was getting a pitch for business in any way. For myself, they were successful in their endeavor; I returned to my job in Oregon with a new respect for the idea of looking at a vendor as a business partner rather than as an adversary. (Though I didn't know it at the time, it was a concept that would impact me in the future in the way I conducted myself when dealing with my own clients.) It was at that moment that I realized Chris had taken this opportunity to show me the big picture. One could say I had led a sheltered life in that I had only worked for the air force and this small hospital located eighty-four miles from anywhere. Chris probably would not have used these exact words, but he knew I got it. I would find myself forever grateful for my friendship with Chris, both professional and personal.

This short seminar at AHS provided me with an unintended outcome: I wanted to join that management team, not just work with it from my hospital. The last time I had that feeling of belonging to a group of motivated executives was when I was part of the Air Force Medical Service Corps (hospital administrators). The one obvious difference between the two organizations is the way they manage executives. In the military, for most, tenure and time-in-rank are strict guidelines for advancement. AHS, on the other hand, advanced its executives based on merit. The company was obviously geared toward giving its executives the opportunity to excel, regardless of age or tenure. I didn't know if anything would come of my new long-term goal of working at AHS, but I definitely looked at my professional future in an even more positive way than I had before.

The seminar was anything but an employee-recruitment tool, yet the management staff of AHS was open to speaking with anyone interested in employment opportunities with the company. For the first time in my life, I witnessed the need for focusing on the revenue side of an operation, where I would work in a for-profit environment. Up to that point, whether working in a military or civilian hospital, I had always worked in a business where the emphasis had been on cost control, as they were always nonprofit entities. Yet everyone I dealt with on a daily basis from outside the confines of hospitals was focused on profit maximization. In other words, by virtue of their own mission statements, the goals for each of these organizations were diametrically opposed to each other.

I still could never see myself as a salesman at the time, because up to that point, my focus had always been on cost containment, not profit maximization. No wonder I did not consider myself a salesman; I was a grown adult with plenty of experience, but one without any exposure to the rest of the story: *profit*. The available employment slots at AHS for the operations side (my area of expertise at the time) were few in number. At the time, I didn't have the confidence or the desire to apply for a sales slot; besides, I wasn't finished with my project at hand. I returned to Oregon with a rejuvenated vigor and a revitalized commitment to do my very best daily in all that I accomplished.

4. A SIMPLE SOLUTION FOR A COMPLICATED PROBLEM

Although the intent of this book is not to educate readers on health-care materials management (MM), I am compelled to introduce an area that will assist you in understanding how we were getting so much attention from other hospitals in Oregon, Washington, and the major medical-supplies distributors serving the Northwest region. If you prefer, you can skip the technical overview about MM and move on to the next chapter. You will miss, however, learning about one of the key aspects of our system that brought others from around the Northwest to see what we were doing.

As we were getting our arms around the ability to minimize the cost of supplies and the processes that supported that endeavor, it became apparent we had to broaden our approach to cost containment beyond just reducing the cost of syringes, needles, and the like. The hospital purchasing groups, such as those at Intermountain Healthcare (IHC) and its subgroups, had perfected the negotiating of contracts with vendors, so bickering over the costs at the hospital level was almost a waste of time. As the task of automating the MM operation was progressing, it became evident that the system required a focus on the time and motion associated with *all* of the processes involved with the movement of those supplies ordered, received, and delivered to the hospital departments. Concentration had to be on reducing the time necessary for performing those tasks; then, and only then, could real savings be realized. Successful reductions in time spent on performing tasks always relates to reduction in labor, which ultimately means reduction in payroll, which is the biggest single expense item reflected on any hospital's general ledger. If properly executed, the reduction in labor would be realized in virtually every department *except* MM.

It may seem as though I was taking care of my own department with little regard for others. Nothing could have been further from the truth. The goal was to take those purchasing- and supply-related tasks performed by the department heads and/or their designated technicians and have my lower-paid "box-kickers" do the work. The ultimate goal was for the MM staff to go to each of the departments' storage areas, scan each of the on-hand quantities, and let the system calculate the respective supply requirements. Other systems on the market were doing all of that. Yet something was missing. The stock supplies were being handled efficiently, but what about the nonstock supplies?

NOT JUST A GLORIFIED PURCHASING SYSTEM

When I looked at MM systems available on the market that were in use at hospitals in the Portland area, it was obvious they were developed with the purchasing module as the focal point (you are probably thinking, *That makes sense*). Yet I was surprised to find that buyers were scanning the warehouse shelves in order to create purchase orders for replenishing stock instead of relying on the computer-generated reorder lists.

My time with the coveralls resulted in a case study on the time and motion related to managing supplies. I realized one important aspect of the entire MM operation: all of the activity begins in the warehouse, and purchasing only reacts to those activities. As a practice, all recurring requisitions (for stock items) are forwarded to the warehouse, where clerks enter the requests into the system and then distribute the supplies to the appropriate departments. There is one very unique distinction that separates our system from all others: our user processes recurring requests for both the stock *and* nonstock items. The normal practice is that recurring requests for nonstock items are forwarded to the purchasing department. You might ask why I am stressing this point. Please read on to get a crash course on requests for supplies normally handled in a health-care setting.

THE MOST FRUSTRATING MM PROCESS
FOUND IN THE MAJORITY OF HOSPITALS

In most hospitals, the clinical staff considers the hospital warehouse to be a place for storing medical supplies used by more than one clinical department (for example, needles and syringes) and the nonmedical supplies, such as pens and pencils, used by all departments. Few look to MM, however, as the source for all of their supplies. One of the most radical approaches we offered the hospital departments was the way we handled requests for the nonstock supplies.

The term *nonstock* is just what it sounds like: supplies not stocked in the hospital inventory. Again from my coverall days, it became apparent that the vast majority of supplies (up to 85 percent in volume and 75 percent in dollar value) were not managed by MM. The implication of these statistics was far-reaching, as it had an impact on the way we designed the concepts for automating the department. Ultimately, we changed the way supplies were ordered, which had an effect on the entire hospital staff. It bothered me that department managers—such as the registered nurses in charge of the surgery department, ICU, and the inpatient wards—were placing orders for supplies not stocked in the warehouse.

Those responsible for ordering supplies at the department level did so on a weekly basis. People working in the surgery department maintained more than 450 different sutures and fifty different stainless-steel staples (which, in this small hospital, were worth more than $100,000). Also, supervisors working in surgery would manage surgical implants, such as artificial hips and knees that were worth thousands of dollars each. Although many of the items were on consignment, the individual managers were still responsible for maintaining a very expensive inventory. Essentially, surgery personnel managed an inventory greater in dollar value than the inventory maintained in the MM warehouse that served the entire hospital. The surgery scenario was only one example of the entire problem associated with the nonstock situation.

The hospital laboratory ordered 750 different nonstock items, such as reagents, on a weekly basis, and the radiology department ordered 500 specialty catheters and guide wires and even stored and ordered all of the radiology film with little help from MM.

The rationale for managing these supplies in the various departments was that they were unique to each and did not require storage in the warehouse, and so didn't require the services of MM. At first blush, one might think of this reasoning as sensible. However, after carefully looking at it, one can find a flaw in the process. It is the responsibility of MM to deal with the replenishment of *all* supplies, which includes ordering, receiving, stocking, and delivering supplies to the end user. When MM did not provide that level of support for all supplies, people making considerably more money than those working in MM were doing tasks that should be performed by lesser-paid employees.

The manual process involved using a multipart form (usually four copies). I found most hospitals with an automated MMIS still used the manual process for nonstock supplies originating in the departments. Furthermore, every item requested was handwritten on the form. The following scenario best describes the convoluted process for handling nonstock supplies that was in place prior to the development of our system.

Consider a head nurse in charge of the surgery department who requires a new type of implant requested by an orthopedic surgeon and does not delegate the task to another employee (normally due to trust and accountability issues). Acquiring the implant (and all other nonstock items) involves the following steps:

- The nurse acquires a purchase-order (PO) number from purchasing.
- The nurse contacts the vendor by phone and places the order, a process that often entails being placed on hold and waiting for returned calls.
- After placing the order, the nurse forwards a copy of the nonstock request to MM for matching with the packing list accompanying the item when it is actually received from the vendor.
- Oftentimes the handwritten orders have generic descriptions

(almost always without the manufacture's number) for the items ordered, and they don't resemble any description on the packing list furnished by the vendor. Such vague documents submitted by the departments can generate follow-up phone calls (and missed calls) for verification of the fact that what was received was indeed the item ordered.

- After the receipt is processed in MM, the nonstock requisition is attached to a copy of the purchase order and the packing slip, and then the packet of papers is forwarded to accounts payable (AP) for processing the check for payment to the vendor.

- Before payment is rendered, the packet is forwarded to surgery to verify that what was ordered was indeed the item that was delivered to the department. That action means the OR director must pull out the copy of the receipt, verify that yes, they have the correct item, and then send the packet back to accounts payable. The AP clerk expenses the item to the using department, which ultimately appears on a general ledger expense report that the end user must review at the end of the month. Remember that at most hospitals, this process occurs literally thousands of times per year (even to this day).

This whole nonstock ordering process was the most cumbersome and aggravating system for everyone involved. The diagram shown on the next page is a graphical depiction of what was just described.

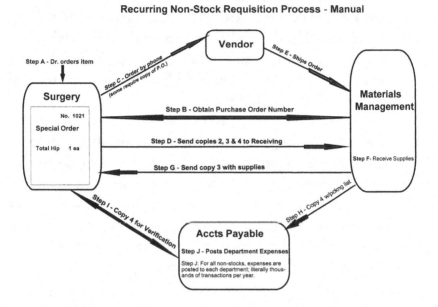

Figure 1 - Nonstock Requisition Process without MMIS

The consequences of this process cannot be overemphasized, as virtually every department manager in the hospital got involved, some occasionally, others spending countless hours on a process that should never have been part of their jobs in the first place. Nobody in the hospital should find it necessary to deal with a vendor when an item has been previously ordered by MM. After the research is performed and product choice and cost parameters are established for placing the first order, there is never the need to type or handwrite a request ever again. Rather, all activities related to acquiring its replacement should be accomplished by the MM department, period. This is not a territorial decision, it's a logical one. The MM staff knows everything necessary for placing subsequent orders.

The process for acquiring stock items from the warehouse is relatively simple:

1. Items are normally ordered from requisition lists and submitted to MM.

2. POs are created for replenishment of supplies.

3. Items are received and the receiving copy of the PO is forwarded to AP.

4. All items are automatically charged to the departments by the system.

When considering the design requirements for the system, there wasn't any reason nonstock items couldn't be handled in the same manner as the stock items, so we combined the two processes into one. Our motto regarding item identification was, "If you can touch it, give it a number." As soon as the item was given a number, only that number and quantity desired needed to be submitted to MM for processing. It was one of those rare opportunities (especially in the early eighties) when we were able to witness right before our eyes a computer saving time on the processing of thousands of transactions.

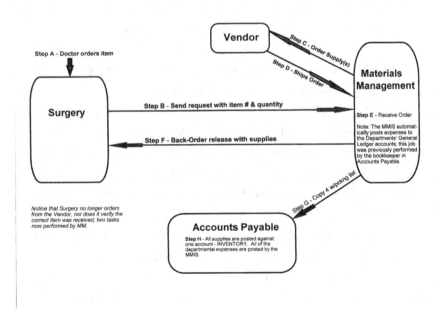

Recurring Non-Stock Requisition Process with MMIS

Figure 2 - Nonstock Requisition Process Using MMIS

BRINGING NONSTOCKS TO THE
WAREHOUSE AS STOCK ITEMS

When Lentz and I brought the system to perform at a high level of efficiency for managing the items in stock (a mere 1,100 items), I began my campaign for acquiring the responsibility for bringing more items into the inventory. Items for consideration were those used at least once per month, both stock and nonstock.

When I arrived at the hospital, my staff was not known for its ability to perform at a satisfactory level. Therefore, it was a gradual process for gaining any kind of confidence by others that my staff could competently manage the stock items in the warehouse, much less the nonstocks. Even after we began to receive high marks from the departments on how well we improved our level of service, managers were still reluctant to relinquish any of the responsibilities involving the supplies they managed. It turned out to be a huge sales job on my part, one department at a time.

Since the biggest consumer of supplies was the surgery department, I chose it as my first candidate for a makeover. Some have asked me why I didn't try working with a smaller department for my first experiment. First of all, MM was getting rave reviews on its improved performance for handling the stock items, and I had no doubt we could do the same for many of the nonstocks. Jane, the OR manager, was a relatively new director for the hospital when she took charge, and she wanted to promote herself as a manager who could work well with others. I seized the opportunity and arranged to meet with her in surgery.

When we finally met, I asked to take a look at her sutures inventory. I was stunned by the amount of supplies sitting in her department. As mentioned earlier, there were more than 450 different sutures (not including the steel sutures). Some individual items would have a quantity of at least twenty boxes, and they were so old the boxes were fading (indicating a large amount of dead inventory). I asked her if I could take on the responsibility for managing the sutures in the hospital warehouse. It was obvious she was apprehensive, but I told her she could keep a working level of sutures in the operating room.

Furthermore, I told her that she could set the reorder levels for all of the sutures moved to the warehouse. What I did not tell her was as soon as the MM system gathered enough usage data, I would turn control of the levels over to the computer. I told Jane if I ever back-ordered a suture for her department, I would personally escort her to the hospital president's office to lodge a complaint. Rest assured, I briefed my staff if we *ever* back-ordered a suture to surgery, *ever*, I wanted to immediately be made aware of the problem so we could correct it. This one project was rather traumatic for both the surgery staff and my own. We had to make room in the warehouse for the new inventory and then make sure we never ran out of supplies. The surgery staff did have their working sutures inventory, but it was one-sixth of what it was before the change. To replenish that inventory, shopping guides were used instead of the nonstock requisitions. By moving the sutures into the warehouse, they became stock items.

After two years of perfecting the system and having the MM staff well trained, we were able to convince other department managers we were up to the task of monitoring their supply levels for them. With their cooperation, we were even able to set levels for their nonstock supplies and began reordering supplies for them. As a result, we made it so the only time a department manager ever needed to be involved with submitting a nonstock request was when requesting it for the first time.

The system produced the necessary pick-lists (that included both stock and nonstock supplies) and in turn suggested purchase orders were created for the buyers in the purchasing section for replenishing the levels of stock in the warehouse and satisfying the requests for the nonstocks. Eventually, reduction in labor was realized in virtually every department throughout the hospital, so much that departments like surgery, physical therapy, and nursing all relinquished 5 percent of their next annual budget so MM could increase its support for them.

That's it! The hospital employees eventually learned that all they had to do when ordering any supply item was send the request to MM and forget about it. It took some time for surgery personnel to get accustomed to the idea, but once they did, they realized they had bigger fish to fry and began to trust the MM staff to take care of their supplies. If the MM staff is competent and provides the proper level of service, that trust becomes a reality. There were a few managers who felt like they were losing control and it took longer for them to accept the new method, but they finally came around.

MAKING BIG CHANGES FOR THE ORGANIZATION

Rules Applied:

5. Be an Effective Communicator   *6. Embrace Change*

7. Lead with Confidence   *13. Be a Team Player for the Organization*

20. Control the Bottom Line ... of the Organization

Unlike most other departments, what we did in MM impacted everyone in the hospital. As a result, I looked to find procedures that would benefit all departments as well as MM. I owed it to the organization to make such improvements a reality.

For me, implementing new ideas was a gradual change. For others, it seemed as if there were too many changes, and they were coming too fast. We all had to focus on the ultimate goal, which was to make improvements for the betterment of the organization.

Surgery no longer used nonstock requisitions for recurring requests, so they did not have to handwrite their requests for items that had been ordered before. It's important to note that the traumatic part of the transition lasted maybe five days; the new process was so much easier for both departments that it set the groundwork for even bigger changes in the not-too-distant future. I don't want to say that it was a "whistle while you work" atmosphere, but the working relationship between both departments was certainly much more amicable. Later on, one of our employees would go up to the operating rooms, gown up, scan the suture shelves, and then place orders for them. The end result was that sutures were being managed by staff members making 40 percent less money than the surgery staff. Within six months, we reduced the value of the suture inventory in the warehouse from $125,000 to $22,000, and we were able to get a $28,000 credit from the sutures vendor for the dead stock they agreed to buy back from us. In addition, during the remaining two years I worked for the hospital, we never ran out of sutures. Every critical item in the inventory had a safety level established that precluded the system from giving it a reorder point of zero. When the system attempted to do so, an exception report would be generated to alert the purchasing agent. The success of the sutures conversion to stock was the launching pad for many more projects to follow. During the three-plus years of developing and using the system, we transferred an incredible amount of supplies from the hospital departments to the warehouse. We increased the number of line items in our inventory from 1,100 to more than 4,800. By doing so, we relieved the other departments from the responsibility of managing the supplies, and we ordered virtually all nonstock items for the hospital.

Later in this book, I will refer to some of the institutions I visited regarding the entire manual process for supporting the acquisition of nonstock items. It amazed me how every hospital handled them in the same manner as just described. Later on, we even extended the application by giving item numbers to services.

5. GETTING SOME EXPOSURE

In early 1983, a little more than a year after we began developing our system, we were getting a considerable amount of attention about it from medical-supply sales reps. Because they visited other hospitals in the Northwest and spoke about our progress, I began to receive calls from materials managers who would ultimately pay us a visit to see what we were doing. While we were getting so much attention, Lentz and I were invited to speak at the IBM users' meeting, which was referred to as the ECHO (Electronic Computing for Healthcare Organizations) conference. It was being held in May 1983 in Monterey, California. The purpose of the conference was to allow members to share software applications developed on IBM hardware that could possibly be of use to fellow users.

Back then, Microsoft's PowerPoint and Corel's Presentations were still in development, so we had to use 35mm slides. I hired a photographer to take pictures of our computer screens, and we needed all of the three months to get ready. Today, it would be a presentation that could be prepared in one afternoon.

During the presentation, the response was overwhelming; there were hospital managers in attendance for both materials management and information systems who were fascinated with our approach to automating the materials-management (MM) department. Our egos were inflated so much, we almost had to rent a larger vehicle to get us home. Although I had plenty of feedback prior to the conference suggesting we had something that could be of value to others, this meeting was the first validation by complete strangers that we were onto something. Needless to say, the adventure could be labeled as nothing less than a great success, and we lived with that sensation for quite some time. We didn't immediately act on that feeling, but the activities that followed in the ensuing months were done with the memories of that meeting in the back of our minds.

TAKING ON A BETA SITE

In late 1983, Gary, the hospital president, called me to his office to tell me the hospital administrator at Tuality Community Hospital was in need of a new MM system. He wanted to know if I thought our system would be of benefit. I informed him that if the MM staff at Tuality was willing to put in the required effort, we could make it happen. I promised to call Tuality's materials manager and see what I could do.

Tuality is located in Hillsboro, Oregon, which is a suburb of Portland located about a hundred miles from The Dalles. I'd never had any reason to know anyone at Tuality until after Gary approached me. When I did call Steve Huson, the director of MM, he would be talking to someone he had never met but had been told by his boss supposedly had something that might be of benefit to him. I had no idea what he was thinking when he answered, but it had to be awkward for him; yet he was gracious and expressed a sincere interest in what I had to say. I invited him to pay us a visit in The Dalles so I could demonstrate the system in action. Think of it—he was going to visit an unknown peer who developed a system in a small rural hospital. To the hospitals located in the Portland metro area, our hospital was a tiny dot at the edge of the Oregon high desert.

Well, Steve made the trip out to see us, and he came with an open mind, expressing a sincere interest in what we had to offer. He also brought Steve Barrett, his warehouse manager, along with him. After the first thirty minutes of the presentation, they were duly impressed and began asking me how quickly we could install the software so they could turn their department around. Unlike my department when I took the job in The Dalles, they already had an automated MM software package in place. It was not one of the best systems on the market, and when he saw what we were able to accomplish, Steve wanted to trash his system and make the switch to ours. Everything happened so fast, I had no idea what I was getting myself into. Supporting another hospital three hours away required flawless software, good documentation, and impeccable on-site training—all of which we had none of. Yet we decided to press forward and make it happen. To be quite honest, it was no way to perform an online conversion, though it certainly showed Steve's willingness to take a risk to make it work. Looking back, if the installation at Steve's hospital had failed, it could have been a career stopper for me *and* him. I never considered that possibility at the time, but it could have been catastrophic.

Within six months, the hospital was up and running virtually without incident. Steve and his staff thanked me many times for the new materials-management information system (MMIS), and the improvements to their operation that came about since its implementation. As a side note, I am thankful for the fact that this hospital was the only one where I personally performed 100 percent of the on-site training by myself. When I agreed to assist Steve and his staff, I didn't know what I was thinking when I thought I could pull off such a stunt alone. That portion of the project had failure written all over it. It was both scary and exhilarating. Had it not been for Steve and his staff's trust and support, it never would have happened. More than twenty-five years later, Steve retired from his position having been a solid user of the software throughout all those years. He knew how to get the most out of what the system had to offer.

The system was up and running in two hospitals now. However, during the beginning months, there was a great deal of telephone traffic between the two hospitals, and it could not have been possible had my own staff not been so supportive.

TESTING THE WATERS

Rules Applied:

5. Be an Effective Communicator   *7. Lead with Confidence*
12. Instill Teamwork

Even though our offices were a hundred miles apart from each other, Steve and I became teammates when it came to getting the software installed and running at his facility. Steve and his staff were open to suggestions for making the transition a smooth one, and our employees also worked well together over the phone.

It was not an ideal acquisition for Steve and his operation, but we were both keenly aware of the fact that, as managers, our credibility was on the line. We can proudly say that the entire experience was a positive growing experience for each of us.

From the success at Steve's operation, after only six months online with our MMIS, the positive reports were overwhelming. It was as if Steve and some of the metro-area medical-supply sales reps had initiated a campaign to promote the system. I received several calls from other hospitals located in Oregon and southwest Washington asking when the system would be available on the open market. Although I was always willing to share what I was doing at my own hospital, there wasn't much I could offer any of the callers, since we did not have plans for selling the system. Some came to visit me at our hospital and usually left taking ideas they said were of help to them, yet it was obvious they wanted more. What was really happening was that I was spending a great deal of time away from my duties at the hospital. We were having fun, but it was also becoming overwhelming; my staff performed admirably in the way they conducted so many tours for others. I won't say the extra activities were taking anything away from them, because they had perfected the way they performed their daily tasks. However, we did spend quite a bit of our time entertaining guests. It was a good feeling to see the staff working with such confidence and pride; quite a difference from when I met them just two years earlier. After about two and a half years, I asked my supervisors to have the staff cross-train into each of the sections within the MM department. Within three months, all of the employees were able to work in the warehouse, receiving supplies and delivering them to the hospital departments; central supply and distribution, where they used barcode scanners to inventory supplies in departments throughout the hospital; and purchasing, as buyers who performed all tasks without assistance. After the cross-training was completed, it became much easier to schedule vacations and take on special projects. Obviously, I was not dealing with a union shop.

BITTEN BY THE ENTREPRENEURIAL BUG

Even though Steve's request at Tuality was a complete surprise at the time, curiosity from other hospitals didn't always happen by chance. Our hospital was a member of Health Futures, a consortium of seven small hospitals from virtually all corners of the state of Oregon. One of the functions of the consortium was to have the materials managers meet bimonthly to review upcoming contracts. All contracts were negotiated by Intermountain Healthcare (IHC)—a supergroup that had many mini-groups like ours hire them to negotiate our purchasing contracts for us. I considered these meetings to be little more than boondoggles, as I believed the majority of the contracts could have been reviewed and approved simply by using the US mail system (e-mail didn't exist back then). The contracts were already negotiated; in fact, an individual from the consortium had been hired to do just that: negotiate contracts. We simply rubber-stamped them to make it official. Aware of the heightened attention I was getting about our software from the vendors, I needed some feedback from other materials managers without them being aware of the fact that I wanted their reactions. The success of Steve's operation at Tuality gave us our first validation that our MMIS had some merit, yet I wanted to see if I could get even more interest from outsiders. Therefore, I made a proposal to my fellow members at one of the meetings.

I suggested, "Instead of always meeting here each time, why don't we rotate the meeting place and go to each of the consortium hospitals to get a personalized cook's tour of each operation?"

Some of the members were not too excited about the prospect, since they lived less than an hour away from the meeting place and lost only half a day to attend. Most of us were required to travel more than two hundred to three hundred miles to attend and lost almost two days in the process. Ultimately, the group approved and voted the cook's tours to be instituted, beginning in July 1984. Nate, a consortium member from Merle West Medical Center in Klamath Falls, was an assistant administrator with many of the same responsibilities I had in The Dalles. We kind of hit it off and usually had lunch together when attending the bimonthly meetings. He was so enthused by the idea of the cook's tours that he volunteered to be the first hospital on the tour. I didn't want to wait any longer, so I made sure our hospital was number two on the list.

Time flew by and before we knew it, we were visiting Merle West, which was located at the very southernmost part of the state, just nineteen miles from the California border. Though the city itself had a population of only seven thousand, the hospital served a much larger population located throughout the surrounding areas. I already mentioned that in The Dalles, we lived eighty-four miles from anywhere, and that at times it was a challenge to conduct business at the hospital. After my visit to Klamath Falls, I got a whole new appreciation for just what it means to be isolated. There is no getting around it: Klamath Falls is in a remote location, because no matter how you look at it, you are almost three hundred miles from anywhere (265 miles from The Dalles, from nowhere to nowhere). It was easy to understand why Nate quickly volunteered his facility for the first cook's tour; he wanted a break from making the long trip.

Coming from the north, the hospital was the first facility you saw, sitting on a hill that overlooked a huge lake immediately across from the highway (actually a 250-mile two-lane road). The hospital was a nice-looking two-hundred-bed facility, operating with an inpatient census at about 55 percent capacity. It was the only acute-care medical facility for more than a hundred miles to the north, south, or east and sixty miles to the west, accessible only by way of a mountain range often impassible during the winter months. All kidding aside about the locale, what struck me most was that it was a beautiful, professionally run facility that was able to attract qualified professionals to work there. At the time, the only real industries were farming and logging; the hospital was the biggest employer in the city serving the area. It was a good feeling when everyone showed up for the tour, especially considering how difficult it was for many (actually most) to get to Klamath Falls. Liz, who was Nate's materials manager, conducted the tour. Nate still went on the tour with the guests, but he let Liz field all of the questions.

They had an automated MMIS that would never have met my needs, yet Liz expressed satisfaction with it. She was concerned about running out of supplies, so the on-hand quantities for many of the supplies appeared to be rather high. Liz's justification was that since they were three hundred miles away from their suppliers in Portland, she had to elevate her reorder points. She insisted the practice was necessary, despite the fact that the hospital had the same contractual delivery requirements for the vendors as the rest of the consortium where, weather permitting, next-day delivery was guaranteed. Nate told me on the side that Liz had back-order problems on items stocked in her warehouse, and he supported her policy of elevating the reorder points. The procedure in place was evident when walking through the warehouse, as she had a bulk storage area that took the majority of the space in the warehouse. As a result, items ordered from the warehouse were being pulled from bulk case quantities rather than from boxes or even by individual units, which would be located in the loose storage area. For example, they would purchase several cases with six boxes of syringes at one hundred per box, no matter how long some of them would sit in the warehouse, rather than pulling, let's say, from a shelf with just two boxes that could have been sitting on a shelf rather than on top of a bunch of cases of slow-moving inventory. There was a special storage area where office supplies were located, with a separate cage to avoid pilferage. Their practice was to purchase items like pens, pencils, and note pads by the gross. With the amount of inventory in that cage, they could have opened a retail office-supply store and competed with the local stores supporting the entire population of Klamath Falls.

Liz said, "By buying in bulk, I am able to get a good price break on almost all of the office supplies."

I felt obligated to ask the question, "Do you think the carrying cost for maintaining excess inventory is justified?"

Again, Nate stated, "Based on our locale, I support her policy." I admired Nate for supporting her in front of the group.

When we took time for a coffee break, I slipped into the purchasing office on my way and asked the two buyers for usage information relevant to office supplies. For the five top usage items, Liz had on-hand quantities that would last the hospital more than four years for each of those items sitting inside the cage.

OUR TURN

In September 1984, two months after the visit to Klamath Falls, it was our turn to host the bimonthly meeting at our hospital in The Dalles. Visitors to our department from outside organizations had become a common occurrence, so the event didn't require any special preparation by my staff. This visit was an opportunity for my staff to strut its stuff. It had been a long three-year journey that brought us to the point where we would be showcased for our peers from outside organizations. The warehouse and central-supply areas were spotless, the purchasing section had all of its paperwork up to speed (in- and out-baskets were empty), and the staff was ready—not just to present, but to answer any questions the visitors might ask of them. At that point in time, it was no longer necessary for me to do all of the talking, as every member of my staff was able to talk about not only their own duty section, but any section within the department. When our visitors first arrived, I asked Joyce Johnson, the warehouse clerk, to give our guests a tour of the place, suggesting she start by first showing them suture alley and then swing by the office-supplies area. All of our guests were surprised we were stocking sutures in the warehouse. Two in the group interrupted Joyce at the same time and looked right at me (so much for turning it over to my staff).

Richard from Rogue Valley Memorial Medical Center located in Medford, Oregon, took the lead. He was very animated and incredulous. "How could your OR supervisor possibly agree to let you keep sutures in the warehouse, and why would you *want* to store them here?"

I explained, "I admit, it was a gamble on my part, but I was confident the system was performing at a level efficient enough to where we could trust it to not let us run out of supplies. Please understand, the OR supervisor was not ecstatic about the idea in the beginning. I let her establish the minimum stock levels for each of the sutures, so the computer would know when to reorder each item. I told her if I ever ran out of a stock suture, I would personally escort her to the hospital administrator so she could lodge her complaint. What I did not tell her was that after the computer had gathered enough usage data—no more than four weeks' worth—I was turning control of the minimum stock levels over to the computer."

The crowd laughed and someone asked, "How well is *that* working for you?"

I replied, "Well, I haven't made any trips to the administrator's office with her yet." More laughter.

I continued, "When the initial load of sutures was transferred down here, there were 448 line items valued at over $125,000, and after six months, that same suture inventory of regular sutures is now valued at about $28,000, with no back orders, *yet!*" Instead of laughing again, the crowd just nodded their heads in approval.

Another person asked, "What did you mean when you said *regular* sutures?"

"The sutures inventory does not include the steel sutures, which have just been transferred to our control." I then pointed to the next set of shelves where they were stored.

One of the guests quipped, "I would never want to have that responsibility. My OR supervisor is another Attila the Hun."

I responded, "Off the record, Jane was just like that until we successfully took over control of the sutures. Now we work well together as a team." All members of my staff were nodding their heads in agreement.

After the sutures discussion, Joyce continued with the tour by heading over to the office supplies.

Nate immediately asked, "Joyce, where are your bulk supplies located for the fast movers, such as pencils, pens, and note pads?"

Joyce calmly looked at Nate and said, "This is it."

Nate said, "No, I mean, where are the bulk supplies that back up this stock in case you have a great demand for some items?"

Joyce beamed as she explained, "We had such an area before, but since the computer manages the reorder levels, and with next-day delivery by our office-supplies vendors in Portland, we no longer need to keep such great quantities in our inventory."

Nate was beside himself and snapped his head around to look at me. "You have only eight number-two pencils on the shelf. How could that possibly be enough to support an institution of this size?"

He asked *me*, but Joyce didn't see that Nate was looking at me when he asked the question, so she responded, "After Tim met with all of the department heads and convinced them to order only enough supplies to last until the next week's order arrived, the departments changed from ordering pencils by the box to ordering by the piece. Now that we go out to most of the departments ourselves and check their stock levels for them, we are able to make sure we only order what they need. If a department head has an abnormal request for supplies, we process the order with a flag that tells the computer to ignore the amount when calculating the minimum stock level. We are able to satisfy any request within one day to satisfy their needs, and since we are maintaining the levels for their stock items, the only time they order supplies from us is when they are ordering new items." I wanted go over and hug Joyce and give her a big kiss, but thought better of it.

Nate looked at me and said, "If Joyce is any indication as to what all of your employees are like, it's no wonder this operation looks so professional. You intentionally had her show us this area for *my* benefit."

I responded, "I know you doubted me when I questioned the need for so much bulk stock at your facility, so I thought, *seeing is believing*. However, we would have shown this area even if you and I hadn't had the discussion at your hospital."

Nate immediately asked, "What would it take for me to have your software in my hospital?" I was unable to give an answer because I just didn't know how far my administration wanted to go with giving our software to other hospitals. It was at that moment I realized that no matter how much support I was getting from my administration, sharing, selling, or even *giving* the system to other hospitals would never be a decision I would be able to make on my own.

TEAMWORK AT ITS BEST

Rules Applied:

5. Be an Effective Communicator   *12. Instill Teamwork*

This event exemplified the fact that my employees worked as a solid team. Joyce's confidence combined with pride in her work represented success in every sense of the word. It was a proud day for everyone on my staff.

MM wasn't my only responsibility at the hospital, as I was ultimately responsible for the overall performance of many of the hospital's support services. The pharmacy, respiratory therapy, cardiopulmonary, dietary, housekeeping and laundry, and central sterile processing departments were also members of my staff—over a third of the employees at the hospital. Fortunately, I had outstanding department directors and supervisors managing the day-to-day operations of those areas. Nevertheless, I made sure I saw all of them on a daily basis, and in return, I had their support for the way I was changing the MM department. They were able to see how MM was affecting all hospital departments in a positive way. I loved managing people, and all of my department directors were great team members. I came to the conclusion that managing people in a totally different environment was an area that appealed to me.

The success with Steve's operation at Tuality broadened my perspective as to the implications of what our system might be able to do for other hospitals. Seeing the satisfaction on the faces of Steve and his staff was such a rush; it was difficult to adequately describe my feelings. I would never have met these people by focusing on just my own operation, and though I wasn't directly involved with them on a daily basis, I saw that we did change their lives in the workplace for the better. As all of this activity was going on, one sobering thought hit me like the proverbial lead balloon: *What would happen if I installed the software in an operation that was not well managed?* For example, what would happen if we *did* give Liz our system? I realized I might find out, sooner than later, because Nate was obviously pleased with the site visit and told me he would be getting back to me. I might be getting an answer to that question very soon.

SURPRISE LESSON FROM AN INDIAN GURU

In 1982, the Bhagwan Shree Rajneesh, a self-proclaimed Indian guru, and several thousand of his followers moved to the Big Muddy Ranch just outside Antelope, Oregon, a small farming community (population seventy-five) located sixty miles from The Dalles. The people who belonged to the cult called themselves Rajneeshes and they renamed the ranch to Rajneeshpuram; they also took political control of the town of Antelope and changed its name to Rajneesh. Many of the followers were wealthy and gave all of their earthly possessions to the Bhagwan when they joined the cult. Some may remember that the Bhagwan bought more than 130 Rolls Royces with the money and was often seen driving them through the community to demonstrate his influence over his followers.

Without attempting to give a complete history lesson on the Bhagwan (easy to find on the Internet), I will summarize by stating that his followers sought election to two of the three seats on the Wasco County Circuit Court. Fearing that they would not get enough votes, they decided to incapacitate as many voters as possible in The Dalles, the population center of Wasco County. In order to do so, they initiated the single largest bioterrorist attack in US history by using a strain of salmonella to contaminate ten different salad bars at restaurants throughout the city of The Dalles. The attack was performed between August 29 and October 10, 1984. Of the 751 people infected with salmonella (my twelve-year-old daughter was one of the victims), 45 required hospitalization. The victims of the outbreak ranged from two days old (just after his mother was infected) to eighty-seven years old. Fortunately, no deaths were attributed to the attack.

To some, the statistics do not seem to be so devastating; however, this small town of about eleven thousand people was supported by a hospital with only a hundred acute-care beds, and imagine what the first couple of days were like after the salmonella had spread throughout the town. When the initial attack took place, the hospital was overwhelmed with patients in the ER, and the physicians had no idea as to what the cause was for so many patients all at once. The ER was impacted so severely, patients were put on stretchers that were scattered in the hallways of the hospital. At that point in time, we in MM were enjoying measurable success with our MMIS and its ability to maintain adequate supplies for supporting our patient population, except I missed one important feature that put us in a bit of a predicament: the ability to react immediately to a major medical event.

During the 1980s, it was common for computer departments to batch major processes to be run during the evening so valuable processor time would not overload the computer during the day. Part of that thinking was probably a carryover from the batch-processing mentality from the days when keypunched cards were used for data entry. Anyway, one of the applications we allowed to be processed during the evening run was the assemblage of the suggested-order list (SOL). At the time, it seemed like a luxury just to be able to get it the very next day; just four years earlier while in the air force, I was accustomed to getting an SOL on a weekly basis. Well, because of the attack by the Bhagwan and his followers, my thinking was altered. First of all, imagine the effects a salmonella outbreak can levy on a community—we used toilet paper at a phenomenally high rate because of the amount of diarrhea and vomiting resulting from the outbreak. In addition, we used one week's worth of isolation gowns and sterile gloves in one day. Under normal circumstances, such an increase in usage would not be of concern if the event triggering the unexpected activity was going to last for just one or two days, especially since we maintained two weeks of supplies on the shelves. Because of this tragedy, I learned the first day of such an event is only the beginning of what's to come, and we needed our system to have the ability to respond to it while it was happening. In other words, the second day of an event is the most demanding for supplies because the hospital is then at full capacity with patients. The day before, patients were still being admitted throughout the day. Therefore, replenishment of supplies must arrive in the warehouse from the suppliers on that second day. Our problem was, we were unable to produce an SOL on the afternoon of the outbreak, which would have created the necessary purchase orders for replenishing the depleted supplies.

Since we were unable to produce an SOL on demand, we were scrambling on the second day to call vendors and have replacement items express shipped to arrive that same day. Our sales reps were very responsive and understood our dilemma, to the point where some of them actually drove supplies to us from Portland in their own vehicles because the company trucks had already been dispatched before we called for supplies. Meanwhile, Lentz was able to respond to my request by noon on the very next day of the outbreak, and gave us the ability to request an SOL on demand. From that point forward, we were able to respond immediately to a major medical outbreak.

LESSON LEARNED

Rules Applied:

5. Be an Effective Communicator   7. Lead with Confidence

The catastrophe that unfolded as a result of the Bhagwan's attack on the residents of Wasco County was, of course, unexpected. The initial response was pure pandemonium, and we found ourselves at the hospital in a survival mode.

After we dealt with the immediate needs of the patients coming through the doors, we had to evaluate what went wrong and what would be needed to keep the same type of situation from occurring in the future.

We learned a valuable lesson from someone we had no desire to be receiving a communication from in the first place.

Even though it took more than a year to prove the Rajneeshes were responsible for the outbreak, the local community suspected them as the reason for the event from the very beginning. Therefore, the voters showed up in record numbers, and the Rajneeshes' attempt to take over the county circuit court was thwarted. For me, I was taught a valuable lesson that allowed us to tweak the system to be even more responsive than before the outbreak.

PLANTING THE ENTREPRENEURIAL SEED

In November, less than four months after the visit by the Health Futures group, Lentz and I went to COMDEX, a computer trade show that was held in Las Vegas. To be honest, it was a boondoggle where we had a great time. On our second day, we went to a fast-food restaurant for lunch. When we first arrived, the lines at the counter were rather long, so while Lentz and I waited at our table, we talked about future developments for our system. When lines at the counter finally dwindled down, Lentz offered to go up and get our lunches for us.

While I waited for him to return, a nicely dressed gentleman who was sitting at the table next to ours said, when I looked his way, "Hi, my name is Bob Campbell. You two seem to be rather excited about your work. What's it all about?"

That simple question resulted in us having lunch together. We met for dinner that evening, and two weeks later, Bob flew Jan and me to meet with him at his business located in the San Diego suburb of Vista, California. Bob owned his own PC hardware and software shop and was looking to see if we might be able to do something together with our project. Unfortunately, because our software was operating on a midrange computer and Bob's company only used PCs, we were unable to form a collaboration. Nevertheless, Bob did infect me with the entrepreneurial bug. The idea of risking my own security and not having a job with the hospital didn't seem as insurmountable a prospect to me. I still had doubts as to my ability to make the move, but not enough to dissuade me from at least considering it in the future. Bob was a small-business owner, but it would have been easy to confuse him with an executive for a major corporation. He was polished, unassuming, and very confident in all that he did. It was an exciting experience. Unfortunately, the timing was not right for either party. Nevertheless, Lentz, Jan, and I credit Bob with confirming our belief that we would be able to do it on our own when afforded the opportunity. The idea that he would even consider looking at us as people he could invest in boosted our own confidence in what we were doing.

I came to realize that no matter how much I enjoyed what I was doing on the job, I could only *suggest*, not *decide* on matters regarding what I could do with proliferating the system, Lentz's availability for working with me, and how I decided to use my own time on the job. It was a sobering thought that left me feeling, well, empty. Up to that point, I thought I knew where I was headed with my position at the hospital, and I certainly could not complain about Mark Scott, my boss, who supported me in all I was doing with the overall plans for the hospital. I definitely enjoyed going to work each morning, but had it not been for the competence of my staff, I would never have been able to work on perfecting the MM system in the first place. My position in The Dalles was good for me as it related to hospital administration, yet even though the ancillary services mentioned above were operating smoothly, they still took time away from what I really enjoyed doing: looking for ways to improve efficiencies of the MMIS. The entrepreneurial seed planted by Bob Campbell was beginning to take hold, and I found myself in unfamiliar territory—that of uncertainty. I knew no matter what decision we made, Jan and I would be looking at some major changes in our lives. She had supported me many times before, but we had finally settled down and acquired some stability in our lives. Anyway, it didn't do much good to belabor the point until there was a *definitely maybe* situation to contemplate in the future.

I decided to continue with the present course of action, tweaking the system while exploring what possibilities might follow. It was important to find out if there was a sincere interest in our system from other hospital MMs. Finding out would confirm it wasn't just my inflated ego that made me think our system was unique and more efficient than systems on the open market. The visit by the consortium members and the IHC rep was a success; we were able to get a group of six materials managers from different-sized hospitals favorably impressed with the system. Although it was a small beginning, all I could do was hope the grapevine would begin to fill with some positive chatter. Only time would tell.

It was a crazy time in my life. Here I was a loyal, hardworking executive for this hospital located in rural America. I had a boss who supported me in all I was doing, and yet for some reason I had this gnawing desire to do something more. I thought I would be working at the hospital for years to come. The only way I saw my situation changing was if something were to become available at a company like American Hospital Supply. I would probably jump at that opportunity.

DO I REALLY WANT TO DO THIS?

I considered myself lucky that Steve and his staff at Tuality were beginning to operate on autopilot and required little of my time for support. Just as I was beginning to relax, Mark informed me that Nate from Merle West had called, and it looked as if we had another hospital in need of our system. Of course, I had a good idea of what I might be getting myself into, but somehow I still looked forward to the challenge. This time, I would be supporting a hospital located 265 miles due south of us, where access was limited to a two-lane highway. It could not have been more inconvenient to get between two different spots on the map. Normally it would be an easy commute, but there was no commercial flight between the two cities, so driving was the most common way to travel. Getting to Klamath Falls required giving up almost a complete day to driving the distance. When I came up with the idea of having the consortium visit each hospital, I never really considered just how much more remote some of the hospitals were than our own. A common phrase flashed through my mind: *Be careful what you wish for, you might just get it.* Since I was a private pilot, I decided to fly down to Merle West and spend only two hours getting to and from my destination instead of the six hours it took to drive.

Although I was comfortable with my position at the hospital, I was beginning to get an idea of what it might feel like to be an entrepreneur. Yet I still had the security of knowing I could rely on a paycheck from the hospital during tough times. In December, just four months after my first visit to Klamath Falls, I found myself back on my way to Merle West to install the tapes furnished by Lentz, and to give the MM staff a two-day seminar on how to build their database. I took our two sons (ages fifteen and thirteen) out of school to fly with me. This allowed me to turn the trip into a father-and-sons event. The training at Merle West was satisfactory; however, I had my doubts as to whether they would be ready for an online conversion in just six months, a thought that haunted me as we flew home.

6. WHAT A DIFFERENCE A YEAR CAN MAKE

It was in early January 1985 that I received a package from the Health-Care Materials Management Society (HCMMS) confirming my appointment as one of the speakers for its spring seminar in Las Vegas at the MGM Grand Hotel. These gatherings gave materials managers a forum for sharing solutions to problems experienced at their own health-care facilities. The package included a seminar agenda with the date and time for the presentation, as well as hotel reservations. I ordered nonrefundable airline tickets with a Saturday night stay-over, so we could afford for Jan to accompany me. Air traffic was regulated at the time, and round-trip tickets from Portland to Las Vegas cost $800 each. In contrast, with a Saturday-night stay-over, a trip cost $350 for both round-trip tickets. Surprisingly, HCMMS agreed to pay the hotel bill for all five days, so Jan and I found ourselves looking at an affordable five-day vacation in the spring.

With confirmation in hand, I had four months to prepare for my presentation. I was able to use some of the slides Lentz and I made for the IBM ECHO conference, but we'd made some significant improvements and updates that prompted the need for even more slides. With more than three years of data in the system, there was credible information and screens that allowed me to adequately demonstrate the capabilities of the system. In fact, I was confident I could have most materials managers salivating over the idea of having so much information at their fingertips.

When Chris Tew left American Hospital Supply (AHS) to go work for a company that specialized in products relevant to eye surgery, he was replaced by Tom Alamano, who was Chris's boss at the time. Tom went back to the field as a sales rep because the job paid more; it was common for good sales reps to make more (much more) money than the executive staff at AHS. When Chris's position became available, Tom took the opportunity to take over a territory Chris had cultivated during his years on the job. Tom obviously had the right experience for the job, and the two of us also hit it off extremely well. During the ensuing two years, Tom was able to see our project mature into a system that was truly performing as intended. Eventually, Tom approached me and said he thought our system was so far ahead of what his own company had to offer its clients that he thought the people from his corporate office needed to look it over. Of course, I told Tom I would be willing to speak with his folks from Chicago.

VALIDATION FROM THOSE IN THE KNOW

Two weeks after I met with Tom from AHS, Mike Hudson called me from his office in Chicago. He was the vice president and general manager of American Data Services (ADS), a division of AHS. He said, "I have heard so much about what you are doing at your hospital, I was wondering if I could come out with some of my staff to see your operation in action." They had their own materials-management information system (MMIS) that operated on Texas Instruments' midrange computers.

ADS was part of a huge corporation that didn't just sell its computer system outright to hospitals, it also gave it to clients willing to commit to purchasing a high volume of medical supplies from AHS in return. Even though I had a lot of respect for the AHS organization, I always referred to this giveaway concept as the same as letting the fox in the henhouse, where the relationship with the vendor was almost *too* amenable.

When I first came to The Dalles, I was at a knowledge deficit when it came to systems on the market. After all, my exposure to materials-management (MM) systems was limited to the system developed by the air force. At the time, I was a career officer, and MM was not my final career goal, so I didn't have a reason to be curious about systems available on the civilian market. The air-force system was based on sound logistics management, but as mentioned earlier, the automated system was always behind the times because it took so long to get enhancements implemented. While we were developing the system at The Dalles, I took every possible opportunity to visit other hospitals that had automated MM systems; I wanted to acquire new ideas for our system. At the time, there were three major companies offering systems on the open market: Enterprise Systems, Inc. (ESI) of Chicago; Continental of Shawnee Park, Kansas; and ADS of Chicago. When I was afforded the opportunity to visit a hospital in Salem, Oregon—about seven months prior to the call from Mike at ADS—I jumped at the chance to look at the system and was given a comprehensive demonstration. To them, I was just another box-kicker interested in an automated system, so the people giving the demo were very candid about their feelings as to what they perceived as the pros and cons of the ADS system. Knowing that I was in the process of developing my own system, they were quick to point out all of the deficiencies of the ADS system, advising me what not to do. It was not until much later that I realized just how valuable my trips to the other MM operations were at the time. During the three-plus years we were developing our system, I had an opportunity to perform site visits at different hospitals with an MMIS from each of the companies mentioned above. I gleaned information I could never have gotten if I had been a vendor competing with the companies that developed the systems I was evaluating. I never walked away with new ideas; rather, I learned what not to do. Essentially, I was able to get an up-close-and-personal look at my competition. Of course, we weren't competitors in the world of MM systems—not at the time, anyway.

Ten days after Mike called, he came to our hospital for a presentation along with five members of his staff in Chicago and Maureen Flaugherty, an AHS sales representative from Southern California. All of them were as professional as the people I'd met on my trip to AHS headquarters two years earlier. At first, Mike's demeanor was rather guarded; however, within the first thirty minutes, he was having a difficult time controlling his enthusiasm. Although he didn't have any MM experience, he did understand automation in the field. After all, he was the top dog (at maybe thirty-five years old) of a multi-million-dollar company that sold automated MM systems. I am of the belief that a decent manager doesn't necessarily need complete technical knowledge of the systems he or she is managing. Rather, I believe possessing overall experience managing *people* is the most important quality of a senior executive. Mike's questions were very direct and to the point; it was obvious he was comparing the various features of what I presented to that of his own system. We spent the entire day together, had a working lunch in the hospital cafeteria, and then at seven o'clock, Jan joined us for dinner at one of the local restaurants. I did the majority of talking throughout the day, but at dinner it was Mike's turn.

Mike said, "Tim, we are all very impressed with what we saw today. I will be contacting your CEO in about six weeks to make an offer for purchasing the rights to the software you developed at the hospital. I need to draft a formal proposal for my boss, who has already told me he will take my recommendation to the board of directors, which doesn't meet until July 1."

It is important to understand, Lentz and I had no rights to the software, because we developed it while employed by the hospital. ADS could come in and essentially take the software with them. If so, I would just go back to being an assistant administrator at the hospital, with nothing further to do with the development of the software.

Mike continued, "It is our opinion that we have just seen the best materials-management software system right here in your hospital; it is far better than what we have today. When I come back with the offer, I am also going to offer you a job for managing a new division of our company that would run on IBM equipment. You can bring Lentz and anyone else with you that would be needed to start up the division. I am certain you will be very busy developing and marketing the software to hospitals around the nation."

It had been a long three and a half years, but it looked as if the effort was about to produce a bonus never imagined at the onset of the project. I remember it was difficult for Jan and me to go to sleep that night, as it looked like we were going to be packing our bags once again. Whenever I was given job opportunities through the years, Jan and I never let geography be the reason for not accepting a job. After all, I was actually given a choice to accept or reject the last three assignments from the air force, and we accepted all of them. We were certain we could find something nice to talk about after we lived in Chicago.

Going to work the next day was a challenge, because I knew it was quite possible I might be leaving everything behind that we had worked so hard to build over the past three and a half years. More important, I would be leaving a group of people I had grown to love and admire; without a doubt, missing them would be the most difficult part of the process. Other than thanking my staff for putting on such a great demonstration, I couldn't really share the potential end result of their efforts until much later. Besides, up to that point, nothing was in concrete. I just had to wait and press on as if nothing was going to change, and of course I needed to prepare for the presentation I was giving in Las Vegas just two weeks later.

URGENT MESSAGE: THE NEW AHS MANAGER WANTS TO MEET ASAP

After the visit from Mike and his staff from ADS on Friday, our world became rather surreal. Jan and I found it difficult to return to work on Monday morning. I had an executive staff meeting to attend, but I didn't have my heart in it; I just wanted time to sit back and think things through. When I returned from the meeting, there was a note on my desk advising me of a call from Pat Noonan of AHS in Yakima, Washington. The message indicated it was important we speak as soon as possible. I knew of him because I had received a notice from AHS announcing that Pat was the new regional manager responsible for both the Yakima, Washington, and Portland, Oregon, regions. I called Tom at the Portland AHS office, and he told me Pat was his new boss and the first AHS manager to be given the responsibility for two regions at the same time.

Pat introduced himself and said he'd heard the folks from ADS paid me a visit, and he wondered if he could also come and see our system. I thought the urgency in his voice was rather odd. However, other than an imposition on time, I didn't have any reason to deny him the opportunity, especially since ADS was already talking about the possible acquisition of the system. Besides, I certainly had the presentation down to a science, and it wouldn't take any real effort to put on another show. Ultimately, we agreed to meet early the next morning.

Pat arrived at 8:30. I found him to be very friendly and professional; in other words, the typical AHS manager I had learned to know and respect. After exchanging greetings and getting acquainted with each other, I asked, "How did you hear about our system while living in Yakima?"

He said, "Working for American allows me to hear quite a bit. Besides, there has been a great deal of talk about what's going on here. Tom Alamano has been keeping me up to speed about the development of your system."

He continued, "Chris Tew has also been talking about you for quite some time. In fact, I just spoke with him yesterday after you and I talked; I told him I was coming to see you today. Chris is anxious to hear from me after my visit with you." At this point, Chris had not worked for American for more than two years.

I didn't quite know what to think about that revelation, but I didn't have time to ponder over it; I just needed to proceed with the demonstration. "How much do you want to see, Pat?"

"I will stay for as much as you are willing to show me."

With the ADS visit behind me, I felt it could not hurt anything if I gave him a serious look at the system. After all, it was quite possible Pat could ultimately be referring potential clients in the future. At first, I gave him a cook's tour of the hospital and took him over to meet Lentz. As I began my normal routine, it became only too obvious he definitely knew quite a bit about the field of health-care MM.

After two hours, he declared, "Tim, you have an incredible system, and it is much better than I imagined."

Once again, I found another fan of our system. Throughout the morning, Pat inquired about my expectations of the possible move to ADS. He then questioned me as to how fond I was of the idea of moving my family to the Chicago area. I had no idea as to where he was leading with this line of questioning, but I decided to just keep on listening to him throughout the day. He kept on referring to the harsh winters and the hot and high humidity summers of the Midwestern states. By the time noon rolled around, Pat invited me to lunch and asked if Jan and Lentz could join us. He obviously had an agenda, since he wanted them to be included.

TRULY UNEXPECTED

At lunch, Pat shocked us by saying, "I think it would be a mistake to let ADS purchase the rights to the software."

Since he was a manager for the parent company of the one I had just presented to only four days earlier, it did not make sense for him to make such a statement. I told him, "We don't have a choice, because the software does not belong to us. When ADS returns with an offer, the decision to sell will not be ours to make."

Pat countered, "That is true only if you do not do something before ADS comes back with an offer."

We all looked at him in disbelief, and I immediately responded by saying, "We don't have the money to purchase the rights to the software, and what would we do if we did have the money?"

Pat then stated the obvious, "Start your own company so you can market and sell the system, just as ADS would."

The three of us sat there speechless, waiting for him to go on.

He obliged. "All you need to do is get enough money together to submit an offer before ADS returns with their own."

With our current positions at the hospital, the idea of giving up all the security we currently had, and the potential opportunity with ADS, seemed a bit over the top. Considering our lack of resources, what Pat was suggesting didn't seem feasible. Pat was the one leading the discussion by asking questions about a possible venture for starting a company from scratch. I taught college courses in the curriculums of business and management, which included discussions about entrepreneurs (defined as the risk-takers of the business world). Yet I didn't have any practical experience to fall back on and only knew of the textbook examples. Jan seemed pretty calm and collected, but I felt she too had to be thinking along the same lines as myself.

Pat made a case that helped my negative feelings dissipate somewhat. "Tim, American's corporate environment would frustrate you to no end. Even as the head of the division, you wouldn't have the immediate access to Lentz you are now accustomed to. Every time you and your staff would come up with new ideas for development, they would require committee approval."

He continued, "I'll bet when you now come up with new ideas for the system, you present them to Lentz, the two of you collaborate, you agree on a desired outcome, Lentz gets right to programming, and you get your desired results in short order ... and you move on. You definitely would not have that kind of flexibility, access, and most important, the quick turnaround time you are currently accustomed to getting here at the hospital."

His argument was oversimplified in that Lentz worked for the CFO and wasn't part of my staff; even so, he was right on the mark. Lentz and I had a special working relationship, and it was very productive, especially considering the fact that we both had other jobs to do. Our administration was very progressive, and I was part of the management team initiating several major changes throughout the organization. Many of those changes involved Lentz and his staff and would take up much of his time away from the MM project. Nonetheless, Lentz and I were devoted to completing our project and found ways to follow our own priorities. I was fortunate Lentz was just as excited about the project as I was; otherwise, my jobs could have been thrown into the projects queue like all the rest and I would just have had to wait my turn.

As Pat spoke, I reflected on the fact that even though I wanted more of Lentz's time, I was pretty lucky with what I already had, and I definitely didn't want to deal with another bureaucracy. I was already fighting to get my way with further developments as time progressed, and I knew I could not possibly afford to slow down the pace. Essentially, Pat was throwing cold water in our faces in a way best described by the popular phrase, "He gave us the rest of the story." When considering the prospects of going to ADS as a future employer, Pat was able to give us a necessary piece of information that could only come from someone who understood the company's infrastructure. Nevertheless, we would be leaving all of the security we had at the time or the prospects for the future with ADS; the idea of giving all that up seemed like the most unlikely choice we would ever make for our family and my career.

Soon, the discussion changed from talking about ADS to looking into the possibility of finding investment money to start our own company. We continued to talk about actions that could possibly threaten our job security—a part of our lives Jan and I had enjoyed for almost twenty years. Pat mentioned he had a friend who was also a regional manager for AHS and might be looking for an investment opportunity. Before we knew it, we were seriously looking at the possibility of leaving our jobs and venturing out on our own. We really didn't have any answers at the conclusion of our meeting, but Jan and I knew that in the very near future, our lives would never be the same.

We all agreed we were dealing with a small window of time. ADS was expected to be back with an offer within five weeks. Of course, we weren't certain the administration would accept an offer from us. However, I thought that if I had a check in hand, they would accept the offer because of that old adage, "One in the hand is worth two in the bush." There was no guarantee ADS would return with an offer (in fact, the hospital executives did not believe it would be back), and with June 30 being the end of the fiscal year, any significant amount of money given to the hospital would give an unexpected boost to the bottom line of its financial status.

The most difficult task at hand was coming up with a figure we thought the hospital might consider appropriate. Mike from ADS never mentioned how much he might offer the hospital, so we really didn't have any idea as to the correct amount. We were shooting blindly at a target, and we ultimately decided on $100,000. Of course, the big obstacle was raising the money, not only for purchasing the rights to the software but for starting and sustaining a business long enough to attain a steady income for covering the overhead.

When Jan and I called her father, Gordon, on Saturday morning to tell him about the outcome of the ADS visit, he was happy for us, knowing it was a goal we both wanted. After Pat called on Monday and requested the meeting, I didn't bother to tell Gordon because, at the time, I thought it was just another scouting trip from an AHS manager. When I called him *after* our day with Pat, it was a whole different Gordon on the other end of the line. He responded, "I agree with him." Somebody he'd never met! "You have too good of an opportunity. Why give the system to a big company like ADS?"

He did a one-eighty from the conversation we'd had on Saturday Jan and I explained there might be some money out there to try to start a company, but we didn't have the means to pull it off. Gordon was not real happy with the end result of our call, but he realized we didn't have a good answer to make it happen. After spending ten years in the air force, I had never networked with anyone living in the world of entrepreneurs. Furthermore, I certainly didn't have any friends or acquaintances who had enough spare money to invest in us.

Just before we were about to leave for Vegas, Jan received a call from her physician who informed her of some lab results that precluded her from being able to travel. To make a very long story into a shorter one, Gordon—someone I admired ever since I met Jan—joined me in Las Vegas.

MORE THAN A PRESENTATION

It was nice having Gordon there, as we were the best of friends and it would have been far too long of a time to stay in Vegas by myself anyway. The two of us had a chance to talk in greater detail about the fact that Jan, the kids, and I could be moving to Chicago later in the summer. Gordon asked if I had given much thought to the idea of not going with ADS and starting a new company like that guy from American had suggested. I explained we did not have the funds, in that we were still recovering from the loss of the money it took to transition from military to civilian life. Furthermore, I explained I didn't know anybody else with enough money who could possibly bankroll such a venture. I truly believed my best bet was to make the move to Chicago and climb the corporate ladder at American. I was going to be starting pretty high up the ladder from the get-go. Gordon said he was finally getting accustomed to us living on the west coast, and as a father and grandfather, he was being just a bit selfish by wanting us to stay. I told him I didn't blame him, but I reminded him that both of us understood geography could not be a determining factor when considering executive job opportunities. He reluctantly agreed and we changed the subject.

Before we knew it, the big event was upon us. The only negative was that I had never given a presentation about the system without the aid of the computer and my skilled staff. Not to mention our showcase warehouse, which provided a great backdrop for a quality demonstration. Instead, I was using just a 35mm slide show as the means for showing a software system.

During the years in which I worked at broadening the scope of the system, Gordon and I had met at least twice a year at family gatherings, and he would listen to me describe the activities related to my job. He always showed a sincere interest in what I had to say. When Gordon informed me he wanted to join the audience for my presentation, I was both surprised and honored. He is a retired air-force officer, and at the time he was an executive engineer with Lockheed who had given many professional presentations throughout his career. It was nice that he wanted to be at a presentation on subject matter that was completely out of his realm of expertise. Nevertheless, I looked forward to getting his feedback afterward.

I decided to introduce myself to each person at the door as he or she entered the room. I then took the microphone and greeted the audience of forty-plus with a hearty "Good afternoon." I found myself ready to dig in and give it my best. The first slide was up on the screen, and the immediate positive response by the audience told me it was going to be a good session. Indeed, it was a *great* session; the audience was engaged, and there was genuine interest in what I had to say. I did my best to describe the basics of the system and demonstrate its various features by sharing the story about the coveralls and lessons learned from the Bhagwan. The idea was to demonstrate that the system was definitely designed from the ground up. I found myself dealing with a friendly crowd and knew within five minutes that all of the aggravation it had taken to reach that point was well worth it. When my time was up, nobody left the room. I continued to field questions about the system. When I did finally end the session ten minutes late, about a dozen people were waiting to speak with me. Most of them took the time to just stop and congratulate me on a good presentation. One man, however, was obviously stalling, standing away from the rest so he could be the last one to speak with me. When Gordon was the only other person standing there, he told Gordon to go ahead and speak with me first, but Gordon said he was with me.

The gentleman then turned to me with a huge smile and outstretched arm, and said, "Hi, Tim, I'm Dave Maclachlan and I want to buy your software." A response I definitely did *not* expect to hear.

As we shook hands, I replied, "Hi, Dave, but the system is not for sale."

He quipped, "Yeah, but it will be, and I would like to be your first customer."

I couldn't say anything about ADS because of our nondisclosure agreement, so I said, "At the moment, I am not at liberty to talk about what could possibly be on the horizon, but there definitely *is* something in the works."

"I'm not surprised, Tim. So when *will* you be able to say something?"

"I should know in about five weeks."

With a sense of conviction, he said, "Okay, I will call you then with the intent of following up with a site visit."

After that exchange, I finally said, "You are obviously in the market for a system, Dave, so how big is Valley Medical Center, and where is Renton, Washington?" (His name tag indicated place of employment).

He said, "Valley is a 305-bed acute-care hospital located just ten miles south of Seattle, and we are operating with a 75 percent occupancy rate. We are not the biggest hospital in the Seattle area, but we are definitely the busiest." Their workload was twelve times greater than what we experienced in The Dalles.

Although I didn't say it aloud, I thought to myself, *Wouldn't it be something if I could report for work on my first day at ADS with my first paying client already in the queue?* Well, that was certainly putting the cart before the horse; at least there wasn't any law against positive thinking. As I was talking with Dave, I could see Gordon standing behind him looking extremely pleased. While Dave and I were swapping business cards, I thought about how I couldn't wait to hear what Gordon had to say.

GETTING IMPORTANT VALIDATION

Rules Applied:

3. Look the Part   *4. Play the Part*

5. Be an Effective Communicator   *7. Lead with Confidence*

8. Be Consistent; Be Decisive

The intent of this commentary is not to be self-serving— rather, it is meant to stress the fact that such an occurrence could never have come to fruition had I not followed and believed in the rules listed above.

Essentially, one could say that I spent at least three years preparing for this presentation. This one event was just the beginning of something that escalated beyond what any of us could have imagined possible.

Although I was knowledgeable about my subject matter, it was definitely a different venue than presenting in front of others on my home turf. Instead, I was presenting in front of my peers on neutral ground, which meant I had to be better than average.

Undoubtedly, I got everything I hoped to get out of the experience and more. The positive feedback was overwhelming, and I was anxious to share the experience with Jan and Lentz. It was obvious our approach to automating MM had definite appeal to other materials managers. Granted, this group was a small sampling on which to base that assumption, but the overall response by the majority of the people in the room was positive enough for me to walk away with that feeling.

Just when I thought it couldn't get any better, there was even more unexpected feedback. After Dave left the room and I began gathering up the surplus handouts, it was Gordon's turn to comment about the previous hour. This distinguished, conservative gentleman who rarely raised his voice blurted out, "Tim, you *have* something here. It has the potential of a new gold mine!"

I stopped to look at him and said, "Thanks, Dad, and let's hope ADS comes through with their offer so I can start digging for that gold."

He replied, "No, Tim. I think this Pat guy was correct; you should convince Lentz to go with you and start a company of your own."

I was shocked yet gratified by Gordon's enthusiasm. It didn't take long, though, for reality to kick in. I said, "Dad, thanks for your vote of confidence, but as I said earlier, I don't have the funds to start a company and still be able to support the family. I just don't see it happening."

It was obvious he was not pleased with my response, but he did not have a comeback other than, "We are going to miss the chance of a lifetime."

I chuckled to myself because Gordon said *we*. I remember thinking, *I really sold Dad on the system.* We wrapped things up, gathered our luggage, and headed for the airport.

AN UNBELIEVABLE GESTURE THAT CHANGED EVERYTHING

When I returned to work at the hospital, it was difficult to focus on anything, as I was in a state of uncertainty. For a brief time after my return from Vegas, time seemed to move in slow motion. It was the Sunday morning after the presentation, and we were having a casual family breakfast when the phone rang. It was Gordon.

He immediately said, "If Jan is there, please put the speakerphone on so we can talk as a group."

I complied, and Gordon and his wife, Sue, were both on the line.

He began, "Tim, as I told you in Vegas, I don't think you should go with ADS and move to Chicago."

I again replied, "Dad, I don't have the funds to do it on my own, and as soon as ADS buys the rights to the system, I won't have any say in the matter."

Gordon said, "I will retire from Lockheed three years earlier than planned and become one of your investors, as well as start working with you full-time in any capacity you think will be of help to you."

I looked at Jan, and we were both in shock. I immediately replied, "Dad, no! We cannot take such a chance. We would not able to live with ourselves if we failed." Jan was nodding her head in agreement.

Gordon quickly responded, "I was in that audience last week, and you had them eating out of your hands."

"Dad, that was only a sample of the materials managers in the field, and I agree, the audience was very receptive to what I had to say. I question as to whether or not it would have been the same if I was a vendor up there trying to sell them the software."

Gordon quipped, "You sold it to Dave from Valley."

"Dad, I love you, but Dave only expressed interest at a conference in Vegas, and we didn't even talk about price or anything of the sort. There are no guarantees he will come back to look at our system."

Each time I came back with a reply, Gordon countered with a statement showing his overall belief in the fact that we could pull it off. He was confident there was only one decision to be made, and that was to form our own company.

Without a doubt, I was taken aback by Gordon's strong reaction to the presentation. I remembered thinking to myself, *Maybe I am cut out to be a salesman.* Yet there were many more questions that needed to be answered before we could continue this discussion with any seriousness.

Gordon then said, "Tim, why don't you set up a meeting so the three of us can meet with Pat, Chris, and Lentz? This is Sunday, so what do you say we meet next Friday or Saturday? I will fly up there tomorrow so we can prepare for it."

I asked them to wait for a minute and then put the phone on hold so I could talk with Jan about what was happening. I said, "Jan, I don't know about this. I'm not sure we are ready."

She then said, "Tim, it seems like you let the genie out of its bottle.

I don't think we can say no. After all, we are just talking. That can't hurt, can it?"

I agreed, reluctantly, and told Gordon, "We look forward to seeing you, Dad."

To me, it was *here we go again* with another whirlwind of activity—and if we *did* start our own company, this time it would be even more traumatic than when we left the air force. Back then, I made a decision that involved leaving a perfectly good job, yet it was a decision I never regretted because it was for Jan's health. This time, we were both gainfully employed and we were considering giving all of that up so we could do, what, create jobs for ourselves?

I couldn't believe what was happening. During the years leading up to this point, I had been hoping to join a large company like ADS. It was not as if I went to them seeking a job. Instead of having to submit a résumé and go through their vetting process, they came to me and said they wanted me. It didn't get much better than that. When I said I didn't have any thoughts about going it alone, I was serious. It wasn't that I was afraid of the idea of starting a company. It just had never crossed my mind, and why would it? The folks at ADS were duly impressed, and it was just a matter of a few weeks before I would receive confirmation they were making an offer to the hospital for the rights to the software. Furthermore, they were going to offer me a position as one of their executives, *and* I would head up a new division created for me (their words, not mine). After they did so, I had no doubt I would perform at a level sufficient to accomplish both my short- and long-term goals. I envisioned being part of that professional team I witnessed almost three years before. Why would I even consider the idea of giving all that up for a career with unknown rewards and certain instability (at least in the short term)? Besides, I didn't have any experience when it came to running a company, not to mention that it would truly be a start-up company. It meant we would be starting from the ground floor. Yet it seemed like everybody around me thought I could pull it off.

I found this idea of starting a business of our own to be a bit ironic. Up to that point, I had been teaching business classes for a local college, and part of the curriculum was to introduce the concept of entrepreneurship. I taught my students that entrepreneurs were known as risk-takers. I made a point of understanding every topic I covered in all of my classes and thought that such was the case with this topic. I was always taking risks related to my job, trying new concepts that had never been attempted before, and the majority of the time the risk proved worthwhile. When I took those risks, they were never so daring that the outcomes could threaten the well-being of my family. I always had the security of knowing I was going to get paid even if I failed (within reason). This was one of those times where I would be learning much more from a practical application than from a book or classroom, even if it was something I was teaching to others. In other words, I realized I had been teaching a concept I didn't fully grasp myself. It wasn't until I found myself considering the idea of risking the financial and job security I had come to enjoy over the years that I truly understood the idea of entrepreneurship. Just four years prior, I had been unemployed for three months after I left the air force, and I never wanted to find myself in the same predicament ever again. I had a wife and three kids whose lives were dependent on me making sound decisions when it came to providing their livelihood.

The next weekend, as promised, a meeting was held, with Gordon, Lentz, Pat, and Chris joining Jan and me in our home. Despite my concerns, I listened to those around me and decided to consider what they had to say. Without bothering you with all of the details, suffice to say all agreed to go forward and follow up with another meeting on June 20 that would include all of our spouses. One side note: two days after Pat returned to his home in Yakima, he wired $25,000 directly to my bank account. I was not expecting it, nor was there anything in writing describing what was expected in return for the money. He definitely demonstrated his commitment to the new venture and his trust in me.

I remember when Pat and I first talked on the phone about a name for our new company. He suggested the name Health-Ware—hoping the name had not already been used—and my first reaction was, "Great idea! I'll share it with Lentz and Jan." The three of us met in my office at the hospital, and as soon as Lentz saw the name, he said, "*Management,* we need the word management to show we are more than just a software company." Jan nodded in agreement, and we all decided on Health-Ware Management Company as the name for our new venture. It seemed to be quite a mouthful, but it flowed nicely when spoken. We later found that Lentz's contribution to the name was rather prophetic, as it wasn't long before we were sought after for consulting to other organizations. At about the same time Pat and Lentz came up with our company name, I came up with the name for our software: Computerized Logistics and Supplies System, or CLASS. This name was also approved by all, and we were ready to go forward with more pressing concerns.

BE CAREFUL WHAT YOU WISH FOR

Pat invited Rand, a fellow AHS regional manager from Memphis, to our first official board meeting. He was well aware of the deficiencies inherent with their own MMIS marketed by ADS. He was interested in getting involved with a new company that had a sound solution for the health-care industry. We met in Portland on June 20, 1985, at the home of Chris and his wife, Susan. Janice (Pat's wife) and Faun (Lentz's wife) also attended; Gordon's wife and Rand's wife were unable to attend. Everyone in the room was excited. We knew it would not necessarily be an easy road in the beginning, but we all believed we had the best product, and once we introduced it to the market the demand should be there.

Prior to the meeting, Jan did her homework by researching the formalities associated with the Rules of Incorporation and procedures for conducting a board meeting. As a result, she volunteered to be the secretary of the board, and ensured strict compliance with the rules and procedures throughout the meeting. At the onset, Jan conducted the meeting, until a chairman of the board was elected. Although her time in control was brief, her assertiveness caused me to take pause and make a mental note about how well she handled herself. She was dealing with proven executives with an adeptness I had only seen in someone with far greater experience. Pat even took notice as he discreetly pointed to her and gave a thumbs-up signal. I was very proud of her.

The board voted to appoint me as the chairman and CEO of the new company. For many, the ultimate career goal is to have one's own business, to be his or her own boss and answer to nobody. This concept, often referred to as the entrepreneurial spirit, conjures up the idea of complete independence. With this new position, I became an entrepreneur; however, I'd never had any great desire for independence or need to be the guy at the top. Granted, I was constantly striving to get to the top of the hospital's organizational ladder, but I was satisfied with the way my career was going at the time. I'd determined that the best way to reach my personal goals was to focus on perfecting the project at hand, so heading up a small business was the furthest thing from my mind. Yet I had been involved with the project from the beginning all the way to this point, and I felt there wasn't time for self-doubt.

It was a good thing I had more confidence than common sense, because we were definitely caught up in our own hype, and I would have ruined the fun for everyone in the room had I expressed my concerns. I always had a high level of self-confidence when working in my own area of expertise. However, I was never known to put that confidence behind something I had never done before, such as running a new company. I was good at my job at the time, where I had the necessary resources—from the hospital—to support my endeavors. I look back with total disbelief at the way I threw all caution into the wind, with my family in tow. It was just four years earlier that I had resigned my commission from the US Air Force, which had really been my only employer. I had never managed a company, much less started one from the ground up. There wasn't a true business plan. There was just blind faith in my abilities from those sitting at the table. Nobody was going to persuade them to change their minds, as there was a thick fogbank clouding the horizon. I was convinced had it not been for the fog, I might never have taken the risk, and I would have missed the experience of a lifetime. There was no doubt that starting a company from scratch with very limited resources would be much riskier than managing a project with the safety net of the hospital covering all of the overhead.

It was not until that meeting that I began to realize just how much responsibility and accountability I had agreed to assume. Granted, it was a small company—in fact, it could not have been much smaller—but for a period of nearly four years, my focus on the system had always been while under the employ of the Mid-Columbia Medical Center. I was given the charter by these people to take our software and sell it on the open market without the safety net of the hospital that gave me a monthly paycheck. In fact, Jan and I agreed to take a 60 percent cut in pay to keep our operating expenses as low as possible. In the beginning, the only way we could afford to live was by moving in with Gordon and Sue. The people around the table believed I could successfully lead the company and were putting their money behind me to make it happen. I willingly accepted the assignment despite the fact we did not have enough money to operate for more than six months, any computer hardware of our own to support CLASS, or anybody who knew anything about running a company. At the end of the meeting, there were huge smiles and high-fives going around the room. One emotion I didn't share with the others in the room was that I had a huge pit at the bottom of my stomach. I felt like I was in one of those dreams where you find yourself standing before an audience ... butt naked.

Health-Ware Management Company was officially incorporated on June 20, 1985. The final outcome of the meeting required immediate action by only three members of the board. Gordon was retiring from his position at Lockheed, and Jan and I were resigning our positions at Mid-Columbia Medical Center. It was difficult to hear Jan read the notes to the board, saying the words, "Tim and Jan will resign their positions, sell their home, and temporarily move their family to San Jose." My stomach did flip-flops, and I was feeling weak in the knees. Much like when I spoke in front of an audience for the first time and the butterflies disappeared as soon as I began speaking, my feelings of insecurity also dissipated as soon as the decision was made to go forward.

Jan was the first one to resign from her job so she could begin packing up for the move to San Jose. Her boss asked her to reconsider, in case we did not make a successful go of it; of course she thanked him, but declined. I, on the other hand, handed Mark two documents: an offer to purchase the rights to the software (contract included) with a check for $100,000, and my resignation with an effective date of August 31. The later date gave me time to assist the hospital with finding my replacement and, most important, to prepare for starting the new company. The contract stipulated that in addition to Mid-Columbia Medical Center, we agreed to support both Tuality Community Hospital and Merle West Medical Center for the cost of expenses only. By agreeing to this, Health-Ware started with three clients under its belt. Besides, ethically, it wasn't really an option to abandon both Steve and Nate, who had put their faith in Lentz and me when they were given the system.

I have been asked the question, "Why give him both papers at the same time? What if Mark didn't accept your offer for purchasing the rights to the system—why take the chance of him accepting only your resignation?"

First of all, the hospital executives did not believe we had anything of worth to put on the market. (Rodney Dangerfield was alive and well when it came to MM.) In addition, there was a quasi-profit-sharing plan in place for all employees that was paid at the end of the fiscal year, which was happening just nine days after I handed the check over to Mark.

Two weeks after I advised Mark of my imminent departure, I received a call from Mike Hudson at ADS. "Hi, Tim, are you ready to move to Chicago?"

"Hi, Mike, much has happened since you were here. Lentz and I joined with others and have purchased the rights to the software ourselves. We are going to market the system on our own."

Without hesitation, he replied, "Congratulations, Tim, I wish you all the best in the future."

"Thanks, Mike. That is very gracious of you, considering all you went through to look at our system."

"Tim, that's just business."

"If you don't mind me asking, how much were you going to offer the hospital?"

"Not at all; it was going to be $160,000."

"Thanks again, Mike. Perhaps we will meet again in the future." Fortunately, he didn't ask me what we paid for the system.

When talking with Mike, I spoke with confidence, but I knew I had just given away security for my family in exchange for a great deal of uncertainty. There wasn't time to belabor those thoughts, though. The decision had been made, and I had enough on my plate the way it was. I just needed to press forward.

DAVE FROM VALLEY MEDICAL CENTER WAS SERIOUS

After our presentation in Las Vegas, I told Dave Maclachlan from Valley Medical Center that it would be about five weeks before I could give him information about the availability of our system. Almost five weeks to the day, I received the most exciting phone call I could have ever hoped for at the time. It was Dave wanting to know if I had any news regarding the availability of our system, and he was hoping to make arrangements for a site visit. I told him we gave the system the name CLASS and that we had just completed the formation of Health-Ware Management Company. He immediately replied by congratulating me and said he liked the names for both our product and our company. He also said he was looking forward to being the first one to purchase CLASS. In the short time we had before his arrival, we were able to acquire business cards and stationery for our new company.

Dave arrived on July 10 with his hospital's controller, the Data Processing Manager, an accounts payable clerk, and Rose Thuney, who was his key assistant from the MM department. Like many times before, my staff gave a professional presentation that wowed our guests. The enthusiasm by all was overwhelming. For me, this time there was a different twist in that it could lead to an actual sale.

Afterward, Dave said the visit exceeded his expectations and he wanted CLASS for his own facility. He asked when I could go to his hospital to give a presentation to his entire staff. I don't know if I can adequately describe the emotions I was feeling at the time; however, I can say that this moment was huge. I remember thinking, *It can't be this easy.*

In August, Gordon and I found ourselves in Renton, Washington, to give the first presentation representing our new company. When we arrived, even before we turned on the computer, all members of Dave's staff were extremely excited to see us and wanted to know what it would take to implement CLASS. It was obvious Dave and Rose did a huge sales job and built up their expectations. Fortunately, we didn't let them down. As I introduced each new feature, Rose and Dave would interrupt me to mention how well it worked, how clean and smooth our operation in Oregon was, and one to emulate.

It was great to have Gordon there for the demo. He had a difficult time containing his excitement, and so did I. We ended the day on an incredible high, and Dave asked me for a formal quote that he could submit to his board of directors for approval on the purchase of CLASS in January of the next year.

ON OUR OWN

The following months were chaotic at best. Jan and I moved our family and household goods to San Jose in September 1985. Fortunately, Gordon and his wife had a six-bedroom home with three vacant bedrooms. Living conditions were not ideal for anybody involved, yet we all knew we were on a mission to make Health-Ware a success and that the living arrangements should be temporary. It goes without saying that Jan, Gordon, and I were all concerned about the future. We were well aware of the fact that the responsibility for the success or failure of the company rested squarely on our shoulders.

When we incorporated, we definitely did not have the resources to acquire even the smallest computer hardware to support our software. In addition, we couldn't afford to bring Lentz on full-time to program on a computer even if we owned one. The plan was for Lentz to work after hours at Mid-Columbia Medical Center until we could afford to bring him onboard full-time. He had access to the hospital's computer system as long as he was employed there. We kind of had the two critical items available to us. Yet we knew that with Lentz's responsibilities at the hospital, this arrangement was not going to be sustainable. He never was and still isn't afraid to put in the extra effort; he was just as committed to our success as the three of us in San Jose. However, we were attempting to sell an expensive piece of software that was going to have an impact on every health-care provider in hospitals that acquired it, which meant we needed Lentz available to support them on an as-needed basis. As soon as we sold it to another hospital, Lentz was going to be stretched to a point where he would more than likely snap.

To further complicate matters, as soon as we had enough money to acquire a computer and to bring Lentz on staff full-time to program it, where were we going to put them? We were working in Gordon's den in San Jose while Lentz and his family lived in Oregon. Health-Ware was incorporated in Oregon, and our move to California with my in-laws was merely logistical. Our first task at hand was to get Health-Ware on its feet. After we stopped blinking, the fog bank cleared just long enough for us to see that we had to become creative and find a way to make it all happen. We really didn't have enough money to start a company, yet we did so anyway. Fortunately, we didn't think about those problems; instead, they were just items on a to-do list that needed to be addressed. We were almost oblivious to the fact that there were major obstacles to hurdle, and the chances of us succeeding were slim at best.

THE TRUE ENTREPRENEURIAL EXPERIENCE BEGINS

After the move was complete, it was time to enact the plans established at the board meeting:

1. I was responsible for acquiring clients and basically growing the company.

2. Initially, Gordon managed the finances of the company (which were virtually nonexistent), and he took on the added responsibility for writing the CLASS user's manual. Eventually, he went on the road with me when I gave presentations; he often joked that he was my Vanna White.

3. Jan was managing the administrative duties, so she was the first point of contact with everyone outside of the company. Not

to belittle her job with Health-Ware, but she was acting like a "gal Friday" those early days; she did a little bit of everything. Later, she would become an expert on the system and find herself leading training teams at hospitals and clinics scattered throughout the country.

4. Although Lentz stayed on at his job in The Dalles, he was on standby for anything related to information systems for our company.

One of the most difficult aspects of starting a business is having enough cash on hand and/or credit to conduct business on a daily basis, especially when it comes to paying for travel expenses. When we started Health-Ware, Jan and I had a personal credit card that allowed payment to be made sixty days after the date of the statement. As a result, we used that card for charging all expenses for airfare, rental cars, and lodging for the company for all eleven years of its existence—a card that often carried a $20,000 balance we paid every month. Although we were personally responsible for payment, it would have been more difficult for us to conduct business without it. It was one expense we *always* paid on time.

INTEREST FROM THE COMPETITION ... SO SOON?

The three of us in San Jose were busier than we could have ever imagined. In the beginning, it was surreal as we took on the task of building the company from scratch.

We had been in San Jose for only two weeks when Jan came to me and said, "Tim, there is a guy named Greg on the phone for you from Continental Healthcare of Overland Park, Kansas; he asked for you by name."

After I answered, we exchanged greetings, and then Greg said, "Our company is interested in Health-Ware and wanted to know if you could visit with us, so you can demonstrate the features of CLASS."

It was a mystery to me as to how anyone from Continental even knew about Health-Ware, much less enough about it to ask for me by name. Health-Ware was incorporated in Oregon, and the phone number in San Jose was only one month old. In the beginning, we relied on word of mouth to promote our product, mainly due to a lack of funds. Anyway, this phone call sparked a fury of excitement among us and a great deal of speculation.

Greg said, "We will pay all expenses related to the visit."

I agreed to fly out the following week, which required three days of my time when considering travel time each way. When I arrived in Kansas City, I was treated like a VIP by the three men who met me when I stepped off the plane. They took me immediately to their office building even though the company was already closed for business. They wanted to show off their offices. Afterward, as we dined, the three Continental folks did their best to sell me on their company. Afterward, they returned me to the hotel and we agreed to meet early the next morning.

I wasn't really prepared to try to sell the company we'd just founded in June and did not really open for business until three weeks prior to my visit. I had to rely on what I used for the presentation in Las Vegas in May as the basis for what I was going to demonstrate. I was not embarrassed about the size of our company, as everyone in the room knew Health-Ware was a new company. The first task at hand was for both me and Continental's chief operating officer to sign nondisclosure statements (the second set of such documents I'd signed in less than six months). In other words, officially, the meeting did not exist unless we both agreed to disclose its contents.

I had been talking for about ten minutes, explaining how CLASS treated stock and nonstock items in the exact same manner, when I was abruptly interrupted by Continental's chief financial officer (CFO), who stood up and chided, "That is the dumbest thing I've ever heard. Anybody knows you can't do that because of issues with the GL [referring to the general ledger]. How can any of you in this room believe that what he did at that small hospital in Oregon could ever apply to anyone else in the country? Even if that fool in Seattle *did* decide not to buy our system, it's his loss."

Of course, with that short outburst, everything became clear as to why I was invited to Kansas. Dave from Valley Medical Center never mentioned he had looked at Continental's system, but I realized his choosing CLASS had something to do with my invitation to Kansas.

It was obvious everyone in the room was afraid of this individual, because nobody was willing to speak up and defend the decision to bring me out for the meeting. I realized by the tone of voice of this antagonist that at best, these folks would purchase CLASS and just put it away on a shelf, never to be seen again.

I offered, "You are right. Maybe someone could show me *your* system. We could look for areas that would be of mutual benefit and go from there."

Surprisingly, someone jumped up and said, "Good idea; it will only take us five minutes to bring the system up and running."

I must have looked sincere when I mentioned we could possibly have a meeting of minds, because the people in the room were only too eager to show me their system (probably so the CFO would leave the room). It became glaringly obvious that an agreement between our two companies was not going to happen. The CFO looked rather indignant as he waited for his staff to show me how a *real* system provides an automated solution for MM, then he left the room after five minutes. I sat through a ninety-minute hands-on demonstration of their system, willingly, and was not impressed, as their solutions were not much different from the solutions offered by ESI and ADS. Actually, I had been given a pretty good look at their system by the materials manager at Good Samaritan Hospital in Portland a year before. I thought I might see improvements in the key areas, but was pleased to see such was not the case. Although the results of my trip were nothing like I had imagined, I was able to acquire a thorough look at one of our competitors.

I knew I had nothing to fear when I went up against Continental in the future. The amazing part of that morning was I never showed anything else about CLASS after they finished showing me their system. That simple outburst by the CFO made it obvious to others in the room they were mistaken to have thought Health-Ware could have been of any use to their company. Instead, we wrapped things up and headed for lunch. Actually, I was able to return home a day earlier than planned. Although the folks at home were disappointed, all agreed the trip was worthwhile in that I was able to see this competitor up close and personal, and all at their expense. I knew I had gained some valuable insight into their company while they, in turn, obtained nothing (other than that *dumb* idea about treating stock and nonstock in the same manner).

After I returned home, I called Dave Maclachlan at Valley. "Hey, Dave, I just returned from a trip to Continental Healthcare's headquarters. You never mentioned you were considering MATKON as an MMIS."

Dave replied, "Oh, did I forget to tell you about those clowns? Just three weeks ago, a shipment with a bunch of equipment from Continental arrived on my loading dock without a purchase order."

He continued, "I called them to say their equipment was sitting outside on my loading dock and the forecast was for rain that evening. To say the least, the folks at Continental were not very pleased with me, telling me my CFO had told them it was a done deal. I told them they were misinformed, that I was purchasing CLASS from Health-Ware Management Company and they really needed to pick up their equipment."

It turns out Continental extended me the invitation to visit them just a few days after that incident with Dave.

After Dave finished his discourse about the incident with Continental, he changed the subject. "I just attended a conference here in Seattle and met Terri Cartier, who is the new MM at Evergreen Hospital Medical Center in Kirkland, Washington, just twelve miles north of here on I-405. She is in the market for a new MM system, so you should give her a call."

Before continuing, an interesting anecdote about Continental: one year later, the three top executives (including the CFO) were indicted for cooking the books and ultimately lost their jobs.

A REFERRAL BY OUR (ABOUT TO BE)
FIRST NEW CLIENT

Our contract with Dave had not even been formalized, and he was already giving us a referral. I complied with Dave's request and made the call. I found Terri to be friendly and easy to speak with as we arranged to meet just a week later.

She did have a unique request: "I am currently the director of housekeeping and laundry, but have just been appointed as the new director of materials management. I am not ready to have anyone from my new staff involved in the process for choosing a new system, so could we meet somewhere away from the hospital?"

A week later, Gordon and I drove the nine hundred miles to Kirkland, Washington, to meet with Terri. Since we drove right past Valley, we also stopped by to say hi to Dave and thanked him for the referral. He was more than gracious and wished us luck with Terri. Making a long story a bit shorter, because there wasn't a conference room available at the hotel where Gordon and I were staying, Terri had to settle with meeting us in my hotel room, where our computer was set up for the presentation. She was a real trouper, in that the hotel room was dark, and I did not have any visual aids other than our computer system.

Terri told us, "I only agreed to see a demo of CLASS as a courtesy to Dave from Valley, but I have already decided on ESI as my system of choice."

"I understand, Terri. However, I plan on changing your mind in fifteen minutes." She gave me a strange look, but she was a good listener. I was wrong, by the way. It took only ten minutes before Terri reacted.

As she was sitting next to me at the computer screen, she bent over with her head in her hands and said, "I don't believe it. I almost made the biggest mistake at my new job, and I haven't even begun working there yet. Thank you, Dave."

She then sat up, looked at me, and said, "I thought you had quite a bit of nerve when you told me you would change my mind in fifteen minutes, but I now understand why you did. Okay, let's go, I can't wait to see what else you have to show me."

Terri was sold, and there was no doubt about it. At about forty minutes into the presentation, she said, "It's obvious you are a fellow box-kicker and label-licker, and I look forward to getting advice from you as I take on the duties of materials manager at my hospital." After just ninety minutes, Terri was discussing plans for the implementation of CLASS in her hospital. It was the beginning of a friendship that still exists today, more than twenty-five years later.

One week after meeting with Terri, I found myself getting on a plane in San Jose. This time I was alone, and leaving for Merle West Medical Center in Klamath Falls, fulfilling my agreement to provide support for CLASS. The system had been installed at their facility almost exactly twelve months before, when I was still working in The Dalles. In July '85, just two months before I moved to San Jose, I took Mindy from my department to assist with the online conversion in Klamath Falls. She was a big help, and it was much easier than when I'd performed the conversion at Tuality by myself. When I arrived at Merle West this time, I found that at best, they were struggling with the system. I recalled my fears about Liz's ability to support the system when Nate first approached me about acquiring it. I realized this type of problem could occur with any organization that purchased CLASS, and it was one of those dilemmas one had to expect in this type of business. The purchasing ladies, Coy and Julie, were both pleasant and seemed to be good at their jobs, yet they were overwhelmed. It was obvious Liz didn't really understand the system and was causing problems by insisting their manual card system be maintained just in case the computer system broke down. Unfortunately, the main computer system was often shut down, with little or no notice from the folks in information systems (IS). When I went to IS to inquire about the shutdowns, I was alarmed at the lack of concern about the incidents. The programmers responded by saying, "That's the way it is, and materials management is going to have to get used to it, just like everyone else in the hospital." The IS department was under a facilities-management contract much like that of Valley Medical Center with Arthur Anderson and their

CFO, where CompuCare was the company providing a manager and two other programmers for operating the department. The manager reported to two bosses, his boss at CompuCare and Wes, who was the CFO for Merle West.

WHEN THINKING OUT OF THE BOX
CHANGED EVERYTHING

I was perplexed when I left the IS department and I just happened to walk by Wes standing in the hallway. He stopped me and asked, "What's wrong, Tim? You don't look so hot."

I was caught off-guard and responded (perhaps too candidly), "Yeah, you wouldn't either, Wes, if you were given the type of shoddy service I just experienced from the folks in IS."

Wes was not expecting such a response, especially about one of his departments; he immediately became defensive (his body language said it all) and replied, "Well, do you have a better idea?"

I did not expect *that* response (actually, I was embarrassed about the way I was so blunt with him). I had a split second to respond, "Sure, hire my company."

That remark really caught him by surprise (me too!), and then he retorted, "What do you mean *your* company? Who do you have that could run the department any better?"

It was obvious Wes was not pleased with his IS department, otherwise he would never have responded with such a veiled plea for help. I said, "Wes, if you fire CompuCare, which includes the IS manager, Health-Ware could assume the contract and I would hire Lentz from Mid-Columbia in The Dalles, who could probably be here in two weeks. Also, with Lentz as their manager, I will hire the two other programmers."

Wes looked at me in disbelief. "You really think you can pull that off?"

"I believe so, Wes."

A VERY LUCKY GUESS

Rules Applied:

5. Be an Effective Communicator   *8. Be Consistent; Be Decisive*

My encounter with Wes was obviously not planned. I was just lucky he was so dissatisfied with the IS department. Although I did not plan on approaching him about a facilities-management contract, I was able to respond with confidence when I discussed my dissatisfaction. Admittedly, I surprised even myself with my off-the-cuff reply, yet somehow I was able to respond with a plausible solution that appealed to him.

It was a brief moment that would ultimately have a profound impact on our ability to grow the company.

Since Merle West belonged to the same consortium as Mid-Columbia Medical Center, it would not have been a politically savvy move for Wes to offer Lentz a job. However, if I was the one doing the hiring, the move would not reflect badly on Wes. Although I didn't think Klamath Falls would be a place Lentz and Faun would choose to move to on their own, I knew Lentz was anxious to come onboard full-time with Health-Ware. I was relatively certain Lentz would accept the new job—after all, Klamath Falls *was* located in Oregon (barely), and the only requirement Lentz stated as a geographical requirement for Health-Ware was that it be located in the state of Oregon.

If Lentz agreed to take the job, the following would happen:

1. Lentz would work for Health-Ware Management Company, a feat I thought would not happen for at least another year.

2. Health-Ware would have three full-time programmers (at the expense of Merle West), not just one part-timer, and Lentz would not be stretched so thin.

3. Merle West would pay all of Lentz's moving expenses, a considerable chunk of change Health-Ware would have had to pay under any other circumstance.

4. Lentz would get a decent pay raise, and Health-Ware would receive a monthly check of $4,000 for the facilities-management contract.

5. In addition to having an IBM System/36 at our disposal, an IBM System/38 with qualified programmers was also part of the package. The advanced computer would give us the needed resources for developing software on a computer platform that could support the larger institutions.

I went back to the MM office to call Lentz. "Hey, Lentz, how would you like to quit your job in The Dalles and come work for Health-Ware Management Company?"

"What are you talking about, Tim?"

"I just spoke with Wes Simonson here at Merle West and convinced him to fire CompuCare and replace them with Health-Ware as their facilities-management contractor. Therefore, I am in need of a director to come here and manage the two new programmers I am about to hire. Are you interested?"

"Are you kidding?"

"Nope, and you get a raise, while Health-Ware gets a $4,000-a-month management fee. Merle West is paying us to move you, so can you be down here by Christmas?"

"I need to tell Faun, but I'm certain you can consider it done. This is exciting."

After I spoke with Lentz, I received a call from the secretary of Dave Arnold, Merle West's CEO, who told me Dave would like me to stop by his office before I left for the day.

When we met, Dave just wanted a status report about how well the MM department was doing with CLASS.

I told him, "Dave, I'm concerned about the lack of progress by the MM department, in that Liz has her buyers using the manual system in conjunction with CLASS. There was a problem with IS frequently shutting down the system during the day without notice, but it should be resolved in short order." With that comment, Dave looked at me and just smiled.

I continued, "Central supply does not have the expertise to perform the tasks associated with getting the distribution part of CLASS up and running."

Dave then asked, "Do you have any suggestions?"

"I might be able to bring a Health-Ware employee in on a full-time basis."

I was thinking about Cortie, a twenty-six-year-old woman who had been working in CS/SPD in The Dalles for the past two years, and had also been cross-trained to work in all sections of the MM department. From the day we hired Cortie in The Dalles, she proved to be a smart and positive addition to our staff. As for her coming to Klamath Falls, she was single, without family ties to the local community, and I thought she might take me up on the offer. Since I was going to be visiting Merle West on a monthly basis, I would be able to visit with her at the same time I came to support the IS contract.

Dave asked, "How soon can you have an answer about the new employee?"

"I should have an answer by the end of the day."

A new chapter for Health-Ware had just been initiated by selling its expertise in the area of management. I remember thinking, *If we can do a decent job with these facilities-management contracts, meeting payroll for new employees won't be as traumatic to the bottom line as first believed.* I didn't really think I would be as lucky with getting Cortie onboard as I was with Lentz, but with her positive attitude about everything, I thought she was the ideal person to manage the task at hand during my absence.

GROWING THE COMPANY
Rules Applied:

1. Use the Management Scale as a Guide   *3. Look the Part*

4. Play the Part   *5. Be an Effective Communicator*

7. Lead with Confidence   *8. Be Consistent; Be Decisive*

When I went to Merle West for this visit, I never envisioned myself being so bold as to suggest that the hospital was in such need of our experience (which I really had not defined beforehand). Honestly, it just happened that I went with my gut and offered solutions to what I considered to be problems with their organization.

No doubt I was decisive when I proposed our services were necessary, but I had faith in those I chose to assist me with the process. Admittedly, I had no idea as to whether or not we could pull it off, but my self-imposed standing of 7.2 on the Management Scale gave me confidence that my decision was a sound one.

Just ten minutes after leaving Dave's office, I was able to connect with Cortie in The Dalles. "Cortie, how would you feel about coming to Merle West to work as my assistant?"

She quickly responded, "You bet, Tim, on one condition. I will do it only if I am an employee of Health-Ware and not Merle West."

"Of course, Cortie, I wouldn't have it any other way. I need you to be my eyes and ears while I am out of town. I need to know what's going on behind the scenes here; I really have my doubts about the competency level here, and I know you are someone I can count on."

Just like Lentz, Cortie gave her two weeks' notice immediately after we finished our phone call.

With all of the good news, it was time to call Jan and Gordon in San Jose. When I reached Jan, I said, "Hi, Jan, would you put Gordon on the speakerphone so he can hear what I have to say?"

Jan said, "We are both here; what's up?"

"I have some good news for our company. I just negotiated a facilities-management contract for Health-Ware. We are now responsible for running the information-systems department here at Merle West."

Gordon asked, "What does that mean?"

"Well, for beginners, in two weeks, Lentz will be an employee of Health-Ware Management Company."

"What!?!" they both chimed in.

"Lentz will be moving to Klamath Falls and will be the director of information systems, but under our employ. In addition, we are hiring the two programmers, who will of course be on Lentz's staff, and we will receive a monthly management fee of $4,000 for our services."

Jan asked, "Are you serious, Tim?"

I responded, "Absolutely. With the terms of the contract, they will pay me to visit Merle West on a monthly basis and visit with the CFO to ensure we are in compliance with the contract. In addition to getting Lentz onboard and having a System/36 to use, Lentz will have access to an IBM System/38 to use for development, so CLASS can be programmed to accommodate the larger hospitals."

Jan then asked, "How is materials management doing with CLASS?"

"Not well, but I have one more surprise: Cortie just quit her job in The Dalles and will also become our employee to assist with preparation for the exchange-cart system portion of CLASS; she will arrive on the job at about the same time as Lentz."

"You have been pretty busy up there."

"I have a lot to tell you when I come home."

"We can't wait to hear the details, Tim? Having Lentz working full-time as a member of Health-Ware is huge." Without a doubt, we were all relieved to be bringing him onboard.

Before the folks moved from The Dalles to Klamath Falls, I found myself in Seattle on December 20 to sign the contract with Valley Medical Center, and I conducted the first phase of training for Dave and his staff.

Lentz and Cortie were both in Klamath Falls just two weeks after I called and asked them to come onboard with Health-Ware. Lentz stayed in his new home and slept on the floor while Faun, his wife, packed up their home back in The Dalles. Their willingness to risk their own security on our company was gratifying and humbling; just knowing others were willing to put their faith in me to succeed was a motivating factor for continuing with our current path. I was amazed that by New Year's Day of 1986, Lentz, his family, and Cortie were living in Klamath Falls only five weeks after that meeting with Wes in the hallway; just a year earlier, I was preparing for the Las Vegas presentation; and it had been seven months since I met Dave from Renton, Washington, who ultimately became our first paying customer. We all reflected on what a difference a year made in all of our lives, and we only wondered what the future had in store for us.

7. THANK YOU, ARTHUR ANDERSON

When Dave from Valley Medical Center made his decision to purchase CLASS as his new materials-management information system (MMIS), I was unaware that he did so against the wishes of his chief financial officer (CFO). During the beginning phase of the contract negotiations, Dave told me there had been some resistance from the higher-ups but never elaborated. He told me there wasn't any need for concern. He did explain however, that the controller who had accompanied him for the site visit in The Dalles had strongly recommended against acquiring CLASS. When looking at it from an objective point of view, one can easily conclude that the controller was spot-on. During their visit to our hospital in The Dalles, Health-Ware Management Company didn't even exist. Nevertheless, Dave and his group were duly impressed with the features of the system, despite the fact that they saw it working in a hospital processing only 12 percent of the workload experienced at their own facility. The controller expressed his appreciation for the efficiencies we gained by using our system, but though he didn't say it at the time, he believed the system was working in a hospital that didn't even remotely resemble their own operation and doubted the system was up to meeting their needs.

Despite the controller's beliefs, Dave bought into the idea that we were doing everything his hospital was doing but with much greater efficiency. By closely observing all the processes demonstrated, Dave realized the system was unique and offered him an opportunity for greatly improving his own operation. Additionally, he knew he would finally be able to get his arms around the problems he was experiencing with nonstock supplies, an area he was never able to adequately address with his own system, or with other systems he had reviewed during his quest for a new MMIS.

The reality of the situation was, had Dave not attended the seminar in Las Vegas, I probably would have taken that job in Chicago. My first impression of Dave was that he knew what he was doing relative to materials management (MM), and his sincere interest convinced me our system was unique enough to gather the attention of others just like him. My downfall was I didn't have any background when it came to marketing the system or the company. I only had what little I learned in marketing classes during my college days as an undergraduate; my graduate work was in the field of management. The true professionals involved with Health-Ware who did have the needed expertise in marketing were only investors in the company and had jobs of their own to contend with. As the saying goes, I found myself flying by the seat of my pants when it came to marketing.

I was fortunate Dave saw me as a fellow materials manager. He said he liked my approach to developing the system in that it started from the lowest common denominator. In other words, Dave understood the significance of the coveralls and how getting down in the trenches allowed me to address all aspects of MM that required automation. He said, "It is obvious the system was designed to provide efficiencies for all using it, not just us clowns in charge. I am amazed as to how well you and Lentz work together; you guys are, without a doubt, on the same wavelength when it comes to CLASS and your company. You two know what it means to work as a team."

It was apparent that Dave was caught hook, line, and sinker; he placed his career on the line when he decided to fight hard to get approval for purchasing CLASS, and from a company without any other paying clients. In a small way, one might say Dave too was an entrepreneur in that he took a huge risk to fight for what he believed to be the correct choice for his department.

Valley had a facilities-management contract with Arthur Anderson, where a CFO was placed to manage the finances of the hospital. Dave's boss, on the other hand, was the CEO, and he supported Dave when it came to choosing a new MMIS. When Dave acquired approval for purchasing CLASS despite the strong recommendations against doing so from the financial executives of the hospital, the CFO (and his other boss, Arthur Anderson) decided it was necessary to put our company and product through an after-the-purchase vetting process. Since the CFO had the resources of Arthur Anderson, he hired two consultants for six months to scrutinize all aspects of CLASS during the setup, installation, and training phases. These consultants reported to the CFO, yet were assigned to work in Dave's department so they could observe all aspects of the installation of the new software system.

SCRUTINY DIRECTED BY THE CFO

Dave got his way and was able to sign a contract for the purchase of a CLASS license at the price of $60,000. Dave first introduced the new consultants to me when I arrived for the first phase of training. The two-day training seminar to explain the basics of the system was conducted in a classroom setting, instructing the staff on how to build their database. I was unaccustomed to having someone question me on every minute aspect of the system, as was the case with the two from Arthur Anderson, but I didn't have a choice. The consultants' perspective was from an information-systems point of view, and they didn't have any MM experience. One was a nurse and the other was a systems expert. As a result, I found myself explaining the basics of the system in far greater detail than I had intended. I endured, even though it was frustrating to spend time I had not allotted for this type of scrutiny. Yet the consultants seemed to be satisfied with my answers, and there was one benefit from answering all of their questions: my intended audience—the people who were actually going to use the system—hung on every word I said and had difficulty hiding their excitement. In addition, they were able to gain a new level of appreciation as to why their boss chose CLASS as their new system and found themselves eager to get the ball rolling.

As planned, it took six months for Dave's staff to build the entire database before the Health-Ware staff could come back for the online training portion of the system conversion. Many would say, why not import all of the data from Valley's old MMIS? At first blush, it would seem like the obvious method for getting the database built. The reason for not doing so was multifaceted. At best, the data was incomplete in their current system and did not contain many fields found in our system. Even using CLASS to modify their current database would have taken longer than just entering the data into the system as new records with the correct information. The recommended process of building the database from scratch was definitely the best course of action to ensure they got the most from their new system. All of our subsequent clients took my advice on even changing and standardizing the item descriptions to make it easier when accessing items. After they completed their file build and had used it for six months, Dave let us use his data as our demonstration database. The results he was getting from CLASS were most impressive, and using the data from his system became an outstanding way to impress new potential clients.

Later on, we could have imported data from future new clients' old databases; however, I was able to sell the idea of creating new databases for all of our new clients throughout the years. I only needed to demonstrate the cleanliness of our own database to convince them of the necessity of enduring the lengthy process. All of them looked at the exercise as a way to get a fresh start on managing their departments. Without exception, all of our clients agreed the process was well worth the effort; their new databases were virtually error free.

Six months later, when the database was complete, Lentz, Gordon, Cortie, and I arrived at Valley for the online conversion. It started on a Saturday morning and entailed performing an inventory of all stock supplies in the warehouse. Our staff of four worked with Dave's staff to complete the task. This process normally took almost three full days for Dave's team to complete, but with CLASS turned on they were finished in only six hours. His crew of twelve (and the auditors) was elated to see the efficiency of the entire process.

The training for the online conversion was a learning process for the Valley and Health-Ware folks alike. If Dave and his staff felt anything like we did, they felt as if they had just been put through some sort of a meat grinder. As our time there was coming to an end, we were thankful there had not been any major issues. Yet we found ourselves leaving with a tremendous amount of notes on ways for improving the process. A look of panic started to set in with many of Dave's staff as we finished with our out-briefs and began gathering our coats to leave for home. Although this portion of the training took eight days, Dave and his staff said they felt it should have been eight weeks (found to be a common reaction at subsequent installations). Nonetheless, our staff was most fortunate, in that one could not have handpicked a better MM staff for our first client. Dave's management style combined with the temperament of his staff made them the perfect first paying client. The contrast between training at Merle West and Valley could not have been greater.

For the first three months following the online conversion, the two consultants from Arthur Anderson went through CLASS with a scrutiny I never had the luxury of employing when we were developing the system. The process was so large in scope, the proper way to develop the system would have been to keep a duplicate database to adequately test all of the features as they were added to the system. Unfortunately, we didn't have the staffing or additional computer resources at the hospital for running a parallel system. Instead, I submitted new ideas to Lentz, he programmed them, he made them operational in our live system, and my staff tested the changes to the best of their abilities, hoping we didn't miss anything. The system was responsive enough that we usually were able to identify problems as they occurred. When we put the system in Dave's hospital, it came from an environment where it was essentially developed as a work in progress. Yes, by the time Dave's department went live with CLASS, it was being used at three different hospitals, but the workload at Valley Medical Center exceeded the workload of all three hospitals combined. The capabilities of CLASS were being challenged at levels never experienced before. There were minor bumps in the beginning, but overall, Dave and his staff were extremely pleased. However, when I visited the Valley staff three months later just to say hi as I was passing through to see Terri Cartier at Evergreen, Dave handed me a document the consultants gave him just prior to my arrival.

THIS HURTS

"Do what you want with this, Tim, it's just something to justify all of the time these bozos spent with us."

It was a list developed by the Arthur Anderson consultants containing 179 items identifying what they considered as problems with CLASS. I was taken aback when I saw the title—"System Discrepancies"—and the length of the document was embarrassing.

My face must have changed color, because Dave told me, "Don't worry, Tim, we are happy with CLASS; it's doing everything we want of a system and more. You have no reason for feeling bad about anything. You know my CFO and his cronies were not happy with me when I decided on CLASS, especially when I did it despite their recommendations against doing so. My boss, the CEO, is happy, so it's their problem, not mine."

He was a prince for going out of his way to make sure I was okay. Nonetheless, I felt like Arthur Anderson had just painted a scarlet letter on our chest, and we could not afford for them to be bad-mouthing our company. When I read the list, I realized many of the items were minor, and I had been aware of most of them for quite a while. None of the items were showstoppers for me at Mid-Columbia (two of the items were misspelled words); I just lived with them because in the overall scheme of things, CLASS was a functioning product. Yet the consultants were correct to identify all of the items on the list as discrepancies; a few of the changes were good ideas that would improve the overall efficiency of the system and were not what I considered major enough to create a great deal of work for Lentz. Easy for me to say.

When I showed the list to Lentz the following week, I tried to soften the blow. "Lentz, Dave is fine with it. He said this is a document the Arthur Anderson folks created to justify their six months with his department."

His reaction was much the same as mine; like me, he was embarrassed, but not defensive. "I will get back to you if I have any questions."

An hour later, he came back with the list and sought my advice on how to approach resolving just five of the items. After we spent about fifteen minutes together talking about the list, I barely saw him during the next week.

The next time I saw Lentz, he informed me that *all* of the items on Dave's list had been corrected and were ready for Cortie and the MM staff to test for accuracy. The end result was that just three weeks after Dave gave me the list, all of the "system discrepancies" were corrected with all of the necessary changes and installed on Valley's computer.

Two days after Dave received the updates, he called to tell me, "The guys at Arthur Anderson have done an about-face when it comes to Health-Ware Management Company. After we received the updates from you guys, their two consultants quickly verified all of the items on the list were addressed, and then they disappeared. This morning, I bumped into the senior partner for Arthur, who said, "Your decision to go with Health-Ware appears to have been a good one. Health-Ware may be a young company, but those guys obviously have a good work ethic in place." Dave continued, "By not being defensive about the list and immediately correcting the problems, you guys made *me* look good, so thank you."

"Dave, it's the other way around; we could never have afforded to pay $100,000 for the consult by Arthur Anderson to fine-tune CLASS the way they did for us. Their determination to prove you made the wrong decision to go with us was only to our benefit. I guess my best response is, instead of thanking Payne Webber, I should be saying, 'Thank you, Arthur Anderson.'"

Dave then finished our conversation by saying, "Just remember, Tim, call me when you are looking for someone to carry your bags for you."

---

8. MAKING A NAME FOR OURSELVES

When we first started Health-Ware Management Company, we had virtually no money, no clients, and no reputation other than what we'd gained at the hospital in The Dalles, Oregon. At that time, CLASS was operating at Tuality and Mid-Columbia, but Merle West was just beginning to build its files, so we did not have much to brag about. When we moved to San Jose, we were truly gambling with our livelihoods, and our first goal was to make a good name for ourselves. Valley was not a sure thing until after the contract was signed in December '85, and then it was six months before they went live with CLASS. That meant it was six months before we could expect any appreciable success attributed to our system. The management contract with Merle West could not have come at a better time for our fledgling company. Lentz was quite comfortable with his new job and made it a priority to improve the customer service rendered to the hospital by the information-systems (IS) department.

In January, it was time for my first monthly visit to Merle West, where I was required to check on the status of the IS department and then report to Wes, the chief financial officer (CFO). Of course Lentz had everything under control, but it was a great way for me to visit with him and Cortie to discuss matters about the progress of our company. They did not have good news about the people in the materials-management (MM) department, saying there was a lack of direction and the MM staff was lost. Unfortunately, because I didn't have any political power over the MM department, I returned to San Jose knowing there wasn't anything I could really do to better the situation at the time.

A month later, in February '86 and the night before I was about to leave for my next visit to Merle West, I received a call from Julie and Coy, the two buyers who worked in the MM department at Merle West. Julie was the same age as Cortie and Coy was my age. They were a good team despite their age difference.

Coy said, "Cortie told us you are coming here in two days, and we were wondering if you could meet with us privately before you come to the hospital. We need to talk about some problems we are having."

"Of course I can, ladies. Why don't you join me for dinner tomorrow night? We can talk then."

The next evening I arrived in Klamath Falls and the three of us met as planned. They were obviously nervous about our meeting. Julie stated, "We are a bit uncomfortable about meeting with you behind Liz's back, but we are concerned about how poorly we are doing with CLASS."

Coy explained, "We think she is overwhelmed with the system, and she is bringing our department down in the process. Is CLASS too sophisticated for us?"

I chuckled and then replied, "Listen, there are people less sophisticated than the two of you who are doing fine with CLASS. Actually, it sounds as if you identified the problem: Liz is in over her head, and in addition to having difficulty with CLASS, she is unable to manage the department. I appreciate you asking to see me about the problem, and I will do my best to correct the situation."

All of a sudden, both of them had a look of panic on their faces. Immediately, I reassured them, "Don't worry, nobody will know about this meeting. But you have left me no choice; I must do my best to correct the problem. You will know when I am taking action, and just the three of us will know why."

I did not elaborate on what I planned to do, because I wasn't exactly sure what I was going to do. Nevertheless, action had to be taken. I wasn't going to let CLASS be blamed for their management problems.

ATTACKING A NEW PROBLEM

Nate was out of town, and since I was about to leave for San Jose, I decided to ask for a meeting with Dave Arnold, the hospital's CEO. When we met, I shared my concerns: "Dave, I believe materials management is in trouble, and a serious look should be taken at the people currently in charge."

"Are you in a position to help me out with the situation?" He was obviously aware there was a problem, because he didn't question my assessment.

"I will need two days to properly evaluate all aspects of the department. I could then give you a formal evaluation."

"How soon can you perform the consult?"

"I could be back next Tuesday and have the formal document ready on Friday before I leave for San Jose."

He agreed, and I was back the next week to look over the department. The consult was just a formality for gathering my findings, as I already knew the department was in trouble and the problem was definitely due to a lack of sound management. Liz was a nice lady who had acquired a job beyond her capabilities; she had been a clerk in medical records prior to getting hired by Nate, who was in charge of the pharmacy and was spread way too thin to manage MM at the same time. He hired Liz as the director of purchasing to assist him; unfortunately, she had no training as a manager. Those were tough words that had to come from an outsider to make it official. After completing my two-day consult, I met again with Dave.

"Dave, unfortunately I believe your two managers, Liz and Rose, are in over their heads. They do not know how to manage people, resulting in a great deal of dissent among their employees. CLASS is not their problem, it just happens to be the vehicle that emphasizes their inadequacies. It is not easy for me to make this recommendation, but I believe you need to remove them from their positions. I would be willing to help you find a replacement for Liz, and I wouldn't worry about getting a manager to replace Rose until after you get a materials manager who can oversee both departments."

Dave asked, "Do you have any suggestions for me in the meantime?"

"If you like, I can work here for a week and give some direction to the staff, and come back here for a day and a half each week until we find the new manager. Cortie is here, and I have complete faith in her. She is proficient with all features of CLASS because I had her cross-trained in all sections of materials management before she came down here to work."

Dave had obviously been concerned about the poor performance of the department *before* I suggested the consult, as he was eager to hire me to perform the evaluation. After hearing my recommendations, he said, "I agree with all of your suggestions, so how soon can you begin?" I was surprised by his response and decisiveness.

I responded, "I need to go back to San Jose and pack up some clothes, but I can be back next Monday to spend the week."

"Good. However, before you leave, why don't you go back to the department and let the two managers know their services are no longer needed, and they need to report to human resources as soon as possible."

I never expected I would be the one to give them the bad news. It was one of those cases where I just had to "shut up and color." It was a task I had to do, whether I liked it or not. I went to the MM department and spoke to both managers. They were obviously shocked and could not believe I had the nerve to make such a recommendation. It was, indeed, an uncomfortable moment, but the action had to be taken. Fortunately, they were ultimately given other positions (nonmanagerial) in the hospital. After all, they had both been with the hospital for some time, and jobs outside the hospital in the down economy for Klamath Falls were virtually nonexistent.

AN UNENVIABLE TASK

Rule Applied:

5. Be an Effective Communicator

I did not take great joy in suggesting Liz and Rose should lose their management positions. However, the weeks leading up to my consult were strong indicators that decisive action was necessary if the department was going to see any improvement. Neither of them knew how to lead, and their employees were unhappy with the lack of leadership. Liz and Rose were reluctant to receive any advice on how to make the transition to CLASS a smooth one; it was unfortunate, since Liz knew that the system was successfully implemented in The Dalles and Hillsboro. If Liz had embraced change, she too could have been successful.

Their style of management was very much a top-down approach, where the employees had little say in the day-to-day operations. Cortie's input was invaluable in that she was able to objectively evaluate the department while working on-site. Cortie knew what to expect from the managers, and she realized Liz and Rose were unable to deliver.

Their need for training was much more than just learning how to successfully transition to our software; they needed training on how to be good managers. Dave and I agreed they were already supposed to be good managers, and there was not enough time to make it an on-the-job training event.

After Liz and Rose left the office, I called a meeting of the department staff and told them what had just transpired—time to shock even more people. I let them know that was the extent of firings, and we had a great deal of work to do to turn the department around. I don't know what made me think I could manage this staff by reporting for duty only a day and a half a week, but at least CLASS was already in place. Besides, it was just a matter of training these folks on a whole new way of doing things, and I had comfort in knowing Cortie had my back. It turned out Julie and Coy were definitely strong employees and were able to quickly grasp new concepts without being negative when doing so.

Regardless of the reassurances I gave the staff, they were understandably nervous about the management shake-up. Cortie was able to help soften the blow; after I left, she talked with the workers, telling them I was an okay guy and they just needed to follow my lead. Her youth was a real plus, as it was easier for the staff to relate to her. With me working there only on a part-time basis, Cortie was essential to maintaining stability in the department. That first week went extremely well; we instituted some major changes in the operation that required reorganizing the inventory as well as making changes in the purchasing section. I will never forget when I asked Julie to help me move the table that contained all of the purchasing cards she used as a backup for CLASS. She thought we were moving the table just across the office; instead, we were moving it *out* of the office altogether, and I wish I had a picture of her face at the time.

Julie kind of stammered, "We can't work without these cards. I use them all the time."

"I know, Julie, that is one of the problems," I told her. "You don't need them anymore. CLASS is up and running fine, and Lentz has made it so the IS department no longer shuts you down during the day. Therefore, you no longer need the cards. All of the information you need is at your fingertips by using the computer. After you are forced to use the computer without those cards, you and Coy will find your jobs to be so much easier. It won't be long before you come to work in the morning only to find empty in-baskets on your desk."

She and Coy both had to contain themselves from choking over that comment. They said in unison, "That will be the day."

Three months later, much to their surprise, their in-baskets were indeed empty when they reported for work each morning. They became extremely efficient users of CLASS.

The staff working in the warehouse was a tougher crowd, and it was there that Cortie proved to be most helpful. Brad was the man in charge of the warehouse—a rather intimidating guy who was a bronco buster traveling on the rodeo circuit during his off hours (he later shared that he only worked at the hospital for the medical benefits). His gruff voice combined with his rough exterior caused many to consider him unapproachable. When one first meets Cortie, it is easy to get the wrong impression; she is cute, petite, and has an unimposing demeanor. Yet when it comes to taking on assigned tasks, she works with the skill of a seasoned manager and a toughness that causes one to take notice. Such was the case with Brad, where his rough demeanor had no effect on Cortie, as (I apologize for using this next analogy) she took the bull by the horns and was able to earn Brad's respect. As a result, it did not take long for him to become an exemplary employee.

BUSY TIMES

During the same time I was in Klamath Falls for the one-week consulting visit, Pat was visiting Yakima Valley Memorial Hospital in Washington, serving in his capacity as regional manager for American Hospital Supply (AHS). He was paying a visit to Tom Bowman, the director of support services, who mentioned his MM operation was in need of assistance and asked Pat if he knew anyone who could perform a thorough evaluation. Pat disclosed that he was on the board of Health-Ware, and though it could look like a conflict of interest, he suggested that I was the best man for the job. Based on his recommendation, I was hired to perform a two-day consult to evaluate the levels of efficiency in their MM department and found myself in Yakima just two weeks later. When I arrived the evening before my two-day visit, both Don and Jim, the hospital's COO, met me for dinner. They expressed a desire for the truth and told me not to hold back when making recommendations for improvement. They didn't give any hints as to what they were hoping to get from me, but it was obvious they were counting on me to give them a comprehensive and truthful evaluation.

The next two days were disappointing, as the place was in total disarray. The directors of MM and purchasing were in over their heads and they couldn't possibly bring the departments to a level of efficiency that would be satisfactory for upper management. When I completed my evaluation, I sent the management team a list of twenty-three items requiring completion in order to meet their desired goals. Unfortunately, the first two items on the list were recommendations for removing the two managers from their positions. The twenty-third item was a recommendation to get a new materials-management information system (MMIS), but not until after the first twenty-two items were successfully completed. I suggested that if it was properly done, it should take more than a year. I mentioned Health-Ware Management Company had an MMIS solution of its own and would welcome the opportunity to compete for their business when the timing was right.

The biggest lesson I learned from the entire experience was that I never wanted our system purchased by a hospital where the MM department was so poorly managed. A sobering thought came to me when I boarded the plane to leave: what would happen if such a thing *did* happen? It made me realize just how lucky we were to have Dave Maclachlan at Valley and Terri Cartier at Evergreen as our first two paying clients. They were competent materials managers and did not need advice on how to manage their departments. A week later, I received a letter of thanks from Tom Bowman in Yakima, and a check for my services.

ANOTHER TOUGH ASSIGNMENT
Rule Applied:

8. Be Consistent; Be Decisive

Prior to my dealings with the people at Merle West, I had never done any formal consulting. After my visit to Yakima, I realized that when an organization calls for a consultant, oftentimes it is a means of getting an outsider's opinion to confirm problems the executive staff had already suspected. If the consultant is able to give credible advice on how to deal with the problems, that is a bonus.

Contrary to what you have already read about me, I am not a hatchet man. I would much rather use the people in place to correct any noted problems. However, if after interviewing an individual I don't believe he or she is capable of making the changes necessary for correcting the situation, I will recommend a change of personnel. I am not averse to training individuals with potential, but I am intolerant of incompetence.

I continued to perform my weekly visits at Merle West, as per my agreement with Dave Arnold. When I was there during the first week of May, Dave asked to meet with me.

When I went to his office, he greeted me warmly. "Tim, we are no longer in search of a new materials manager, so we are pulling the ads."

"Why, Dave? You need a capable manager to run that operation."

"We already have one, Tim: you."

"Dave, I have a company to run, and I need my freedom to make it a success."

"Look, Tim, the department heads all agree the quality of service coming from materials management is at an all-time high, and it has happened in just three months. I have a proposal: I want to bring you in as our full-time materials manager, knowing full well you have Health-Ware as your primary job."

"Dave, I need to be able to travel without having to get permission from you or anybody else."

"Not a problem. I just want the security of knowing you are in town when you are not on the road and are able to respond to the needs of your staff. What you have been able to accomplish by being here only a day and a half each week has been remarkable. I can only imagine how much better it would be if you were living here full-time."

Of course, I called Jan and Gordon before I accepted the position, and in less than three weeks, we moved our family to Klamath Falls. Dave agreed to allow me to have a Health-Ware phone extension added to the MM phones in the hospital, and I was able to use the MM folks to answer the phone for me when I was unavailable. It was a sweet deal all around; Health-Ware had more financial stability, and within a year, Cortie and I were able to turn the MM department into another one of our showcase clients. I still traveled often for our company, giving presentations and adding to our client base. Just like in The Dalles, my staff was totally cross-trained so that any of them could work in any section of the department. I had learned so much during my time in The Dalles. Managing and training the Merle West staff was an easy process, and having Cortie onboard with her experience and loyal support didn't hurt either.

At about the same time we moved to Klamath Falls, Pat resigned from AHS to help with the formation of another small company. After bringing that company to a successful completion in October '88, he offered to come onboard as the sales and marketing rep for Health-Ware. He worked out of his home in Portland. Everything was happening all at once, and it was all positive.

BACK TO THE SEATTLE AREA

Two months after Jan and I moved our family to Klamath Falls, it was time for the online conversion at Evergreen.

Gordon, Jan, Lentz, and I were at Evergreen to conduct the seven-day online conversion. After we performed the inventory with Terri's staff, the real training began to take place, and Virginia, who was the purchasing agent, was having difficulty with accepting the new way of doing her job. In the middle of her training, she stood up and stepped out of the office. When I mentioned my concern about her demeanor and whether or not she was going to be able to make it through the training, Gordon also left the room. I looked outside and saw Virginia sitting on the steps, sobbing. Gordon approached her and sat beside her, and it was obvious he was consoling her. Ten minutes later, the two of them returned to resume her training. During dinner, I asked Gordon what had transpired when he spoke with Virginia.

He told me, "Virginia was scared, Tim. She said she was going to lose her job because she was never going to be able to learn how to use CLASS. I told her when I was first being taught about the system, I had the same feelings, and that after just a few days, I was no longer intimidated. I told her, if an old fart like me can learn how to use the system, she certainly should have no problems." Gordon gave Virginia the one-on-one training she needed, and by the end of the week you couldn't beat her off the computer with a stick. She became a successful user who we were able to later use as a reference on the benefits of CLASS.

AN EXCEPTION TO THE RULE

The remainder of the training went quite well, and much like the staff at Valley, Terri and her staff thought we should have stayed longer. Nevertheless, we left confident we had another client that would be one we could point to as a success in the near future.

An incident occurred shortly after Evergreen's online conversion that has prompted me to provide the following explanation before I share the actual event with you. This is another place in the book that you might want to skip; it is a technical discourse that is needed to understand the reasoning I used when suggesting a particular action to Terri. It was the only time such a drastic move had to be taken for one of our clients; nevertheless, being able to do so demonstrated the power of our system. If you want, skip to the section entitled "A Flood of Activity."

During the online conversion, clients are taught how CLASS calculates the minimum stock levels (MSLs) for items when they are given automatic control. However, we advise clients not to turn over control for four to six weeks. We tell them to wait for the following reasons:

- On the first day, the system begins to log the daily usage. It normally takes from four to six weeks to collect valid data for controlling the MSLs. The usage for every item—stock and nonstock—is stored for the previous forty-two days; it is from this data that the average daily usage is calculated.
- The rationale for storing that much usage for each item was to allow for the ability to adjust the sensitivity for replenishing the inventory. In other words, if we used all forty-two days to calculate the averages, the system would respond much more slowly when adjusting levels set at fourteen days.
- If one looks at the patient census over the previous six-week period, it becomes apparent that what occurred six, four, or even three weeks ago has no impact whatsoever on what is happening in the hospital today. Accordingly, I reduced the number of days for calculating the average daily usage to fourteen. Ultimately, all of our clients throughout the years subscribed to the same logic for managing stock levels at their own facilities.

Based on the logic presented above, it is easy to understand why I ignored the typical economic order quantity (EOQ) formulas that took into account purchases and receipts for the past year for calculating reorder levels.

In each item's master record, the user defines how much stock to keep on the shelf by designating what we called *days of stock,* which is translated to a quantity that is derived by multiplying that field times the average daily usage rate for each item. With most vendors, given next-day delivery for the majority of their items, most clients chose to set the field at seven days.

Our formula was simple: the MSL (minimum stock level or reorder point) = days of stock times the average daily usage. For example, if a box of fifty syringes is moving at a rate of thirty per day, seven days times thirty would equate to an MSL of 210 syringes. When the on-hand quantity becomes equal to or below that level, the system then uses what we call the response formula to calculate what to order to bring supplies up to an optimum level.

Another reason for waiting four to six weeks is that big mistakes are usually made (and not corrected soon enough) in the beginning weeks after the online conversion. A good example is when the user confuses the amount requested for an item and issues twenty boxes of fifty packs of an item instead of just twenty packs. Not only does the inventory get distorted, but the usage for that item is increased by one thousand packs rather than the twenty requested. For some, the mistake is not so evident at the time, and it can be days before corrections are made. Because of these two factors that can alter the perception of how well the new client is doing, we are normally very conservative with our recommendations.

Two weeks after we completed the online conversion at Evergreen, I decided to call Terri and check on how they were doing.

She was rather pensive. "Well, it's working, Tim." The tone of voice said much more than her words.

"What's the matter, Terri?"

"Well, the system is creating pick-lists and purchase orders, but we are running out of supplies. We just never have enough supplies on hand to take care of the hospital; it's very frustrating."

"Have you had a spike in census since we left you?"

"Yes, just five days after you left, we had a flu outbreak up here and our census has been unseasonably high."

"Terri, if you think you and your staff have a good handle on correcting any issue problems, you need to list your top two hundred items that are your most active supplies that you seem to be running out of, and then turn control over to CLASS to adjust the minimum stock levels for those items."

"You told me to wait four to six weeks, Tim."

"I know. That is the rule of thumb for normal circumstances; but from the sounds of it, Terri, your situation is anything but normal. Just give it a try, and I will call you again tomorrow to see how things are going."

The graph shown in figure 1 demonstrates what happens to one item when the usage accelerates unexpectedly and how it impacts the purchasing activity. It is a good example of what happened to Terri's shop when the flu epidemic hit the hospital. Notice the first two weeks show where the MSL is static. The computer did not have automatic control of the MSLs. Also, note the increase in daily usage after fourteen days, which accounts for their stock outages. Since she had been online for two weeks, turning the individual switches on was the only logical answer.

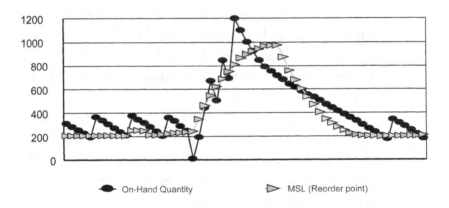

The following describes what figure 1 depicts:
- It is easy to tell that the control switch was turned on just as they were about to run out of the item; the actual on-hand quantity was nine each.
- The on-hand quantity spiking upward indicates receipts for the item.
- Control was turned over to the computer just before the item reached its lowest level (nine each).
- Notice how high the quantity jumps to get ahead of the unusually high patient activity, and then how it gradually falls in line with the lower activity.

I called Terri at about eleven the next morning to see how things were going. "Hi, Terri, what happened?"

"Wow, it worked all right. We have supplies coming out of our ears. Understand me when I say that I'm not complaining, but I had to get extra help; they are still receiving the supplies as we speak. With just a little more than two weeks of being on the system, is it going to suggest too many supplies for subsequent orders?"

"I doubt it, Terri. You might be overstocked for four or five days, but as the patient census begins to drop, so will the inventory. All I can say is, welcome to automated materials management."

One last remark about what differences take place when the number of days for calculating the average daily usage is increased to thirty days as shown in figure 2.

- Notice the on-hand quantity for that item (and many others) dropped to zero, and the hospital would not have been able to satisfy all of its requests with the number of days set to thirty.
- Also notice that the item had been ordered eight times to try to keep up with the demand.
- Twice the amount of work would be required by both the purchasing and warehouse sections of the department. The last thing an MM department needs during an abnormally high amount of activity is an unnecessary increase in activity because of an inefficient computer system.

I always found this type of phenomena fascinating.

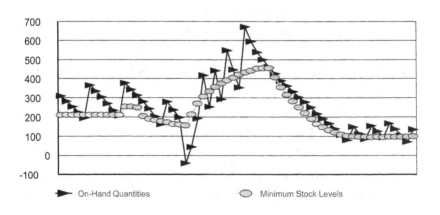

Terri and her staff became outstanding users of CLASS, and having her as a reference was a privilege, as she was a huge supporter of our company. We had many memorable times over the years.

A FLOOD OF ACTIVITY

Dave Arnold at Merle West kept his promise by letting me run my company while concurrently managing his MM department. During the next eighteen months, we signed contracts for the purchase of CLASS with the following hospitals:

- *Redlands Community Hospital of Redlands, California*

After Mary Yahnke (the MM) was given a presentation, she claimed she would purchase CLASS only if we agreed to develop a surgery-case cart system according to her specifications. She agreed to pay for the new system, but insisted it was the only way she would sign a contract with us. Mary was involved with the renovation of her central supply and processing department, and the way it connected with the warehouse and the OR; it was so successful that she hosted site visits by many hospitals in the Southern California area. She was a manager who knew what she wanted and was an incredible negotiator. The responsibility for developing a surgery-case cart system would fall squarely on Lentz's shoulders, so I called him with Mary's proposal. As usual, Lentz agreed, and after six months of working with Lentz while they were concurrently building their database for CLASS, Mary and Lentz developed the case cart system according to Mary's specifications. The simplicity behind its design was most impressive.

- *Hemet Valley Medical Center of Hemet, California*

Hemet was our first client to use the IBM System/38 (and later the AS/400) version of CLASS.

- *Flagstaff Medical Center of Flagstaff, Arizona*

After Brenda Munns visited Redlands Community for a site visit, she was so impressed by what she saw, she told me she wanted to become the Mary Yahnke of Arizona. Just one year later, her wish came true.

- *Grays Harbor Community Hospital of Grays Harbor, Washington*

Henry Pratt and his staff became very successful users of CLASS, only to have to give up using it three years later because his administration replaced all of their software with a complete hospital information system (HIS). Without a doubt, these solutions were the answer to George Orwell's *1984*, a solution referred to as the gray-suit syndrome, where the HIS software answered all of a hospital's problems, just poorly.

This type of situation became a problem for our company, as hospitals looked to a one-system solution rather than choosing the best system for each software application. For example, five years later, when St. Vincent Medical Center of Portland, Oregon, was acquired by the Providence eighteen-hospital system, I was told by the senior VP of finance at Providence Medical Center in Portland, who was in charge of the new hospital's finances, that he knew we had a better materials system, but he wanted to have to deal with only one IS vendor. He said he was willing to accept the lesser quality software in exchange for consistency throughout the hospital. The fact that we were able to successfully interface with multiple systems had no impact on his decision.

- *Island Hospital of Anacortes, Washington*

This hospital was the smallest one to purchase CLASS to date.

- *Josephine Memorial Hospital of Grants Pass, Oregon*

Another small hospital tucked away in a community situated in the middle of the Cascade Mountains.

- *Loma Linda Community Hospital of Loma Linda, California*

Neil Hartwig and his staff successfully implemented CLASS while situated virtually in the shadow of Loma Linda University Medical Center.

- *St. Francis Hospital of Santa Barbara, California*

Sal Ramirez was the director of MM who took more of an interest in our company than just our product.

During his online conversion to CLASS, he said, "You know, Tim, you guys are putting in long hours during this process, yet you all seem to be having so much fun. I wouldn't mind trying it out myself."

I responded, "What do you mean?"

"I think I would enjoy training others on how to use CLASS."

"You know, Sal, you just gave me an idea. If you are anything like me when I worked at my last hospital, I bet you have at least a month of paid vacation accumulated." He held up two fingers. "What if I paid you $100 per day plus all expenses to join us for nine days to help train a new client with us? You have seen all that we do, so you wouldn't require any additional training. I always know six months in advance of when we are training a new client, so it wouldn't be a short-notice request. What do you think?"

"It sounds like fun. Let me know when you need me and I will work it into my schedule."

About a year later, when Sal and his staff had become solid users of CLASS, he joined us for the online conversion at Casa Grande Regional Hospital in Casa Grande, Arizona. The experience had a four-pronged positive benefit I never expected:

1. Derek, who was the MM at Casa Grande, shared with me how much he appreciated having another user of CLASS training him and his staff. He said it gave him access to an outsider's perspective about the system *and* our company.

2. Sal said it was a good experience for him to see how someone else dealt with similar situations he had back at home.

3. It was a true bonding experience among all three organizations.

4. I did not need to worry about paying benefits to Sal while he worked with us, since he was already insured by his own employer.

You will learn later in the book how Sal was the pioneer responsible for getting other clients to become members of our part-time staff. All of this activity was going on while we renovated the MM operation in Klamath Falls and began to accumulate some very successful results.

IN NEED OF A PLACE FOR A SITE VISIT

As mentioned earlier, Klamath Falls is not the most convenient destination, no matter how you travel to get there. After having been there for eighteen months, we finally had a need to use Merle West as a place for a site visit. I had given a presentation to the MM staff at MultiCare Medical Center in Tacoma, Washington, a 750-bed hospital, and Gerry, the materials manager, liked what he heard and saw. He asked where he could go for a site visit. He dismissed The Dalles as too small of an operation to use as a comparison and said he had visited Valley Medical Center, but wanted to see another site. I think he just wanted to get out of town. The only place I felt comfortable using at the time was our operation at Merle West in Klamath Falls, which was running as efficiently as the operation in The Dalles. To a person, the staff had become quite capable. After flying out of Seattle and changing planes in Portland, Gerry arrived in Klamath Falls accompanied by Todd, one of his buyers, and Christine, his boss, who was the executive vice president of the hospital. Christine was an extremely sophisticated and classy executive who actually looked out of place as she visited the MM operation in the hospital. Nevertheless, she wanted to be personally involved in the approval process for one of her departments that was going to spend over $200,000 for a new software and computer system (a considerable price tag at the time).

Each time I demonstrated CLASS, I started in the warehouse, because for the most part, purchasing reacts to what happens there. The actions of receiving supplies into the warehouse and issuing them to the hospital departments are the activities that are actually responsible for creating the purchase orders. I escorted the group to the receiving desk, where Brad was standing in front of the computer terminal with a small box in his hand. When I introduced him to our guests, he stepped away from the terminal so he could shake their hands. In trying to set the stage for the reader, imagine a stocky man sporting cowboy boots, a huge belt buckle, and a handlebar moustache being introduced to an executive who is an attractive, petite woman wearing a white dress.

After they shook hands and exchanged greetings, she asked him, "Are you a cowboy?"

He proudly replied, "Yes, ma'am, I am on the rodeo circuit during my off time."

Christine immediately changed the subject by asking, "What are you doing with that box?"

Similar to the way Joyce handled Nate during his visit to The Dalles three years earlier, I was no longer in control. It became Brad's show.

When he stepped away from the computer to say hi, Christine had stepped up to the terminal as she asked questions of Brad. She had her back to him now.

Brad answered, "Well, Christine …" While he was talking, he put his hands on her waist and very gently moved her to the side so he could use the computer to answer her question. Christine was slightly startled when he moved her, but just smiled when she realized what was happening.

Brad continued, "This item is an artificial hip, and in order to receive it, I pull up the purchase order on the screen and enter the quantity received."

As he demonstrated the receipt process, Christine asked, "How did this hip get into the system in the first place?"

Brad said, "A special-order request from surgery was sent to purchasing so it could be given an item number and put into the system."

"Do I now go to purchasing to see how that is accomplished?"

"No. We have all been cross-trained to work in all sections of the department, so I can go ahead and show you the purchasing process."

It was one of those times when you realize you are only as good as the people who support you. Brad was amazing with Christine and literally took charge of the site visit. I could not have done a finer job myself; in fact, Brad did a *better* job than I would have done.

It was actually Health-Ware's first site visit, and it proved to me I should not be the person demonstrating CLASS. The potential client wants to see how a current client is doing, without the help of the vendor that is selling it.

After their visit to the hospital was completed, Cortie and I took our three guests to a late lunch at a local restaurant prior to seeing them off at the airport. Christine could not stop talking about their time with Brad.

"Gerry, if a bronco buster like Brad can be so proficient with CLASS, I am certain your staff can do the same. That was a very impressive demonstration." CLASS was installed at MultiCare three months later.

TEAMWORK COMES THROUGH AGAIN

Rule Applied:

12. Instill Teamwork

As far as management is concerned, the best outcome of the site visit was how it emphasized the need to instill teamwork among members of the staff. Brad's participation in this visit was not planned—he just happened to be standing in the way at the time. Prior to that visit, Brad never before had a reason to carry on such a conversation with an executive like Christine. Yet because he was given the proper training and was treated like a valuable member of the team, Brad had the confidence in himself to do exactly what was necessary.

Such a performance should make any manager very proud. I know I was.

A LESSON FROM A NEW CUSTOMER ON HOW TO BETTER PRESENT CLASS

When marketing CLASS during the first eighteen months, our strategy was simple: find materials managers in need of an MMIS. One would think I just stated the obvious. I certainly thought so, until I met Marshall Brogie in mid-November 1987 (just one month after the site visit by the folks from MultiCare). He was the materials manager at Barton Memorial Hospital, a seventy-one-bed hospital located in the resort town of South Lake Tahoe, California. Because a world-renowned orthopedic surgeon had established a thriving practice in the town, it was a very successful hospital with plenty of cash in the coffers. Employees joked about the ski slopes having a direct path into their operating rooms.

Marshall said he was about to purchase a system from Enterprise Systems, Inc., but felt compelled to ask for a presentation to make sure he was making the right decision. Gordon and I found ourselves in front of Marshall and his staff, and for the first time the CFO, Jim— who happened to be Marshall's boss—was in attendance. I gave the normal presentation with a brief background about the development of CLASS and then began demonstrating how it handled the day-to-day MM activities. The MM staff appeared interested. Forty-five minutes into the presentation, with Jim still in the room, I began discussing the way CLASS handled nonstock supplies and how it eliminated the need for an accounts-payable (AP) clerk to post any journal entries relevant to departmental expenses for the nonstocks.

Jim stood up and interrupted me. "What do you mean the system *eliminates* the posting of journal entries?"

Up until that point, he had been sitting quietly in the back of the room and hadn't participated in any of the discussions. Suddenly he became extremely interested in what I had to say.

I answered, "The system automatically expenses all items, both stock and nonstock, to the departments as the receipts are processed; therefore, AP does not get involved."

"Who gets charged for the invoice?"

"Jim, they all get charged to one account: inventory."

He was incredulous. "What? How?"

"Jim, when nonstock items are received, they are part of inventory for a nanosecond and then are immediately issued to the departments; so when the departments receive their month-end usage reports, all items are included, not just the stock items. Since it is the job of the buyer to verify pricing for all stock items, it is only logical that price verification would also be done for the nonstock supplies. As a result, accounts payable no longer needs to be concerned with that activity as well."

Then, as if a light bulb turned on, Jim slowly sat down, saying, "Of course." He immediately stood up again and asked, "Can we be online by January 1?"

It was my turn to be incredulous. "You mean in *six weeks*? It normally takes six months, and it would require training during the holidays."

Jim was determined. "Our fiscal year is in conjunction with the calendar year, and I don't want to deal with two different types of postings to the general ledger for the upcoming year."

He was insistent, saying he wanted CLASS and wanted it soon. In addition, he was requiring a tall order during the six weeks before the first of the year. We eventually worked it out to where we hired a part-time employee to assist with their file build on-site during the six weeks. In addition to paying the living expenses for my staff members for training over the holidays, he agreed to pay for their families to stay as well. It was not a perfect online conversion by any stretch of the imagination; however, because of the commitment by Marshall and his staff to making it happen, they became solid users of our system.

Every presentation became a learning experience, ultimately allowing me to do a better job the next time. From that point forward, when we arranged for presentations, we told our prospective clients we had to have the CFO attend the presentation, explaining that doing so would be of benefit to all. Many of the CFOs' reactions were similar to that of Jim, and we usually found an unexpected advocate in our camp that oftentimes made it an easier sale. After my meeting with Jim at Barton, I also changed the format of the presentation such that I gave an overview of the system and addressed the treatment of nonstock supplies during the first fifteen minutes. By doing so, I was able to get the attention of the CFO and guarantee no more than thirty minutes of his or her time would be required. We found a normal CFO's attention span did not last much longer when it came to subject matter centered on MM; some stayed longer, while many left immediately after the overview. Nonetheless, the changes we made not only accommodated the CFO, it allowed for a smoother presentation overall for the entire audience. Jim's reaction to CLASS changed our strategy for all subsequent presentations. We described its uniqueness and impact on the finance department within the first thirty minutes.

9. SEIZING THE MOMENT

I received a call from Paul Jordan of Bergen Brunswig Medical Supplies, someone I had not spoken with in three years. When I left my position in The Dalles, Paul was Bergen's northwest regional vice president. Bergen was a major medical-supplies distribution company that sold to hospitals throughout the western United States. It was our business relationship that brought the two of us together. I couldn't imagine why he was calling, although it was always nice to hear from an old friend. We spent a total of perhaps eight hours meeting during my four years there. I heard he had been promoted to president of the company and had moved to its headquarters, located in Orange, California.

He told me he'd had to track me down, not knowing that I had left The Dalles. He expressed relief in finding me because he thought I might be able to answer a question regarding the Health Futures purchasing group. I did have the answer he was seeking.

After I answered his question, he politely inquired, "What is Health-Ware all about?"

I replied, "In May of '85, American Data Services, the software division of American Hospital Supply, tried to buy the rights to the materials-management system Lentz and I were developing in The Dalles. Instead, with some private investors, we purchased the rights ourselves and started Health-Ware Management Company."

"How are you doing?"

And out of the blue, it struck me: I had a once-in-a-lifetime opportunity and just couldn't let it slip away. I knew that CLASS users were giving optimum service to the hospital departments, which meant the service levels Bergen was rendering to its hospitals also had to be at optimum levels. Instead of giving reports about our company that wouldn't mean much to him, I decided to ask a favor of him that would tell him how well we were really doing.

I took a chance and suggested, "Paul, let's end our call now, and afterward do me a favor. Have your operations chief check the service levels your company is rendering to these three hospitals: Merle West Medical Center in Klamath Falls, Oregon; Tuality Community Hospital in Hillsboro, Oregon; and Valley Medical Center in Renton, Washington." I used Merle West instead of Mid-Columbia as one of the three hospitals because of its higher patient activity. "If Bergen's service levels for these three hospitals are not higher than all of your other clients," I continued, "and it turns out to be a waste of your time, you don't even need to bother calling me back. Otherwise, call back and we can continue our discussion about Health-Ware Management Company."

It's amazing how the mind works sometimes; in a flash, I realized the worst that could come from my request was I never heard from him again. Nevertheless, Paul was polite and agreed, not really understanding how or why I would make such a request. We said our good-byes and left it at that. I was certain that if Paul was intrigued enough to do what I asked of him, and if I was correct with my assumption, I would hear from him soon.

Here was my rationale for interrupting our phone call: I was confident the capabilities of our system were more than hype. We had the best materials-management (MM) software system on the market. Though a questionable move on my part, it would be a unique way for comparing the performance of CLASS to our competitors' products (one might consider this method as a backdoor way of doing so). I can't say I actually expected a return call, but I remembered thinking it would be incredible if he *did* call back.

THOUGHTS BEHIND MY ACTION

This is a good place to explain what I was expecting to happen if, indeed, my assumption was correct. At the time, Bergen was attempting to become more than just a regional medical-supplies distribution company—it wanted to be the best in the business. Although Bergen did not manufacture supplies like American Hospital Supply (a national company), it was still a formidable competitor in the regions it did service, mainly west of the Mississippi. When the two companies went toe-to-toe competing for a hospital's business, Bergen was at a disadvantage when AHS brought its own software system as an added value to those hospitals in need of one. As with any supplies vendor, Bergen's goal was to have every hospital sign a prime vendor agreement, meaning the majority of supplies were purchased from them. Their pricing structure was competitive, especially considering the fact that they would sell their products in different units of issue (i.e. case, box, or each). Executed properly, our companies could mutually benefit if CLASS was the materials-management information system (MMIS) used by all of Bergen's clients. In addition to cementing relationships with its clients, Bergen would have them ordering supplies with maximum efficiency, which would also mean fewer peaks and valleys when clients placed their orders. In turn, Bergen would gain efficiencies when processing the orders for supplies from clients that were using CLASS at the hospitals and clinics.

If Paul *did* call back, I was hoping we could get him and his staff intrigued enough to want to further explore a possible collaboration. There was no telling what kind of arrangement could come of my on-the-spot request of him during that phone call. It was definitely a gamble, yet the potential rewards were intriguing.

The next day, I received a call from Paul, who was incredulous over the results of my request. "How did you know? Without having access to my management reports, how could you possibly know our service levels would be not just high, but the highest for the hospitals you mentioned?"

Wow, I'd hit a home run. My faith in what we were doing was not only beneficial to our clients, but it reached beyond to the organizations selling supplies to our hospital clients. At that moment, I knew all we had sacrificed up to that point was well worth it. There was no telling what this call could mean for us.

Paul asked, "How *did* you know? And what do we do, Tim? Where do we go from here?"

I was prepared for his questions. "Paul, our early successes with our software have confirmed my belief our system is powerful and the most responsive system on the market."

I was obviously wearing my sales hat. I continued, "When we were in the early stages of developing our software in The Dalles, which we now refer to as CLASS, I received accolades from various sales reps about the credible ordering of supplies from my purchasing department. Your folks in Hillsboro actually told me your service level to our hospital here in Klamath Falls was the highest in the region; I heard that same comment when I was in The Dalles. I took a chance and named the only three clients with enough data for making comparisons. We have six more clients, but they have not been online long enough to have gathered enough credible data."

"Tim, it's amazing that all three of them are at the top."

"Paul, we have a reorder mechanism—we call it the response formula—that is uniquely in touch with the daily patient census. Our system produces suggested orders for only what is needed, with few peaks and valleys—a supplier's dream come true. I honestly believed this premise could only result in high service levels for all suppliers. That's the reason I asked you to check on the levels for those hospitals."

It was my faith in this design philosophy that caused me to lay down the gauntlet for Paul, so to speak, and to believe he would be calling me back. The ensuing months brought an adrenaline rush that lasted for quite some time. The entire episode proved that oftentimes a moment of inspiration occurs when one least expects it, and seizing it at the right time usually involves a very small window—even the span of a short phone call. It became apparent at that moment that our lives would never be the same.

TAKING A CHANCE

Rules Applied:

5. Be an Effective Communicator   7. Lead with Confidence

From the moment Paul first called me, I had to speak with confidence that I made the correct decision when I left my job in The Dalles. When I asked Paul to cut the conversation short, it was a gut-level reaction on my part that could have backfired.

I took the lead with the conversation, and fortunately I posed the request in such a way that he wasn't offended. It was a moment in time where all of my leadership skills fell into place.

Paul and I agreed it would be best if I went to visit him at his corporate headquarters in Orange, California. I called Pat in Portland and asked him to join me for the big event. Even though Pat and I lived three hundred miles apart at the time, we were able to prepare for such an important occasion. His enthusiasm was infectious, and since he came from AHS to represent Health-Ware, he furthered our credibility as a professional company. It was obvious Paul was just as serious about the meeting as we were, in that he made sure that all of his executives were in attendance. His regional VPs flew into town, and he invited Lottie Poe, the top sales rep, and some of the other local reps. It was very rewarding to see that Paul spared nothing to ensure the meeting came off without a hitch.

When the time came to strut our stuff, we were ready. We only had nine clients at the time, but it was our goal to convince our audience we were the natural choice as the up-and-coming company to have as an affiliate. Even though we represented a small company, it was important our audience did not get that impression; we went all-out to give the most professional presentation possible. Although Lentz wasn't able to attend the presentation, he was able to give us everything we needed to get the desired outcome, providing us with a complete database from Valley with twelve months of data. As a result, we were able to give actual purchasing and usage data to our audience. I was able to show online graphs representing line-item usages as they correlated to the actual patient census and the quantities purchased from the vendors. When our audience was able to see purchases and hospital usage side-by-side with mostly equal quantities, they could not contain their excitement. I emphasized that it was this type of control over inventory that put Valley at the top of the list of the highest service levels rendered by Bergen. It was fun, as many of them asked me to show some specific high-moving items; the oohs and aahs were frequent throughout that part of the presentation. I emphasized it was the client that dictated Bergen's service levels, not the other way around. When the client ordered supplies based on demand by the number of patients in the hospital, their ordering of supplies would always be credible, thus requiring high service levels from their vendors.

MOST IMPORTANT PRESENTATION TO DATE

The presentation was a success. It was by far the friendliest audience we ever had before us. Their enthusiasm was driven by the idea that if CLASS was the MMIS being used by all of their clients, it only made sense their service levels would also rise. When I demonstrated how well CLASS was able to purchase items in line with the actual patient census, many in the audience expressed their amazement. Abruptly, the demo changed from being a one-person demonstration to an interactive exchange where many in the group felt compelled to participate. I emphasized that ultimately, Bergen's own inventories required to support those hospitals using CLASS would be reduced while they concurrently increased the service levels for each. They became enthusiastic about the prospect of having a means for endearing their clients to them with a new offering that could be promoted as a trendsetting approach for automating MM.

At first, although there was indeed excitement in the air, it was apparent some in the audience were dubious about all that I was throwing at them. I asked for feedback and/or criticism and sought out one man in the audience who definitely seemed intimidated by what he was hearing. He almost seemed relieved when I called upon him, even though he had not raised his hand. It turned out he was one of Bergen's sales reps who came from the field, and he was concerned about how much he would need to know about selling such a complex system. First of all, I stressed that the complexity was in the programming of the system, and we made it as simple as possible for our end users. I further explained that his job was to just find us clients in need of an automated system, and as soon as we got the lead, we would take it from that point on, and they would not be involved at all with the sale of our software.

There was an obvious sense of relief for many in the room as the chatter and excitement elevated to a dull roar. People became more animated, in that they were laughing and challenging each other as to who would get the first qualified lead. They were so receptive. When sales came about because of their efforts, I realized that I never wanted to disappoint anyone at Bergen, ever.

Pat and I looked at each other across the room, and we both had that look of satisfaction, knowing we had indeed accomplished what we set out to do. I then looked at Paul and his three vice presidents standing at the back of the room. It was obvious they too were very pleased with the event that had just transpired. I remember saying to myself, *It would be nice if Jan, Lentz, and Gordon were here to be a part of this event.*

Almost overnight, we raised the prominence of our company. Later that evening, we all went to dinner, and I only wish I could have captured the mood of everybody in the room. You would have thought everyone had just won the lottery. There was no doubt that, ultimately, we would have an agreement beneficial to both of our organizations. Then I remember having a sobering thought amidst all of that jubilation: *I think we're going to have more work than we can handle.* Of course, anyone attempting to grow a business would always welcome such a dilemma. Nevertheless, we were in for a huge growth spurt, and we needed to be ready for it.

After the lawyers got involved, it took more than three months for us to finalize the five-year marketing agreement to officially get the ball rolling. Lottie was not about to wait for an official contract before she actively promoted CLASS to her clients, though. As a result, we were able to have a signed contract with St. Vincent Medical Center, which was one of her clients located in Southern California, before we had an agreement signed with Bergen. Even with the lawyers doing their thing, Paul and I weren't patient enough to wait for them. He was so excited he invited me down again, this time to meet with his public-relations firm, including photographers and graphic artists.

In an afternoon, we worked on photo shoots and drafted designs for brochures and flyers that the Bergen sales force would disseminate to the field. Paul approved the purchase of expensive flyers and pamphlets for promoting our collaboration. They put my picture on one of the pamphlets as the president of Health-Ware, so there wasn't any confusion as to who was selling CLASS. With Bergen's two hundred sales reps scattered around the western United States, we were given free exposure that would have cost us a fortune. After the agreement, we did not need to hire salespeople of our own to make cold calls, as the Bergen folks kept Pat extremely busy just following up on their leads. The ensuing months involved an onslaught of activity with the Bergen reps, as their enthusiasm was infectious. We formed a bond of mutual respect and admiration that lasted for the years that followed. A side note here: we never asked or let Bergen pay for our expenses when traveling to and from Southern California. We never wanted to stress our small size in any way.

POTENTIAL CLIENT WITH NAME RECOGNITION

After we finally had a formal marketing agreement with Bergen, Pat came to my office and told me he had a lead we might want to jump on: the Mayo Clinic had recently opened a clinic in Scottsdale, Arizona, and was in search of an MMIS. Pat received a call from Richard, who was the Bergen sales rep for the clinic. Richard had mentioned their collaboration with Health-Ware to Don Thompson, the director of purchasing, who expressed an interest in seeing what we had to offer. We were amused at the idea of potentially being able to put the Mayo Clinic on our list of clients, but knew it had to be a long shot.

Two weeks later, in September '88, Pat and I went to Scottsdale to give a presentation. It was the first time I presented in front of a potential client with Pat in the room. Sue, who was a representative from Mayo's corporate office in Rochester, Minnesota, also attended; she was there to determine whether or not we had a credible system. Although Don was told by his administrator to look for a system of his own, without Sue's stamp of approval, Don would not be able to acquire CLASS as his MMIS. The response by our audience was quite favorable and we left for home with a pretty good feeling about the possibility of getting Mayo as a new client.

On the flight home, Pat dissected the quality of my presentation. I had sold nine systems up to that point and was, at first, not very receptive to Pat's criticism. In fact, I was quite defensive. After listening to him for two hours during our trip home, though, I realized I was receiving a quality critique of my presentation skills and could only benefit from his input. After all, he had been part of an organization I had grown to admire because of the professionalism exhibited by its executives. As a result, I looked forward to Pat's critique after all of our subsequent presentations, and I received an education that could only improve my ability to capture the attention of an audience. We found ourselves driving to many hospitals in those beginning years, and Pat took every opportunity to make it a learning experience for me. I recall one trip when I was driving, and Pat pulled out the book *Swim with the Sharks Without Being Eaten Alive* by Harvey Mackay (1988). It is a very easy read, and it turned out to be the first of many books Mr. Mackay has written. Pat and I discussed various aspects of the book, and I considered our times together to be a valuable extension of my education.

A SURPRISE INVITATION

When we returned home, we waited for Don to get approval to purchase CLASS; meanwhile, Pat went back to work looking for new clients. He arranged a presentation for Gerry Gardner, the materials manager at St. Charles Medical Center in Bend, Oregon. You might remember I met Gerry seven years earlier when I gave my two cents in front of an audience in Seattle; he took issue with a statement I made without me knowing anyone in the crowd. When Pat told me about the scheduled presentation, I had to confess the mistake I had never forgotten. Nevertheless, I had to face Gerry and hoped all would go well, thinking maybe he did not remember the incident. St. Charles was an impressive hospital situated in a resort town of Oregon's high-desert community (four-thousand-foot elevation). Gerry was just as impressive as when I'd met him in early 1982; he was very professional as he welcomed the two of us.

The presentation went like many others. Gerry and his staff were engaged and became quite enthusiastic as we progressed with the presentation. Afterward, Gerry invited us to have lunch with him. When he and I were together alone, he shared, "You know, Tim, I misjudged you in the past, and I am glad I have had this opportunity to get to know you better. You know what the hell you are doing, and I look forward to becoming one of your clients."

I didn't need to ask him to elaborate, because the only time we had ever met was at that meeting in Seattle. He had not forgotten. This meeting was the beginning of a professional friendship that lasted throughout the remaining years of our business relationship.

MAYO COMES THROUGH WITH APPROVAL

In December, Don of the Mayo Clinic in Scottsdale received approval to purchase CLASS. Five months later, Don and his staff underwent their online conversion with CLASS. They became extremely efficient users, and the Mayo Clinic Scottsdale became a great reference for us throughout the years. As the operation grew, Don hired Bethany Krom as his chief buyer, who had moved from the Mayo Clinic in Rochester, Minnesota. She was responsible for overseeing the growth of the department, as the clinic literally doubled in size over the first five years. In fact, although the clinic did not have any inpatients, we were called upon to assist them with adding handheld scanners to use with inventory control and patient charging. You will hear more about Bethany later on in the book.

A LITTLE FRIENDLY COMPETITION

Not long after Mayo signed the contract to purchase CLASS, we received a call from Jim Mayhill, the director of purchasing at the Wichita Clinic. He asked for a presentation, saying, "If CLASS is good enough for the Mayo Clinic, it must be good enough for us." Our presentation went well and in November 1989, I trained our new client on how to build the database. Jim and his staff were enamored with the system from the very first day, and we scheduled the online conversion to take place in early May, 1990. A month before we were due to arrive for the training, I received a call from Jim saying they were going live with the system in two days, without us there to train them. I tried to talk him into waiting for us in May, but he felt the manual and screens were self-explanatory and assured me they would be fine. We expected a ton of phone calls during the ensuing month, but we were wrong. The staff at the Wichita Clinic did an incredible job, and when we spent the week there in May, it was similar to a vacation for all of us, because they really did not require much education. Throughout the years, the Wichita Clinic was a dream client in that they were on autopilot and required minimal support. The majority of support from us came when we sent them new updates.

AN UNEXPECTED CALL

After returning to Klamath Falls and amidst all of the excitement related to the Bergen agreement, I received an unexpected phone call.

"Tim, my name is Ken Eakin. I am the materials manager at Yakima Valley Memorial Hospital. I am now on item number twenty-three of the list you gave Tom Bowman almost two years ago, so I am looking for a new materials-management software system and wondered if you would be interested in giving us a presentation?"

Two weeks later, I found myself back in Yakima, Washington. This time, it was a pleasure to visit the MM operation. Ken was correct; he'd completed the first twenty-two items on the list. The department did not look the same, and it was obvious Ken took everything to heart when he tackled the list. I was competing against Enterprise Systems, Inc. and American Data Services for the contract, and three months later, we installed CLASS in Yakima. Ken and his staff became solid users of our system and had it not been for the remoteness of Yakima, they would have been a good site visit for future clients.

A WELCOME COINCIDENCE

Six weeks after our trip to meet with the Bergen folks in California, I received a call from Larry, who was Bergen's southwest regional vice president working in their Phoenix office. I met him when he attended that first presentation in California (marketing agreement still in the hands of the lawyers). He told me he was recently given the responsibility for managing the kit-packaging facility (KPF) that was located in Hillsboro, Oregon, ten miles west of Portland. It was an organization responsible for creating and selling customized patient-admission and maternity kits to hospitals (each kit is a plastic tub with a toothbrush, a tube of toothpaste, a small box of tissues, a comb, and various other sundries specified by each hospital client). These kits are given to patients when admitted to hospitals as inpatients. Larry said he lacked the expertise to properly evaluate the operation, and Paul suggested he give me a call to see if I would be interested in evaluating their operation for him. He also asked me whether or not I thought CLASS could work with their assembly line as well as be able to manage their inventory. I told him I could perform the consult for him and would assess the feasibility of using CLASS after I saw the entire operation. Larry agreed to pay for a consult, and I was in Hillsboro four days later. I was truly gratified that Paul believed enough in me to have Larry seek my advice.

DELVING INTO A DIFFERENT TYPE
OF SUPPLIES ENVIRONMENT

I didn't know what to expect to find when I visited the KPF. I was just thankful to have another paid consulting gig. Bergen's northwest operation occupied a building that was divided into two sections: the supplies distribution center on one side of the building, and the assembly line with its own supplies necessary for supporting the KPF on the other. The offices, break room, and warehouse space could have easily accommodated an operation twice the size of the KPF. As for the operation itself, the only way to describe it was to call it a mess; walking from one side of the building to the other, the difference was like night and day. Management from the very professionally run supplies-distribution center had no authority over the poorly run KPF, literally a few feet away. When Larry took over the responsibility for the KPF, it was as if he'd inherited the neglected bastard child of the company. The on-site manager was completely overwhelmed by his responsibilities of overseeing the staff that operated the assembly line and who were responsible for maintaining adequate levels of supplies to support the KPF. Those working on the assembly line exhibited total disrespect for him, and the inventory was so disarrayed that it looked as if it was maintained by a group of five-year-old children.

Providing Larry with an evaluation of the operation at the KPF was easy—the place was in dire need of a new manager. There was no established methodology for maintaining adequate levels of supplies, and the people supporting the assembly line were unsupervised. It was anarchy. Unfortunately, the wrong person had been chosen as the manager; he did not understand how to manage people or supplies. Paul and Larry both knew they had a problem, and that is why they sought my advice.

As far as the computer system was concerned, it too was inadequate. After speaking with Lentz about my findings, we agreed CLASS could definitely support the inventory, but he would need to write some new code to support the assembly line and billing system. Essentially, he would convert it to a point-of-sale system that interfaced with CLASS for supporting the inventory, and Larry would need to purchase one of the new smaller IBM System/36s to make it happen.

MAJOR CHANGES ON THE HORIZON

I sent a written formal review to Larry after I returned to Klamath Falls and waited for his reply. Meanwhile, two days later, United Airlines announced its intent to close its operation in Klamath Falls within ninety days. At the time, it was by far the easiest means for me to travel to other cities south and east of the area, and without that commercial air travel available to San Francisco, we could no longer stay in Klamath Falls if we wanted to grow our business. To say we were in a dilemma was an understatement.

When Larry called me after he received my evaluation of the KPF, he said the report was very thorough; it gave him an objective review of the operation. He agreed to purchase an IBM System/36 and pay for a rewrite of CLASS. He said according to reports by the distribution side of the building, my evaluation of the manager was spot-on.

Larry then asked, "Tim, I need your help. Could your company take over the management of the KPF?" I almost choked when he asked the question; I tried to answer him slowly, so as not to sound too eager. I told him Lentz and I would need to move our families to the Portland area in order to make it happen, and we would need to use the vacant office space in the KPF building. He readily agreed, and we found ourselves getting ready to move again.

Just two months later, in May 1988, Lentz and I moved our families and our company to the Portland area to work out of the extra office space adjacent to the offices supporting the KPF. In addition, we had an office for Pat, and he became a full-time member of our staff.

We were able to use the new computer for operating the KPF as well as supporting further development of the System/36 version of CLASS. Two months later, we leased an IBM AS/400, which gave us the stability we needed for supporting the larger hospitals.

The two programmers we'd hired when we took on the contract with Merle West had no desire to move to Portland, and the folks at

Merle West hospital hired them to maintain the information-services department. Unfortunately for us at Health-Ware, Cortie did not move with us; while living in Klamath Falls, she found the love of her life (she and Jim are still married today). We definitely missed having her with us, because during the two years she worked for Health-Ware, she was essentially my assistant MM at the hospital. She also assisted us with installations of CLASS in California, Washington, and Oregon with unbelievable competency. Cortie was a most reliable employee and a very good friend to us all. She was definitely the best hire I ever made, and conversely, the employee who was the most difficult one to say good-bye to. She was a great member of our team as well as a good friend. We have only the fondest of memories of our times with her.

Our contract for managing the KPF was similar to that of the facilities-management contract we signed with Merle West. Bergen paid for all of our moving expenses, we received a monthly fee for managing the KPF, and we had plenty of office space to accommodate us as we grew our company to a staff of fourteen during the next five years—all resulting from an inspired moment during that original phone call with Paul Jordan.

After six months of managing the KPF, my traveling demands increased substantially, and I found myself being stretched too far to adequately manage the operation anymore. Therefore, I asked Jan to take on the responsibility for managing the staff at the KPF. The move proved extremely beneficial on two fronts: it gave her further experience as a manager, in which she turned out to be quite successful, and it gave her the opportunity to become very proficient with CLASS, an attribute that would prove to have profound benefits for Health-Ware in the not-too-distant future.

EVERYTHING FALLING INTO PLACE

Rules Applied:

5. Be an Effective Communicator   *6. Embrace Change*

Some have said that it seemed as if things just seemed to fall into place when we needed them the most. I believe our success was a result of our management practices. If I was unable to confidently communicate the need for change in many of the situations, the nuances would never have presented themselves to us. Also, if Lentz, Jan, and Pat had not been willing to embrace change and adjust themselves to each of the new environments, we never would have been able to successfully manage the challenges before us.

SHOWING THE FLAG

Shortly after our move to the Portland area, Paul Jordan called and asked me whether I could join them in their booth at the trade show for the Arizona Medical Association.

A month later, I joined Paul and his group and set up a display with my computer to give a demonstration of CLASS to anyone showing an interest in what we had to offer. I found this method of promotion to be a poor way to spur interest, as serious candidates for an MMIS would not attempt to look for any type of real presentation in such a public setting. At best, people would ask for a brochure and had little interest in seeing a demo of our product. Of course, there is almost always one exception: in this case, Tom Frith, who was the MM at Sun Health in Sun City, Arizona. He came up to me and asked very specific questions about CLASS.

He inquired, "How does your economic order quantity (EOQ) formula work to drive the automatic purchase-order process?"

"I don't use an EOQ; rather, I developed a formula based on the patient workload."

He was incredulous. "You can't do that!"

I quipped, "Oh, I forgot to read the rule book."

Rather than be offended by my remark, Tom was challenged and wanted to know more. Unfortunately, he did not have enough time to devote to the discussion, so he took my business card and wanted to know if he could call me later and talk about the way I designed the system. Tom called me several times during the ensuing months, and we became good friends over the years. Although I did not acquire any potential leads from the experience, I did find a good friend and colleague.

THE KPF EXPERIENCE

Our time at the Bergen facility, which was located just ten minutes from Tuality, was a great opportunity for us to focus on growing our company. We added three full-time IBM AS/400 qualified programmers (Patti Kelm, Larry Taylor, and Stan Poole) during our first year. We also hired Tom Halverson as a part-time programmer for personal computers (PCs) and made him responsible for programming an order-entry program that would take purchase orders from CLASS and send them electronically to the appropriate vendors. Tom was a qualified IBM AS/400 programmer and was able to program the interface between the computers.

We also hired Mindy from Mid-Columbia Medical Center as a customer-service rep, and we hired Steve Barrett from Tuality as our first trainer to assist Jan on the road with new CLASS installations.

In just two years at the KPF, Jan managed the reduction in inventory by 63 percent (from $675,000 to $250,000) and concurrently increased the level of production of admission kits by 15 percent. Because the KPF looked so much more attractive as a business, Bergen's corporate office decided to sell the business a year later and was able to incur a sizable profit. As a result, we worked ourselves out of a job, because of the great work that was accomplished. When the KPF was sold, we became tenants for the first time in our five years of existence and started paying rent to Bergen (a nominal fee). In less than a year, Bergen was bought out by Owens and Minor, a company located in Richmond, Virginia.

The executives informed us they did not want to align themselves with any particular software company, and we were homeless.

After the buyout, Bergen's entire operation moved to another suburb of Portland, about thirty minutes from Hillsboro. We ended up moving our offices from Hillsboro to an office building in Portland. For the first time, we were officially on our own and no longer worked in someone else's building. At the same time we were moving, Larry Taylor and his wife were both offered and accepted jobs with a company in California. Tom, on the other hand, came onboard as a full-time programmer. He and Patti both moved with us to our new office in Portland.

Although we did not have a contractual relationship with Owens and Minor, the sales reps who were originally with Bergen continued to give us sales leads for years to come. In fact, our two largest clients, Ohio State University and Washington Hospital Center, came to us as a result of our relationship with the Bergen reps, four years after their company was sold to Owens and Minor.

10. A DIFFICULT LESSON TO LEARN

John Guju was the director of materials management at Harrison Memorial Hospital of Bremerton, Washington, who became a new user of CLASS after going through the normal acquisition process. The transition process at Harrison was no different than for any of our other clients until after I visited John during one of my trips to the Washington area. They had gone through their online conversion about two months prior to my visit, and he asked for a modification to the system in a response to a request from his chief financial officer (CFO). It was a reasonable request, so I called Lentz and asked him to dial in and make the change for me. He agreed to do so; however, Lentz told me he did not like dialing in because he always wanted changes to be tested before they were ever sent out to the field. Lentz reluctantly made the change, John was pleased, and I went on my way.

WE HAVE A PROBLEM

Six weeks after my visit to Bremerton, John called and said his CFO was upset because his general ledger (GL) was out of balance. We did not have an answer for him, especially since they had the same version of CLASS as all of our clients who were not reporting any problems. Unfortunately, four more weeks passed by and we still believed the problem was due to user error, and we did not offer any solutions. The CFO called me and said it was not an internal problem and I needed to send someone to balance their GL immediately. There wasn't a choice; that afternoon, Jan took two of her training staff with her and spent three days auditing two months of transactions. While Jan and her staff were in Bremerton, Lentz and his programmers scoured through the programing code in our office and found nothing wrong. However, Jan reported that the GL was out of balance and she could only attribute it to something CLASS was incorrectly posting to the ledger. After she determined it was somehow our fault, Lentz immediately went to Bremerton so he could look at the code on-site. It took him another day, but he did find the error. It was a single letter placed in the code that threw everything out of balance, and it occurred when he dialed in and made the custom change for me eleven weeks earlier.

ADMITTING OUR MISTAKE

After Lentz told me what he discovered, I immediately went to meet with John's CFO to admit the problem was our fault. I told him how the error occurred and why we had incorrectly assumed it was an internal problem. The CFO thanked me for responding to his demands so quickly and for my honesty about what happened. He then informed me he no longer wanted our services. I understood we were at fault, but after we pulled out all stops to correct the situation and admitted our mistake, I was surprised that he essentially fired us.

I wish I could say we were the only casualty of the incident; unfortunately, John lost his job because he was not more forceful with us when the GL problem was first discovered. Admittedly, John should have put our feet to the fire. However, with all of the positive reviews he received from Dave Maclachlan at Valley and Terri Cartier at Evergreen, he believed us when we said the problem had to be an internal one. John never harbored any ill feelings toward us and said he realized the error was a result of something he asked of me when I was visiting with him. John said the CFO was a loose cannon, and he was not surprised by the man's actions. John was subsequently hired as the materials manager for a group of medical clinics in Washington and requested a presentation about CLASS at his new organization. I wasn't sure we deserved it, but I was gratified by his loyalty, especially considering the problems that happened at his previous place of employment.

MADE A MISTAKE

Rule Applied:

8. Be Consistent; Be Decisive

I would like to blame the incident on the CFO's inability to forgive us after making the mistake. However, the change to the code that skewed the GL was not the mistake; rather, it was us not checking into John's original complaint that got us into trouble. If we had requested copies of the GL so we could search for the error in the beginning, we could have short-circuited the problem and perhaps kept them as a client. More important, John would not have lost his job because of one of our mistakes.

There is no denying the fact that it was a painful lesson to learn.

The entire debacle was a wake-up call for all of us. First of all, I no longer asked Lentz to dial in to a site and make custom changes to CLASS on the spot. Future requests for customization were put through a rigorous testing process before they were ever released to the client.

The incident just described actually occurred shortly after we finalized the marketing agreement between Bergen and Health-Ware, and after we moved to the Portland area. I shared the event with Paul Jordan of Bergen so he would not hear about it from someone else.

The problem at Harrison was caused by my desire to please our client, and it backfired on me. The CFO could have hurt us badly with future potential clients; if he did so, I was unaware of it, since we signed several other clients in the state of Washington subsequent to the event at Bremerton.

———

11. A BUSINESS PARTNER WITH CLOUT

Our software operated only on IBM hardware: specifically, the System/36 for the first two years, the System/38 for the next two years, and the AS/400 from then on. Lugging the PC/36, the PC/AT, and the monitor was becoming a real drag; however, at the time, it was the only way for us to demonstrate our wares. Later we acquired a PC projector, which at the time cost $6,000 (today about $350). It allowed us to present to larger audiences, yet we were inhibited by having to switch back and forth from the System/36 to the PC so we could use the PC for managing the presentation. We did the best we could with what we had, but it was definitely not professional enough for my satisfaction.

Today, we often hear big corporations being vilified. Well, I have a story about the biggest corporation in the computer industry that showed us *big* at its best. In the early '90s, IBM enhanced its Business Partner Program, through which they gave reputable small businesses selling software on IBM hardware access to their executive conference centers for presenting products to prospective clients (the program has changed significantly over the years). These centers were located in cities throughout the United States; the only caveat from IBM was that the software must work well on IBM hardware. These rooms were always state-of-the-art, with executive-quality furniture, an overhead projector, a large presentation screen connected to the AS/400 (and all of the other computer systems), a PC, an overhead projector, and anything else we might need to successfully present our software—and, most importantly, IBM's tacit support. When scheduling a presentation for a hospital, we would contact the IBM office closest to our prospective client and arrange for the use of its executive conference center. I would always arrive at each destination the day before, introduce myself to the rep at the IBM center, give our tapes for loading on the AS/400, go through a dry run, and then meet with the prospective client the next day. We were responsible for providing any snacks to our audience, but even then, oftentimes the local IBM rep would assist in that area, just so we could be assured of providing a successful demonstration of our software. On the day of the presentation, we were able to enter the conference room with complete confidence, knowing we were prepared. The IBM rep would often sit in on the presentation and observe the response by our prospective clients. After we'd used these facilities a few times, the IBM reps for subsequent presentations always graciously accepted me when I arrived. We would never have had the resources to present in such an expensive setting.

COOPERATION TO THE MAX

The most interesting presentation I ever made at an IBM center was when, in the fall of 1994, I met with Terry Jones, the VP of materials management (MM) at Ohio State University Medical Center (a 1,500-bed facility). After reviewing our promotional material, he said he was going to a meeting in San Diego and wanted to know if I had a site visit in Southern California. I suggested I give him a personalized presentation at the IBM building in Los Angeles and visit the folks at Glendale Adventist Medical Center afterward.

He agreed, so I made the arrangements with the IBM office in downtown Los Angeles; they had no problem with me presenting to an out-of-state organization. When I met Terry for the presentation, it was rather surreal, in that it was just the two of us in the huge executive conference room that could comfortably seat an audience of fifty. Terry had already checked with some of the clients I gave as references and was eager to see CLASS up close. Just forty minutes into the presentation, he informed me that he had seen enough, and asked me how soon I could make it out to Columbus, Ohio, to give a presentation to his staff. I was shocked to hear he had more than two hundred full-time equivalents (FTEs) on his staff, which meant he had more than 275 employees on his payroll to cover multiple shifts and part-time employees. I did not care how big of an institution we were dealing with; I believed he had way too many people to get the job done. I knew if he had CLASS as his materials-management information system (MMIS), Terry would be able to incur a considerable reduction in staff.

A full presentation usually took about two hours to complete, but Terry was very decisive and felt he had more than enough to warrant a presentation at home. It ended up that he did not go to the site visit in Glendale. A week later, Terry called from Ohio State and extended an invitation to demonstrate CLASS at the IBM center in Columbus. He asked me to give two presentations in one day because he wanted various department heads to attend, and all could not be there for an early-morning presentation. He said more than seventy employees from throughout the organization would be in attendance throughout the day. I arranged for the use of the IBM center in Columbus; we used their facilities a second time for presenting to the same organization. Along with the invitation for the presentation, Terry asked that I visit with him the day before, so he could give me a cook's tour of the medical center. The facility was huge, and putting CLASS there was going to definitely test our concepts for operating MM in a massive complex. After the tour, Terry invited me to his home for dinner, where I met his wife and children.

The next day, Terry stayed for only the first ninety minutes of the day and apologized for leaving early. He told me he was certain the day would go well, and he would be contacting me to arrange for the next step of our relationship. Before leaving for Columbus, I remember telling my staff, "The only way I could lose this sale is if my fly is down during the presentation." This a true story: after I completed the day and was outside of the IBM building standing on the sidewalk in downtown Columbus, I panicked as I realized I had forgotten to check my zipper … no worries, it was up. At the time, the sale to Ohio State University Medical Center was the biggest for Health-Ware and elevated our status even more with a 1,500-bed medical center under our belt. For IBM, Ohio State purchased two AS/400s to meet its needs.

ONE REQUIREMENT: BE A REPUTABLE COMPANY USING IBM HARDWARE

Many times, our prospective clients already had an AS/400 in their hospitals and did not require additional hardware. Yet the folks at IBM never objected to us using their facilities; it was enough for them to know their client was satisfied enough to be adding more software to their IBM hardware. Of course, there were times when we added a new client for whom acquiring new hardware was indeed part of the process. We even received a nominal commission when a sale of hardware did occur. Sometimes our share of the sale provided us with a decent paycheck when some of the larger institutions required equipment that cost nearly half a million dollars. We chose not to sell the equipment; rather, we let IBM deal with the client in that area. Our specialty was software, and we knew it.

We were thankful for everything the people at IBM did for us through the use of their Business Partner Program; they gave us the ability to present our software in a professional manner, regardless of the size of our company. When we presented to our prospective clients, they were able to evaluate CLASS for what it was: a quality solution for operating MM in a health-care environment. An interesting fact about us being able to use the IBM facilities was that prospective clients rarely expressed concerns over the size of our company. It appeared as if IBM and Health-Ware were actual partners, an illusion that worked to our benefit. Yet if we would have ever disappointed any of the IBM reps, our relationship would have been short-lived. Although the program was for showcasing IBM hardware, for us it was much bigger in that it provided us as a small business with the means to compete against those who had the resources to do so on their own. I was able to give presentations in IBM centers at such places as Los Angeles, California; Dayton, Ohio; Columbus, Ohio; Portland, Oregon; Augusta, Georgia; and Silver Park, Maryland, to name just a few. Our thanks go out to the folks at IBM—with them as a true business partner, our successes were definitely increased. Imagine how expensive it would have been to rent such facilities—the cost would have been prohibitive for our small company.

A GREAT RELATIONSHIP

Rules Applied:

3. Look the Part   4. Play the Part   5. Be an Effective Communicator

There is no doubt we would never have been taken seriously by anybody representing IBM if we were unable to give a good presentation. In addition, we always looked our best and acted as if we belonged to their team. We had to be true professionals.

---

12. EVERYBODY'S JOB: MAKE THE CLIENT #1—NO EXCEPTIONS

The majority of our sales presentations were engaging and invigorating; as soon as I received the nod from the prospective client that I had a new sale (usually within the first hour), I switched my role from salesman to fellow materials manager. Oftentimes, the trust I seemed to gain from what I had to say to these very new clients-to-be was gratifying. One of the more interesting times was when I presented to the materials management (MM) staff of Merritt Peralta Medical Center at the IBM building in Oakland, California.

The 450-bed multihospital system was in need of department restructuring before it could even begin to upgrade its materials-management information system (MMIS). The presentation began at nine o'clock and continued until late afternoon. Within the first hour of the presentation, I cited as an example the time I successfully quadrupled the number of items stocked in our warehouse. At first, they were dubious about the idea that they could add even one more item to their inventory.

I responded with a conviction of someone who believes in what he is saying, "With proper organization, combined with the use of our system, you will not believe how many more stock items you will be able to add to your inventory."

I emphasized that quantities of most items would go down significantly as new items were added. Greg Van Riper, the director of purchasing, asked if it would be possible for me to go to the hospital and take a look at the warehouse immediately after I finished with the presentation. I was on a tight schedule that day, but I was already packed to leave for the airport, which was only twenty minutes from the hospital. I agreed, and afterward I followed him and his staff to the hospital for a quick run-through to assess the situation.

The way the warehouse was organized, they definitely did not have room for any more supplies. The department had doubled in size when the two hospitals merged into one, and they did not have the expertise at the time for combining inventories. Although they did need a new MMIS, I strongly recommended that they reorganize the warehouse before they acquired it. I said if they performed the reorganization in a specific manner, they could ultimately increase the number of line items while concurrently reducing the overall amount of supplies maintained on the shelves. They were a bit skeptical but realized I believed in what I was saying. Greg said they wouldn't know where to begin to make it happen, so I volunteered to send them a diagram for reorganizing the shelving if they sent me a layout of the warehouse with all of its dimensions.

When I returned to my office the next day, a fax was waiting on my desk with the layout I'd requested. I spent four hours on the project and sent a proposed layout that depicted what I would do if I were in charge of the project. There were no guarantees I would get a signed contract from them, but I didn't care because I had just made a friend who could use my help. If nothing else came of it, maybe I would at least get some good PR as a result of my efforts. Ultimately, Greg and his staff did purchase CLASS.

When I visited the hospital four months later to give the initial one-day training session that launched them on their way to going live with CLASS, I was able to see the results of my proposed changes to the warehouse. The workers were proud of their accomplishments, and rightfully so.

GOING THE EXTRA STEP

Merritt Peralta became a fantastic client, and it was always great to receive calls from the folks there. On one occasion, Jan took a call from Greg, and when he told her to say hi to our staff, she responded by saying, "Here, say hi to them yourself. Lentz, Tom, and Tim all happen to be in the main office." Jan then punched the speaker phone, and after we said hi, Greg mentioned that he thought it would be nice if the next release had a certain field added to the purchase-order inquiry screen. Jan pulled up the screen for me as he was speaking and pointed to where Greg thought it should be added. Lentz was also looking at the screen while I described to Lentz what Greg was requesting.

While Greg was talking, I whispered to Lentz, "That's a valid request, and it's an easy one to accomplish, isn't it? What are the chances you could give it to him tonight and not tell him you are doing it?" Lentz rolled his eyes and said I was correct, it would be easy, and he would do it. (Of course he would.)

The next morning, Greg called again. "Imagine how surprised I was when I signed in to the purchase-order module only to find my idea that you said would go in the next release up and running *today*."

I told him, "It was a good idea, Greg, and we just wanted to surprise you."

"You guys are amazing!"

It was incidents like this that gave us a sense of satisfaction at the end of the day.

MAKING AN IMPORTANT POINT

Another incident showed that not all our employees had embraced the concept of going the extra mile for the client.

Stan had been with us for four months, after coming from Josephine Memorial Hospital of Grants Pass, Oregon, which was one of our clients. We had known him for a year and found him to be a likeable and organized programmer. He worked incredibly well while ensuring the installation and online conversion of CLASS at his hospital went off without a hitch. When he let us know he wanted to move to Portland, it was an easy decision to hire him, as we were in need of another programmer. On one occasion, I went to our programmers' office, and Stan was the only person in the room at the time, sitting at his desk across the room with his back to me. He was just ending his call with a customer, and he did not hear me enter the room. I was just waiting for him to finish.

After listening for about thirty seconds, I heard him say, "Linda, you just need to call your data-processing department and someone there will be able to assist you."

After he completed the call, he turned around to see me standing behind him, and he looked *guilty*. I had heard enough of the conversation to know that it would have taken Stan just a few minutes to help Linda with her problem.

I asked him, "Hey, Stan, was that Linda Underwood from St. Helena Community Hospital?" (We had only one client named Linda.)

"Yes."

"Couldn't you have helped her take care of her problem in about five minutes?"

"Yes."

"Why didn't you just take care of her problem? Why put her through the hassle of having to call data processing and relay her problem all over again? She might even need to deal with missed calls, since it happens to be lunchtime right now."

He looked me straight in the face and said, "It's not my job."

I had to turn around and leave the room. I was proud of myself for not blowing up, because I truly believed I had every reason to do so. Evidently, by the time I reached my office, I was flushed beet-red, because Pat saw me pass by his window and immediately came out to ask me why I looked so upset. I explained what had happened and said I just couldn't believe how Stan was so matter-of-fact about it. Pat then asked, "What do you want to do about it?"

"Pat, do you know that United Airlines commercial where the general manager of a company walks into the main office?"

"No, I have never seen it, what's it about?"

I did my best to recap the story:

The general manager of a company—Ben—walks into an open office and begins to talk in generalities about how conducting business has changed from giving the personal touch to their clients. Instead, they use telephone calls and faxes for communicating with them. The boss goes on to say, "Well, I just received a call from our oldest client, who just fired us." (While he is talking, his secretary passes out United Airlines tickets to each of his employees.)

Ben continues, "We are going to change the way we do things from now on, beginning with personally visiting each of our clients."

One of his employees says aloud, "Ben, that means over two hundred cities."

Then the secretary hands Ben an airline ticket.

Another employee asks, "Ben, where are you going?"

Ben responds by saying, "I'm going to see that old friend that just fired us."

It had played on TV so often, I was surprised when Pat told me he had not seen the commercial. I mumbled, "I only wish I knew when United was going to play that commercial again in Portland."

"Why?"

"If I had a tape of that commercial, I would call an employee meeting and share it with everyone."

Pat could see I was serious and quipped, "Boss, let me make a few phone calls, and I'll see if I can find out for you."

About thirty minutes later, Pat came to my office and said that after being passed on to four different secretaries, he finally connected with one who could talk about the commercial.

Pat said, "When I asked her if she could tell me when that commercial would be playing in the Portland area, she said she couldn't possibly get that information for us."

My heart sank.

Pat continued, "Then she said, 'But I can do better than that. I will contact our PR firm, and you should have a copy of the tape in your hands by tomorrow afternoon.'"

Pat really came through for me, not to mention United Airlines. I immediately called Jan and asked her if there was a day anytime soon when all of our employees would be in town. Much to my surprise, she said the following Wednesday was available, and it was the only day with everyone in town for the next three weeks. I asked her to inform everyone there was a mandatory meeting at two that Wednesday.

At the time, we didn't have any reason to keep a VCR (DVDs were not on the market yet) or TV in the office, so Jan and I brought our own to the office for the meeting. While we were setting up the room prior to the meeting, some of our employees arrived a little ahead of time. For the first time ever (and the last), I didn't greet the employees in my normal friendly manner. Instead, I was rather subdued as they were arriving. I had asked Jan to do the same, just so we could set the tone of the meeting as a serious event. We weren't rude, just busy without time for small talk. When comments like "Where's the popcorn, and are drinks provided?" were made, we simply responded with polite smiles.

After everyone was seated, I stood up and said, "Heaven help us if it ever gets to the point where I need to give such a speech to you."

With that said, I turned out the lights, and Jan played the one-minute commercial for us. At the end, one could hear a pin drop. There was an eerie quiet that overcame the group. Jan noted that Pat had tears in his eyes. I understood, because even today, I choke up every time I try to recap the commercial for others. I identify with how one would feel if his business had ever come to the point where it would lose a client because of a feeling of despair on the client's part. It was at this juncture that I swore we would never take a client for granted, and we were going to make every one of our clients a success story of their own. After all, Health-Ware Management Company only existed because of the successes our clients enjoyed with our system. When a materials manager and chief financial officer made the decision to purchase our software, they did so because they believed that they too would reap the benefits CLASS had to offer. I made a promise to myself that I would turn this negative into a positive by showing the entire staff how serious I was about quality customer service. I took it for granted that everyone knew how I felt, and I realized that as our company grew, in-service training would be vital to our success. The majority of the employees responded favorably to the commercial and understood the reason for the meeting. Stan just sat there looking stoic and rather uncomfortable. Unfortunately, instead of turning him into the type of employee we required, it just made him resent me even more. I realized hiring him was a mistake, and I was disappointed in myself for not seeing that part of his personality *before* offering him a job. I needed all of our employees to be as customer-service minded as the rest of us. It was imperative that every staff member at Health-Ware treat our clients the same way they treated me. If they did so, I knew we had a prescription for success. Stan never saw it that way. Just four weeks after the staff meeting, he chose to go work as a programmer in a hospital where he didn't need to worry about interfacing with clients.

GETTING A POINT ACROSS

Rule Applied:

11. Define Expectations

It was important to address my concerns relative to providing quality customer service soon after the incident with Stan. I needed to communicate my desires so other staff members understood my commitment to providing outstanding support for our customers. Pat, Jan, and Lentz were the only other staff members I told about the reason for the staff meeting, and when we did show the tape, I never referred to Stan or the incident.

I did not plan on firing Stan, and I was surprised when he decided to quit working with us. However, it was better that he leave if he could not live up to our standards.

Even though the incident with Stan was the impetus behind the meeting, I realized it would not hurt for every member of the staff to see just how important it was for us to give quality customer service. After discussing the matter with the management team, we made a point of sending each of the programmers on the road for an installation. At first it seemed like a luxury we could ill afford, but I considered it to be worth the effort. We began sending all employees, one at a time, to a facility so they could interact with a client in the field. I cannot adequately describe just how much such a move improved the morale of each of the employees. Afterward, it was only too evident that attitudes changed for the better. They always returned with a different perspective, and when they answered the phone, there was a special pep in their voices when speaking with the client, especially if it happened to be the client they visited on-site. The overwhelming benefit that came from this whole fiasco was the positive impact it had on the client base, as I always received positive feedback from the clients afterward. Not only was our staff able to personalize the connection, but the clients were also able to identify with them when they called the office.

We were able to take a negative and turn it into a positive. They say a picture is worth a thousand words—well, seeing someone in person can be worth several thousand.

―――――――

13. AN INCREDIBLE PROSPECT

We never said no to a lead from anyone at Bergen, even if we considered it to be an impossible sales opportunity. After all, they gave us the lead to Mayo Clinic's campus in Scottsdale, Arizona, and we thought that was a long shot before the sale came to fruition. You can imagine how exciting it was when Pat walked into my office and told me Lottie Poe of Bergen had just given us our best lead to date: a group of fifteen hospitals. The potential client was Adventist Health Systems (AHS) West, which was headquartered in Roseville, California, a suburb of Sacramento. With news of that magnitude, we always brought Lentz and Jan into the loop, as they too were owners and would welcome the adrenaline rush. Our first response was one of excitement—it could mean a large influx of income and a decent bump to our monthly maintenance money. Nevertheless, our emotions were reserved, since it was just a potential lead and a slim one at best. Anyway, the four of us had fun talking about what such a potential lead would bring to us if we ever made it happen.

We looked at any hospital or clinic as something our system could handle, regardless of size. However, we had a few concerns when it came to the idea of taking on a hospital chain like some of our competitors were doing:

1. The support for our current clients could be compromised if we took on a group of hospitals all at once. We enjoyed being able to give our new clients individual attention when we assisted them with their online conversion with CLASS. I remember when we were courting a potential client, I called Debbie Auchterberg of Sierra View District Hospital in Porterville, California, to ask

if I could use her as a reference. I received a response from her I will never forget: "Will I still get the same level of support from Health-Ware when you are driving a Mercedes?" From that point on, I always thought of her response each time I provided a list of references to prospective clients. Accordingly, I realized just how important it was that when we took on new clients, we continued providing support at a level equal to or better than before.

2. We were well aware of our small size compared to our competitors, and although we openly discussed the possibility of taking on a group when we formed our company, we agreed it was probably something for us in the distant future. Remember my premise: we were operating in a fog. Well, looking back while I write this book, I realize that some of the time that fog bank was impenetrable. There we were, thinking about attempting to take on a group of fifteen hospitals when at the time, we had a client base of only eighteen hospitals and two clinics, and we were supporting that client base with a staff of six. The last thing we wanted to do was to take on a project that could cause the wheels to fall off. Not only would converting this lead into a client require scores of steps, it would take us into unfamiliar territory, such as the need for adding and training a considerable number of new staff members quickly. Also, the possibility of having to manage concurrent online conversions would be a new challenge. It wasn't going to be the first time we would find ourselves delving into the unknown, but we didn't need to concern ourselves about such a possibility and put the cart before the horse.

We'd met Lottie when Pat and I first went to Bergen's headquarters in Orange, California, to meet with Paul and his executive staff two years earlier. Lottie was the lead sales representative invited to attend, and it became obvious as to why she was number one when we later had opportunities to work with her. She was the most hard-working, positive, and professional sales rep I had met from *any* company. Therefore, it was no surprise when we learned that of all the Bergen sales reps, she had the most and the largest hospitals in her assigned territory. She did an amazing job of familiarizing us with each hospital before we arrived, always ensuring we were ready.

We were presenting to one of the AHS/West hospitals located in Simi Valley, California. Dick Meyers was the director of materials management and a devout member of the Seventh Day Adventist religion, as well as a senior employee of the Adventist organization. Furthermore, he had been employed by AHS his entire adult life, mostly in the field of materials management. Although he wasn't managing one of the bigger materials operations in the corporation, Dick had enough experience in the Adventist system that his opinion on matters concerning materials management was well regarded. He admitted he wasn't in charge of one of the larger hospitals of AHS/West, but he was indeed one of the most vocal of its members.

Dick told us the folks at the AHS/West corporate office were searching for a new automated materials-management information system (MMIS) to replace an outdated one that had been acquired from a company no longer in business. The corporate data-processing department (today known as information technology or information systems) was supporting the software and found it difficult to meet the needs of the hospital materials managers (MMs). As a result, they were looking for a solution from another company, or at least that's what we were led to believe. Dick had heard about us from Lottie at Bergen, and after reviewing our promotional materials, he decided to extend us an invitation so he could see what we had to offer up close and personal.

Dick greeted us with open arms, and his warmth and sincerity were obvious from the outset. He said he was receptive to new ideas and anxious to look at our system. Although the chief financial officer (CFO) didn't show up for the presentation, we decided to give the full show anyway. We wanted Dick to have enough information to share with the folks at his corporate office. Dick had a difficult time containing his enthusiasm, and he became an instant ally throughout the entire presentation process. It was a relationship that would have a profound significance in the near future. He admitted that even though he would express his thoughts and desires to the corporate selection committee, he was a small fish in a big pond; a few of the hospitals in the group were three times the size of his own.

The group would be the perfect size for us. However, since we only had twenty clients at the time, I didn't consider our chances to be very good. Dick's operation was typical of a 150-bed hospital, and it was obvious we could help him in a big way. We brought our PC/36 with us and gave the presentation to him and his staff in his office. It wasn't a typical demonstration of our software, in that it was about as disorganized as it could be. People were coming and going, and phone calls were being accepted by almost everyone in the room; it was difficult to finish a sentence without an interruption. Nevertheless, Dick was engaged and duly impressed, assuring me he was going to get the word out to the right people in his organization. I liked Dick, but I left with the feeling I was unable to give it my best.

Well, evidently the Simi Valley demo *was* good enough, because not long after our meeting, Pat received a call from Dick who told him to call Brett Spenst at AHS/West system headquarters. Brett was the project manager appointed to facilitate the process for finding an MMIS for his company's fifteen hospitals. We didn't meet him for about two weeks, but when we did, like Dick from Simi Valley, Brett made us feel quite welcome and at ease. When we met him, he was a young executive in the organization—even younger than I was—and also a lifelong member of the Adventist religion and organization. He worked in the field of finance and was appointed by Terry Burns, who was the assistant CFO and the VP over data processing (now information systems) as well. Terry was a tough, no-nonsense individual who obviously had a great amount of responsibility when dealing with the management of the computer operations of a multi-hospital organization located in the states of California, Washington, Oregon, and Hawaii. Brett was the perfect person to serve as a buffer between Terry and the vendors involved with the acquisition process.

I must digress for a moment and share the fact that, prior to giving a presentation to the Adventists, I knew nothing about their religion. My first demo to an Adventist organization was three years earlier to the materials-management department of Loma Linda University Medical Center, a prestigious institution with such acclaimed surgical operations as "Baby Faye." Dave Russell was the director of materials management. When we shook hands, I knew I had met him before, I just didn't know where.

I greeted him with, "Hi, Dave, you look familiar."

"No, I'm sorry. I don't remember you."

I could have stopped there, but no, I continued with, "Maybe we had a drink together at a health-care conference somewhere."

He curtly responded, "No, that wasn't it." He didn't look offended, but let's say *annoyed* best described his demeanor.

"Oh well, maybe it was over a cup of coffee."

"No, that wasn't it either."

Well, I couldn't have blown an introduction prior to turning on the microphone more than if I had intentionally wanted to sabotage my own delivery before it even began, and I was totally oblivious as to why. Pat kindly pulled me aside and filled me in that Adventists didn't eat red meat, consume drinks with caffeine or alcohol, or use tobacco.

It was a classic example of inserting one's own foot into one's own mouth. It was that presentation that convinced me to do my homework prior to every presentation and not *during* it. By the way, the reason Dave looked familiar to me was that he had been the director of materials management at Portland Adventist Medical Center prior to his current assignment, and we had met before at a conference in the Portland area, but not over a drink or a cup of coffee. The presentation went well, but it was obvious Dave and his staff felt we were too small of a company to be able to support his operation. Besides, we didn't have much to show in numbers, as we had only a few clients at the time. In the end, Dave chose Enterprise Systems, Inc. (ESI) as his new MMIS vendor.

A year later, it turned out I would have a reason to be in the backyard of Loma Linda University Medical Center. I was invited by Neal Hartwig, the MM of Loma Linda Community Hospital, a 150-bed hospital that was located virtually in the shadow of the University Medical Center's campus. Neal was in his midthirties and wanted to better his organization while remaining autonomous from the medical center's materials-management operation. He needed to automate his department, and although Dave at the medical center had offered to bring Neal's department online with their system (the PC-based system from ESI), Neal wanted no part of it; he didn't want to be an MM in name only. Although his hospital was loosely attached to the University Medical Center as a staff organization, there was no line authority between the two facilities; it had its own executive staff and operated with its own budget and mission statement.

When Dave heard Neal had decided to go with CLASS as his MMIS, he invited Neal to visit with him and attempted to persuade Neal to change his mind. Nevertheless, with the backing of his CEO, Neal was given the go-ahead to acquire our system, a decision that bothered Dave for some time. I never saw Dave throughout the entire process when I visited Neal at his hospital, but Neal always gave me updates after he had the opportunity to show off his progress with CLASS to members of the University Medical Center's MM staff.

AN ATTENTIVE AND ENTHUSIASTIC AUDIENCE

Back to the AHS/West presentation. We presented at its headquarters in Roseville, California, on a Wednesday morning. When I first met Terry Burns, he told us he was in the process of hiring a corporate director of materials management and thought he should have one in place within one or two months. Actually, I was relieved he did *not* have a materials-management director in place; it meant I would have one less ego to contend with. Terry explained we were one of three vendors being considered for their MMIS solution. The other two companies were ESI (a company with a PC solution and over five hundred clients at the time), which was presenting on Thursday, and the AHS/West data-processing department (IS or IT), which was presenting on Friday morning. All fifteen hospitals were represented by their respective directors of materials management, and the CFOs were also in attendance—a fact demonstrating just how serious they were about evaluating a new MMIS.

The sizes of the hospitals in the group ranged from ten to 450 beds.

I looked forward to the idea of putting CLASS in all of their hospitals, regardless of size—something I had always believed possible. Instead of taking the PC/36 with us, we were allowed to put our software on their IBM AS/400 used at their corporate office. Lentz included enough security that we were not worried about them getting a workable copy. I knew within thirty minutes I had the majority, if not all, of the materials-management directors very interested in what we had to say. There was a myriad of questions from the audience attempting to apply the radical new approach to their own hospitals.

After I demonstrated how CLASS treated nonstock the same as stock items and how it eliminated the need for manually posting the general ledger expenses for nonstock items, I had the attention of everybody in the room.

To stress my point, I shared a saying with the audience I used regarding our treatment of supplies: "When looking at an item to be purchased, one will ask, 'Is it stock or nonstock?' Our response, 'We don't care.'"

I will never forget when Tally Dorn from Glendale Adventist Medical Center stood up and said, "Don't you think 'we don't care' is a rather dangerous motto to be espousing as a vendor?" The audience (and I) got a good laugh from his comment. Tally came up to me afterward and said, "Tim, it is obvious you *do* care."

When I shared the story about convincing my OR director to let us stock the sutures in our warehouse, many in the audience told me there was no way their OR directors would ever approve turning over control of items such as sutures to materials management. I responded by saying, "I did not gain the trust of the surgery manager overnight. I first had to prove I could manage keeping adequate amounts of lap sponges and customized lap packs in our warehouse. I do not want to tell you what she said to me when we once back-ordered lap sponges to her. Afterward, I knew that was one item I would never run out of, period."

The presentation to the Adventist organization was an invigorating experience, and I felt I had just gained a group of believers in our system.

After more than four hours (which included a vegetarian lunch), I thanked everyone for their attention.

I was about to leave the podium when Terry stood up in front of the group and said, "I think we should end Tim's presentation by saying *amen!* He truly spoke the gospel about materials management in a way that we have never heard with such conviction."

For a brief moment, I was uneasy, and then the entire audience jumped to their feet and gave me a standing ovation (even the CFOs). To say the least, I felt *very* good about the way the demo had gone. Brett immediately stood up and extended his hand to thank me for the time and effort and told me he had received an overwhelming amount of positive feedback from many of the attendees during the course of the day. He told us he did not see how ESI could possibly captivate this tough crowd the way I did, and he looked forward to calling us on Friday with good news. In addition, the majority of the MMs came to me and thanked me for the day. It had been, indeed, a very good day. We were looking at a possible $400,000 sale, and just as important, a decent monthly maintenance fee. We were trying not to count our chickens before they hatched, but it was difficult to not feel so confident.

It was no surprise there was some excitement in the air when Pat and I returned home. Pat always took good notes during all of our presentations (a valuable tool for critiquing an event), and he said he could not believe how positive the entire group had been throughout the day. We knew we didn't have a contract, but we were pretty good at predicting a sale or rejection. Every indication was we had a sale.

You can imagine the shock felt throughout the office when Brett called us that Friday afternoon (as he said he would) to tell us the Adventist MMs unanimously chose their corporate data-processing department as the vendor of choice for their new system. That call confirmed my belief that Fridays are reserved for giving both good and bad news. If you look back at what day of the week layoffs, promotions, or the awarding of contracts occurs, you might be surprised to find they usually happen on a Friday. Unfortunately, the folks from Roseville reinforced my belief in this phenomenon.

We were devastated by the news, and it was a very long afternoon, as we were in total disbelief. I had a difficult time believing they decided to not go with CLASS as their system of choice. I tried to show a positive face for the rest of the staff, but I admit I was devastated. I knew I had the vast majority of the MMs eating out of my hand, so what happened?

THE REST OF THE STORY

When we returned to work on Monday, we shook off the rejection we received on Friday and went back to work with what we were doing before. On Wednesday, I received a conference call from two of the Adventist MMs: Dick Meier from Simi Valley and Jim Duncan from Feather River Community Hospital. Both of them were obvious supporters of CLASS during the presentation of the previous week. Dick was calling from his hospital bed, where he was recovering from an emergency surgery, and Jim was calling from his office in Paradise, California. They advised me not to be surprised when I received a call from Brett in a couple of days. Of course I was a bit confused, but they quickly clarified the reason for the comment. Jim recapped the following:

"All of the AHS/West CEOs went to a management retreat last weekend in Sunriver, Oregon, immediately following the last MMIS presentation, where they were planning their strategies for the upcoming fiscal year. The corporate CEO asked Terry Burns to share the results of the MMIS search with all of his CEOs. Terry announced they had a unanimous decision by all of those who attended the presentations and chose to have the corporate data-processing department develop a new MMIS rather than buy a system from an outside company.

"George, who is my CEO, had spoken to me Thursday evening just before leaving for Oregon to attend the retreat. I told George everyone agreed CLASS was exactly what they needed. When George heard Terry announce the results of the vote, he immediately left the conference room so he could call me at home. He told me, 'Jim, I thought you were enamored with that CLASS system, so why would you vote for the corporate DP department?' I told him I still wanted CLASS, but Terry met privately with his CFOs prior to voting for an MMIS and strong-armed them into voting for his department to develop a new system instead of going with one of the others. He suggested they get the MMs onboard with the idea. When they returned to the open meeting to vote, many of the CFOs in turn applied pressure on their MMs to vote with them. Most MMs worked for them and felt compelled to do so, regardless of what they wanted. When only a few renegades like Dick and me voted for CLASS, Terry said, 'Come on folks, let's make this a unanimous decision.' I told George, 'The other holdouts and I raised our hands to make it unanimous. After all, we had to work with Terry in the future.'

"After I finished my recap, George was livid and returned to his meeting with the CEOs. He asked if he could have the floor; of course, the corporate CEO acknowledged George to hear what he had to say. George then volunteered the true story behind that unanimous vote. George told me the corporate CEO was visibly upset. After he looked at Terry Burns, he turned to the CEOs and stated, 'This was a choice for the MMs to make, not the CFOs.' He told the others to leave the meeting room and call their MMs to get a true count regarding their system of choice, and not let the CFOs desire affect their response. All of the CEOs were released to make the necessary calls and reported back with their results. Fourteen of the fifteen CEOs came back with a vote in favor of CLASS as their system of choice. George said the CFO of that one hold-out told her MM he could not change his vote."

Wow, what a phone call. The bottom line was that if Jim had not kept George apprised of his desire to acquire CLASS the night before the "unanimous vote," and if George had not felt compelled to call Jim at home from the CEOs retreat, the decision would never have been reversed. Jim said Brett Spenst had informed him that Terry was instructed by the corporate CEO to correct the situation and to notify the folks at Health-Ware Management Company they were going to be the new MMIS vendor. Of course, we were elated and almost in disbelief (this time in a good way). One could not script such a chain of events, and because Jim and Dick advised me of all that had occurred, it put me in a very good position when it came to negotiating the terms of the contract.

Brett did indeed call me on Friday and invited me to return to Roseville so Terry and I could negotiate the terms of the contract (again, reinforcing my belief Friday is the day of the week for receiving bad *and* good news). When Terry and I met the following week, he was very professional; however, he looked as if he would rather be passing a kidney stone than sitting with the guy who was taking responsibility for a project he wanted to manage himself. Nevertheless, we sat down and penciled in an agreement. Instead of going to each of the facilities for a day and a half to train for the initial file build, we agreed I would meet with his MMs at their corporate office in Roseville for three biweekly sessions. I would train a third of the MMs at each meeting and anyone else they deemed necessary.

AN UNUSUAL REQUEST

Terry then threw a curve at me by saying, "Tim, as part of the contract, I want you to personally visit each of our hospitals and assess the capabilities of my materials managers."

He saw my questioning look and immediately volunteered, "Look, Tim, there is no doubt you know materials management, and you have already won the hearts and minds of my materials managers. I want you to visit them, evaluate their current environment, and give any advice you deem necessary for ensuring their conversions to CLASS incur as little trauma as possible during the process. I will notify them of your impending visits." I was flattered, but I must admit I did not envision this stipulation as part of the contract. Nevertheless, it couldn't do any harm, and it would be a preemptive way to avoid obvious problems.

The negotiations process was rather frustrating for Terry. He could not understand why I was so stubborn when it came to negotiating the terms of the contract. Of course, he was unaware of my discussion with Dick and Jim prior to being notified about the debacle with the "unanimous vote" scenario. When he told me he would only pay $360,000 for a site license for all of his hospitals (the equivalent of the cost for three licenses), I told him that was fine, but he was leaving out the fee for on-site training, and I could never agree for my staff to do all of the installs for the amount he proposed, telling him it would be $10,000 plus expenses for each of the hospitals. I stood firm and would not budge each time he attempted to negotiate that part away. We broke for lunch and after we reconvened, he informed me he had a solution: the training expenses would be incurred by each of the hospitals, and we were to bill them on an individual basis. Of course, I didn't care who paid the bill, I just needed to ensure we did indeed get paid for our efforts. With our previous sales, I never separated the expenses for training from the license amount, but it worked out well in this case. Terry was able to feel as if he got what he wanted by being creative. As a result, we signed the contract.

One odd aspect of the entire AHS/West experience was that the very next week, after the contract had already been signed, several of the Adventist MMs wanted a site visit for seeing CLASS in use at a hospital. Although we had a couple of AS/400 clients, none of them had been online long enough to use as a site visit. We did have a clean operation in Klamath Falls, but it was three hundred miles from anywhere, and the MMs said they did not care what platform it was operating on, provided all of the same functionality was offered on both platforms. Since the majority of hospitals were in California, asking Mary at Redlands Community was an easy choice, and she never said no to us. I hate to say it, but seeing CLASS in action at Mary's facility was almost an unfair advantage for us, because she had such a flawless operation—not to mention the fact that Mary was a most impressive MM and could answer any and all of their questions. She was able to provide many anecdotes highlighting the features of CLASS. The eight MMs who attended walked away in awe and could not wait to get to work.

The first of the three initial training seminars convened six weeks later at the corporate headquarters in Roseville. When I arrived, Terry met with me and informed me that he had just hired a new corporate MM. All right, guess who he chose. I spent some time talking about my earlier encounters with him, and if you haven't guessed it yet, Dave Russell from Loma Linda University Medical Center was Terry's new guy as the corporate director for materials management. Terry told me Dave would be attending the second training seminar. I told Terry I was acquainted with Dave and told him I thought he was a good choice. To be honest, I really had no idea how good of a choice he made, although Dave certainly had the necessary credentials for the job. Besides, it certainly wouldn't be my place to say anything to the contrary.

I had a great time at that first seminar; the attendees were eager to learn and were very enthusiastic about going online. At each of the sessions, the MMs brought their purchasing agents and/or buyers with them. Since I had people attending the training seminars who had not seen my presentation, it became obvious that I needed to explain much more than I usually did in a training session. I made it known that I would need the full two days to conduct the sessions, and all agreed it was necessary. Besides, all of the MMs said they wanted to hear the presentation again, saying it could only be helpful to them. Since it was a two-day seminar, it was a good opportunity for me to meet with the folks outside of a business setting. We all went to dinner together the first evening of the seminar and had a chance to get to know one another. The next day, we had to make a decision about which hospital would be the first to have CLASS installed. Jim from Feather River and Dick from Simi Valley were in attendance, and both wanted to be the first candidates with the software installed. However, when Brett suggested Portland Adventist would be the logical choice since Health-Ware's office was also located in Portland, Jim and Dick both said they understood and reluctantly agreed.

WE MEET AGAIN

Two weeks later, it was time for the next training seminar, and to meet with Dave Russell in his new position as the corporate director of materials management. Discussions were cordial, but he was someone who did not exhibit a great deal of emotion. If Dave had not been an Adventist, he would have been a great poker player, as he was very difficult to read. I could not let that fact deter me from my mission as I began conducting the seminar.

We began at eight o'clock and took a ninety-minute lunch break so the MMs could contact their offices and put out any fires requiring their involvement. At the beginning of the second day, Dave came up to me and invited me to join him and his wife for lunch at the break. Of course, I accepted.

After we sat down and ordered our lunch, Dave muttered, "You know, I realize I owe an apology to Neal."

Even though it had been two years since the sale to Neal at Loma Linda, I knew exactly what his comment was regarding. Nevertheless, I acted as if I didn't know what he was talking about and asked, "What do you mean, Dave?"

"When Neal Hartwig chose to go with CLASS, I told him he was making a mistake, that he should join me at the Loma Linda University Medical Center and use ESI for running his department. I now know why he chose to go with your company. You have given a tremendous amount of thought to CLASS and from what I have seen, you have thought of everything. When you are presenting, you back up all of your claims with very believable anecdotes. I understand why all of the MMs are so excited to get your system, and I am looking forward to seeing our hospitals go online."

Dave did not need to share that information with me, which was a clue I should be able to count on him always being fair with me even though he was a difficult read. Dave's comments were very complimentary, and I knew we could not disappoint him or his MMs.

Well, we wanted the contract, we got it, and there was no doubt we had our work cut out for us. I left the restaurant knowing that many were counting on us to provide them with a successful transition to using CLASS.

Having Portland Adventist as the first AHS/West hospital to go live with CLASS was a blessing. It didn't take long for us to discover that Myron Krause was (and still is) a solid manager and extremely well organized, a fact evident in all aspects of his operation. Despite the fact that he was so organized, he was always open to suggestions and new ideas. Within just one year, Myron and his crew became one of our best clients. In fact, his operation became our best place for showing off our IBM AS/400 version of CLASS. Later, representatives from major medical centers around the nation came to visit with Myron and see his staff in action. I considered it a tribute to Myron's professionalism and that of his staff. After leaving the hospital, the visitors would always ask me if the people they had just visited were on my payroll. Just like those who had visited Mary at Redlands Community Hospital, people walked away from what they had seen at Portland Adventist Medical Center in total awe.

It turned out Terry's part of the contract requiring me to visit with all of his MMs on-site was necessary. When CLASS was finally installed at the subsequent facilities, those who had attended the training seminars had understandably forgotten much of what they had been taught months earlier. Therefore I conducted a mini–refresher training session for each of them during my visit. In addition, I was able to advise those that needed to reorganize their operations in preparation for when they went online with CLASS. Some required many changes and, admittedly, some were resistant in the beginning. However, I was persistent, and none of them wanted to be seen as failing because they were unwilling to take advice from the guy who had successfully won approval of their peers. At times I was relentless when giving advice. First of all, I did not want any of them to fail, and second, I did not want to go back to Terry with any negative reports on his MMs. To the person, every MM took our advice and ultimately was successful with the implementation of CLASS.

After I visited each of the hospitals, Jan took on the task of training the new clients, and I became involved only when she felt it was necessary. It turned out to be a true challenge for Jan and her staff; there were a few of the smaller hospitals with materials-management departments requiring quite a bit more training than the other hospitals. Nevertheless, all of the materials-management people were extremely easy to work with, even during the most stressful of times. If we could have handpicked a hospital group to take on as a multi-hospital system, it definitely would have been AHS/West. It was an extreme pleasure and honor to work with them over the years.

14. THE BUBBLE BURSTS

For six years, it seemed as if we could do no wrong, as if we were leading charmed lives. We started with virtually nothing, and had grown our company to a point where it had become a formidable force in the world of automated health-care materials management (MM). We started in a spare bedroom in the home of my in-laws where Jan, Gordon, and I were the only employees. Four months later, we were able to bring Lentz and Cortie onboard and five months after that, Jan and I were able to move our family back to Oregon. We had grown at a fast pace, and just two years after signing the contract with the Adventist group, we found ourselves with a staff of fourteen and a monthly price tag of $40,000 for payroll, taxes, and benefits. At the time, the amount of staff was necessary to handle the Adventist installs and other sales that occurred during the same period of time. Getting all of the Adventist installations up and running took about ten months and for the most part, I can honestly say the new hospitals were doing well with CLASS.

We had grown at a fast pace, and two years after signing the contract with the Adventist group, we found ourselves with a payroll we were not going to be able to sustain. It became obvious that unless we increased our sales, we would soon lose the ability to keep the additional staff we had acquired. After signing with the Adventist group, we had taken on a sense of invulnerability; we believed we could do no wrong. I knew we had the best materials-management information system (MMIS) on the market, and it was just a matter of introducing CLASS to those hospitals in need of an MMIS. As the sales and marketing guy, it was Pat's responsibility to generate new prospects. With the buyout of Bergen by Owens and Minor, new leads were drying up, so the need for Pat to get new leads was paramount if we were going to continue to succeed.

TOUGH TIMES

In June 1991, our leads were dwindling, and it became obvious we were not going to be able to support our overhead. Drastic measures were necessary if we wanted to remain solvent. As with most companies, the biggest percentage of any budget relates to payroll, and I had to look at invoking pay cuts and/or layoffs. Up to this point, I'd never believed that could happen to us. I called a meeting with Pat, Lentz, and Jan to discuss our dilemma. I informed them it had become necessary to trim our staff to bring expenses in line with revenue. Pat suggested I wait and give him a chance to get the sales to a point where we could avoid layoffs. I believed we had to be proactive and countered with the idea of the three officers in the room (Pat, Lentz, and I) taking a 50 percent pay cut until we brought our cash reserves back to the level where we could cover six months of projected expenses.

All agreed and knew the reduction in pay would be in force for some time. I told them the results of the meeting needed to be confidential and the staff did not need to know what we had discussed. I did not want the others to know about our pay cuts, as they didn't need to worry about our woes, especially if we changed our financial posture for the better.

Unfortunately, our situation did not improve. Pat was unable to generate any more leads during the following months, so I found myself in the unenviable position of telling Pat we could no longer afford to keep him as an employee. It was one of the most difficult decisions I had to make, especially since he was one of the original founders of our company.

BITING THE BULLET

Rule Applied:

7. Lead with Confidence

Dealing with Pat was one of those times where I had to just "shut up and color." The difficult part of the decision was that if it hadn't been for Pat, we would never have started our company, and I probably would have ended up in Chicago working for American Data Services. Pat was a professional and taught me a great deal throughout our years together, which made my action even more difficult. Nevertheless, I made the correct decision.

THE WALLS COME TUMBLING DOWN

As if the situation wasn't bad enough, at the same time I gave Pat his notice, we had just put out a release to all of our clients that had a serious bug in it. Prior to the release, the number of service calls coming in to our office averaged about five per day; afterward, it increased to more than one hundred per day. Unfortunately, the bug was buried deep, and we were so busy answering phones that there was no way we had enough time to get to the root of the problem. We could not change the hospitals back to the older version of CLASS because the new one had required a database change. Life had definitely become complicated; we were overstaffed and overworked, and we did not have enough income to sustain our level of overhead.

After two weeks of putting out fires, it was obvious we were in serious trouble. I met with Lentz and Jan to ask if they saw any light at the end of the tunnel. They told me the bug was causing a great deal of inconvenience to our clients in that it was creating more work than before, but it was not affecting their general ledger (a very important distinction). However, the clients were still calling and wanted a fix to the problem.

Regardless of the troubles the bug was causing, Health-Ware was also in the midst of a financial crisis. It became obvious I had to lay off two of our employees. Even with Pat gone and the layoffs, our future was not looking good at all. When we started our company and signed contracts with our clients, I did not include wording for increasing the cost of the monthly maintenance fees (which included new releases). For example, our first two clients, Valley Medical Center and Evergreen Medical Center in Washington, were paying the same fee they were paying when they first purchased CLASS in 1986. We were in a catch-22 situation where we had to fix the problem with our software, but we did not have enough money to remain solvent. We were without any new leads. I didn't care, because we were not giving adequate support to the clients we already had. Besides, we were in no position to be showing our software to anybody else at the time.

I had to come up with a solution, or we would have to close our doors by February of the following year. Our expenses amounted to $20,000 per month, while our monthly maintenance fees equaled only $12,000. I decided the only way we could get out of this mess was to be honest with our client base and increase our fees. Therefore, I wrote the most difficult letter ever and sent it to my clients in November '91. In order to avoid tedious rhetoric by providing the entire two-page letter, the synopsis below highlights the key points:

I was so busy trying to generate new sales I forgot what was truly important: taking care of the clients who made it possible for us to succeed in the first place. I apologized for the problems we had caused them by putting out the bad release, but asked them to live with them until we sent out a new release. In the same letter, I told them about the dilemma with the maintenance fees. I told them that, in order to deal with the issue, I had one of two choices: close our doors, or ask them for more money by increasing their maintenance fees. I included a new maintenance-fee agreement with each letter, in which some incurred a 300 percent increase (still less than our competition). I further stated that, if they all returned a signed contract, I would promise three changes in return: I would not make another sales call for six months, we would provide them with a bombproof release by April 1, and I would keep them informed of our progress.

It was quite humbling to send such a letter, and I had no idea how our clients would react. The first response came just one day after the letter was sent, and it was from Dave at Valley Medical Center (our first client) in Washington,

"Tim, what took you so long? The signed contract together with a check for the new fee is in the mail."

I was shocked by his response. "Dave, what can I say?"

"You said it all in the letter, Tim, and I thank you for that. Your company has exceeded all my expectations, and I am certain all of your clients feel the same way."

He was the first of many who made similar comments, and when it was all over, all but one signed the agreement. Jim Mayhill from St. Charles Medical Center in Bend, Oregon, told me he and his boss (Gerry Gardner) decided they no longer wanted our support. Their IT department decided to maintain the software from that point forward. Despite the overwhelming response by the others, there was a pit in the bottom of my stomach. I didn't care about the lost contract, rather I was bothered by the fact that we had failed a client—Gerry was the one who originally decided to purchase CLASS—who had put his faith in us and what we represented. I cannot adequately describe just how bad I felt at the time.

There was one other exception to the overwhelming positive responses from our clients: Terry Burns from AHS/West called to say, "I received your letter, Tim, and I will sign the new contract; however it will be good only for a period of six months." After the call, I told Lentz and Jan, "We just received a six-month stay of execution."

For the short term, it was good news, but without making any sales calls for those six months, we would be facing this same problem all over again: not enough income to support our operation. It did not matter, because we had to fix the problem with our software and get our clients back to the point where they were proud to have CLASS as their MMIS.

PUTTING THE WALLS BACK WHERE THEY BELONG

Although we were working with a smaller staff, everyone had more time to work in the office and fix the problems we were having with CLASS. Of course, it didn't hurt that I was not bringing in more work as a result of new sales. Under normal circumstances, we'd send out a major release once a year, normally during the month of September. Our clients were only expecting a fix to the software in April, but we soon realized we could have it done in six weeks. Instead of sending out just a fix, we decided to send out a new release and not wait until September, a release that included many new enhancements we had in the queue for the next one. Productivity was at an all-time high, and the synergy among all was incredible. We worked long hours, found the problem with CLASS, and had it fixed by January 5—just seven weeks after the letter was sent out to our clients. As they all worked on the system, I created a newsletter entitled "CLASSic News." In that letter, I announced our first users' meeting, to be held in September. I was fulfilling that promise I made about keeping our clients informed about our progress.

When we decided to provide an entire release, not just a fix, I decided to meet with Lentz with an important request. A couple of years earlier, I was driving Lentz crazy with my last-minute requests for new enhancements, and he finally called me on it. He told me, "One would think you are still a materials manager, because you come up with more ideas than when we worked at the hospital in The Dalles. You know I never want to say no to you, but there has to be a limit, and you need to know when to say *stop*—no more add-ons for the next release."

Lentz made a good case, so I agreed to assign a stop date for new ideas when creating new releases. At this juncture, however, I believed an exception was necessary, and I put a full-court press on Lentz. I wanted to sell him on the idea. We wanted more than forgiveness from our clients: we wanted them to remember why they chose us in the first place, because we were better than our competition. I loved presenting new ideas to him and conceptualizing as we went. I always presented ideas to him from the viewpoint of a box-kicker and label-licker, explaining in detail each process we would be adding or changing so he could understand its significance. When he felt it was necessary, he would counter with alternative ideas; sometimes he thought of the difficulty behind the programming and would provide solutions that would not take as much of his time for completing the task and would give me only a partial solution. I admit the majority of the time I did not relent and asked Lentz to give me what I originally requested. It was because of my attitude in this area that Lentz requested that we agree on a stop date for new ideas. He always believed in what we were doing, all the way back to when we started the project in late 1981. I should have known the hard sell wasn't necessary this time. Instead of objecting, he was as excited as I was about going the extra mile, so he listened intently to my new ideas—and yes, I got everything I wanted from him.

Lentz always stepped up to the plate, and this time was no exception. It was no surprise when he saw to it that all enhancements were completed by February 15. It was then Jan's turn. She and her staff immediately performed quality control on the release and tested all of the enhancements for accuracy. She worked closely with Lentz and the programmers to correct any problems they found in the process. In addition, Jan brought Gordon up to Portland so he could update the users' manual with all of the changes.

Any credible software company would admit that even though their updates are created and tested prior to being dispersed to their clients, when a client finally does receive the new update, mistakes will be found. Therefore, the best way to avoid problems in the field with new updates is to have a quality beta site for testing anything new with the software. In order to improve our quality control, I needed an IBM AS/400 client as a beta site for testing new updates to our software. Prior to having Myron's operation at Portland Adventist up and running, we didn't have such a client any closer than three hundred miles from our office. He had become such a solid client, I decided to contact Myron and ask him if he would agree to let us use his department as our beta site. I agreed to have my staff on-site to install the updates and train his staff on how to use the enhancements. The agreement was extremely beneficial for us, and ultimately for all of our clients. After our agreement, new releases never went out to the field unless Myron and his staff signed off on them being error-free.

Our new release was ready for Portland Adventist by February 20, and although it had only been two weeks since Lentz's staff made it available for testing, Jan and her staff worked countless hours doing their part. When Myron was up and live with the new version of CLASS, Jan and Patti spent an entire week at Portland Adventist, ensuring the release was working well and that Myron and his staff were trained on all of the changes. The accolades from Myron and his staff were welcomed by all of us. After ten days with the update, Myron gave his okay for us to disperse it to the field. In turn, Jan and Patti had the new release, with documentation, out to all of our clients by March 15.

Admittedly, it was a rather quick turnaround from where we had been just four months earlier, but we were confident we had sent out a quality upgrade to the field. All we had to do was sit back and wait—and wait we did. Phone calls from our clients diminished to virtually none. It had been three weeks since the release went out to our clients, and other than a few exceptions, the phones were silent. We were all in the office discussing the new silence when Jan and Lentz started wondering out loud, "Maybe they are not as happy as we are hoping."

Jan asked, "Tim, Lentz and I were wondering if you would make some phone calls to find out how our clients are doing."

Jokingly I said, "This sounds like a trap, but I will do it."

I chose Brenda Munns from Flagstaff as the first client to call, as she was quite upset with me in November and I thought I might as well step into the fire with both feet. Brenda answered with a cheery voice and said, "Hi, Tim, I haven't spoken with you in quite some time. How are you doing?"

I was surprised by her demeanor (in a good way) and responded, "Well, Brenda, the last time we spoke you weren't too pleased with me, so I need to ask, how are *you* doing, especially since you have had the new release for about a month?"

"Oh yeah, I guess we were having some problems before. You promised to have them fixed by April 1. Instead, you sent out a new release by March 15 that not only fixed the problem, but gave us capabilities we thought we *might* see in September, and new ones we weren't expecting at all. I guess you could say we are quite pleased, Tim. Hats off to you and your staff."

I could not wait to tell the others what Brenda had to say, and after telling them, I said, "If Brenda is any indication as to how the rest of our clients feel, maybe not hearing from them is a good sign after all."

I called a few others with pretty much the same results. In the ensuing weeks, we discovered our clients were indeed satisfied, and as we had hoped, our relationships with them became even better than before all the problems.

RIGHTING A WRONG

I was meeting with Lentz and Jan and told them, "Despite all of the great feedback, I can't help thinking about the fact our clients are so happy with us while the folks at St. Charles are still using that broken version of CLASS. It doesn't seem right."

Jan simply asked me, "Why don't we just *give* them the new release?"

Lentz and I both looked at her and nodded our heads in agreement. I was embarrassed that I hadn't thought of it. It reminded me of that popular commercial, "I could have had a V-8!" I went back to my office and made a phone call that was, admittedly, a difficult one to make. I didn't know how well I would be received. Instead of calling Jim, I decided to call Gerry, the guy who originally put his faith in us when he purchased CLASS. Remember, Gerry was that man I first encountered in Seattle when I made a fool of myself, and yet he ultimately chose CLASS as his MMIS. Gerry's secretary answered the phone and asked me to wait while she checked to see if he was available.

When Gerry answered, his voice was, at best, skeptical. "This is Gerry."

I began, "Gerry, before I say what I need to say, I want you to read my lips over the phone. There are no strings attached to what I am about to tell you. Instead of just fixing CLASS, we decided to put out a major new release that is getting rave reviews from our clients. All of us at Health-Ware are not comfortable knowing you are saddled with a broken-down version of our software. Therefore, we want to give you our latest version and three months of free support so we can assure your people receive the necessary training for using all of the new features.

Again, no strings attached. I do not want anything in return, just the satisfaction of knowing we fixed something we broke—mainly your trust in us."

There was a long pause before Gerry replied, "Tim, what an incredible gesture. Thank you. I will tell Jim and have him get back to you to make arrangements for the release."

The release was applied without a hitch, and the MM staff at St. Charles was extremely pleased. Six weeks after my call to Gerry, Jim called and asked me to send him a new maintenance contract.

I immediately replied, "Jim, that wasn't my intent."

"I know, Tim, but how could we go on and miss out on any more outstanding features you folks might come up with in the future, and not to mention, your outstanding support."

The folks at St. Charles were once again loyal clients of ours. What a relief we were back in their good graces.

WE SURVIVED

Rules Applied:

5. Be an Effective Communicator   *6. Embrace Change*

7. Lead with Confidence   *8. Be Consistent; Be Decisive*

11. Define Expectations   *12. Instill Teamwork*

We pulled ourselves out of a very deep hole when it looked as if there was no way out. It was important to communicate our problems with our clients and live up to the promises we made to them—and, if possible, exceed their expectations.

We had to redefine the way we treated our customers and be decisive about it. We did not have the luxury of worrying about the possibility of losing the Adventist group and had to focus on the problems that were impacting all of our clients.

As far as giving the update to St. Charles Medical Center … even if they had not asked for a new contract, it was the right thing to do, and it felt great.

AN UNEXPECTED INVITATION

Two weeks after I spoke with Gerry, I was talking with Jan and Lentz in our main office when the phone rang. Jan answered the call: it was Bonnie from AHS/West, who said she wanted to speak with me. Bonnie was Dave's secretary, and I decided to take the call while standing at Jan's desk.

As always, Bonnie was very pleasant. "Hi, Tim, I am filling in as Terry Burns's secretary today, and he would like to know if you and Lentz would be able to come down to meet with him on May 29?" (Remember, Terry was the client who agreed to sign the new maintenance contract that was only good for six months.)

I asked Bonnie to wait while I went back to my desk to look at my calendar. I knew my schedule was open because I was not traveling anywhere at the time. I put her on hold and told Jan and Lentz, "We don't have the money, but Terry Burns wants Lentz and me to meet with him in Roseville on May 29."

I continued, "I don't want to spend the money, but we can't say no to our biggest client. I really have no choice but to say yes." They both agreed.

I went back to Bonnie, who was waiting on the phone. "Sure, Bonnie, we will be happy to come down."

Before I could say anything else, she chimed in, "That's great, Tim. I will put your airline tickets in the mail today and make hotel reservations for both of you for arrival on May 28."

I thanked Bonnie, and when I gave the phone back to Jan, I must have had a puzzled look on my face, because Jan and Lentz asked together, "Tim, what's wrong?"

"You know our six-month maintenance contract with AHS/West is up on the first of June, so is Terry Burns paying for us to go to Roseville so he can officially fire us?"

After that comment, Jan and Lentz both looked puzzled, so I explained our airfare and lodging were being paid by AHS/West. We were in such hot water with them just five months earlier—there was no way I could even venture a guess as to the reason for the meeting.

The month went by quickly and before we knew it, Lentz and I were on a plane to California. Howard Becker, the VP over systems, met us at the airport and acted as if he was our long-lost friend. When it was appropriate, we asked him if he knew what the meeting was about, and he responded he did not know. He offered to meet us for dinner that evening and insisted on paying the bill, since we were his guests. He picked us up from the hotel the next morning, and when we entered the building at AHS/West headquarters, we were warmly greeted by everyone we encountered. We were ushered to their conference room, where many of the programmers were sitting, as well as Dave and some of his staff from materials management. To say it was surreal as we waited for Terry to arrive wouldn't adequately describe the situation. All Lentz and I could do was wait patiently for Terry with the others and engage in small talk.

While we were talking, my back was to the door, so when Terry entered the room, I could not see him as he slammed the door against the wall, making a huge bang that startled all of us. Before I could turn around to see him, Terry stated loudly (almost shouted), "Tim, I don't know how you did it, but you caused our very vocal materials managers to finally shut up. Now all they can do is sing high praises about your company. All I can say is thank you, and I am very pleased to tell others we have CLASS as our materials system. Don't ever hesitate to call me if you ever need our assistance in the future when dealing with our hospitals." He came over to us and shook our hands. "I look forward to a long and continued relationship with you and your company."

It was just six months earlier that Terry called to tell me he was signing the maintenance agreement, but for only a six-month extension. I remember thinking, *He is just delaying the inevitable, where we would not have enough money to keep the doors open afterward.*

We didn't have the luxury of worrying about it at the time because we had to fix the problem with CLASS that was having an impact on *all* of our clients. Who would have thought that by staying focused on an issue not directly related to the finances of our company, our actions would ultimately be the solution to our money problems? We were not only forgiven, we were praised for the way we corrected our mistake.

Terry spent about $2,000 to bring us down to tell us we were his MMIS vendor; it was the most gracious effort by a client I ever experienced throughout the years at Health-Ware.

It is important to close by saying I never had a bad experience with anyone at AHS/West; even during our worst times ever as a company, we were always treated with respect. I never had the feeling that we were just the vendor. It was their positive attitude that made our relationship special with the folks at AHS/West.

15. LARGER INSTITUTIONS SHOW INTEREST

In April 1993, I received a call from Gary Goldsboro, the assistant director of purchasing at the University of Oklahoma Medical Center, a multi-hospital system that was located in Oklahoma City. He told me he saw an ad about CLASS and asked me for promotional literature. That first phone call lasted about fifteen minutes, and it was obvious he was in search of a new materials-management information system (MMIS). He asked all of the right questions. His pleasant personality was obvious, and it didn't take long to realize he was the most likeable man you could ever meet over the phone.

Gary called back a few days later, this time with Jerry (his boss) on the line. They reviewed the materials I sent them, and they called to ask me about the features of CLASS. We talked for forty-five minutes, where I ended up giving them a mini-presentation. At the end of our discussion, Jerry asked if we had a good place to recommend as a site visit. Normally a potential client asks for a presentation of our system first before inquiring about a site visit; Jerry said he wanted to see a client using our system in the way the literature claims it works. I suggested Portland Adventist Medical Center as the best place for him to see CLASS fully operational. I told them since they would be in town anyway, why not let me give them a presentation of the system? Afterward, I could take them to the site visit. They both said it sounded like a good idea and that Gary would get back to me about the dates regarding their visit.

Gary called back the next day and informed me that, because of budgetary constraints by the state, they had to fly in on a Saturday to take advantage of the airline fares associated with Saturday-night layovers; oftentimes I did the same when scheduling presentations, depending on the time and savings involved. Gary said Jerry and Aaron from the information-systems department would be arriving with him early Saturday afternoon and would not be leaving until Wednesday afternoon. I told him they did not need to rent a car—I would meet them at the airport, take them to the hotel, be their tour guide for the weekend, and show them many of the local sites. Gary replied, "That would be great. Do you have any good places to go fishing? We plan on bringing our gear with us." I was surprised by the request, but told him I should be able to accommodate them.

When I told Jan about the folks coming from Oklahoma, I asked her if she would be interested in joining us for the weekend. That was a rhetorical question, because Jan and I both loved visiting the sights, especially when it came to showing people who were visiting the area for the first time. Three weeks after Gary first called me, Jan and I were waiting for the folks at the airport. We stood there having no idea what to expect, just hoping we would all get along, especially since I volunteered our time for the four days.

Gary was the first of the three to step off the plane; he was wearing a Greek fishing cap and carrying his fishing pole. All three of them sported huge smiles, and our first impressions indicated we were going to have a good time. Like we did with all of our clients, Jan was first introduced as an employee of Health-Ware and not as my wife (she even had business cards with a different last name). I thought it was important she be treated as a valued employee of Health-Ware instead of the wife of the company president.

We became quite adept at not saying "honey" or "dear" or anything of the sort so we didn't let our prospective clients think we were related in any way. Jan was an incredible member of our team in her own right, so clouding the issue with our relationship would only be counterproductive. I introduced Jan as the head of the training staff and told them she volunteered to come with us for the weekend. In fact, when we all got in the car, she joined two of the three in the backseat, telling them there would be more room for everyone. After we took them to the downtown Marriot Hotel (same place we held our users' meeting), we went to dinner and then called it a day.

IT WAS LIKE A MINI-VACATION

We could not have asked for nicer weather for the entire weekend, as it was absolutely beautiful. Jan and I returned to the hotel at eleven the next morning to take them on a tour of the surrounding areas. To begin, we took them to see Multnomah Falls, the number-one tourist spot in Oregon—dual falls with the upper one at 542 feet feeding into the lower falls of sixty-nine feet. No matter how many times we visit the falls, we are always impressed by their beauty. Afterward, we went to the Oregon coast to see the sights and ended our day with a late lunch overlooking the seaside. (It was Aaron's first time ever seeing an ocean.) The entire weekend was enjoyed by all, and we had an opportunity to learn about each other and our individual work environments. The weekend was indeed unique; our potential clients would normally come to town for just one day and not get such individual attention. However, their situation was one of a kind, and I would not have felt right if they came into town on Saturday just to visit with us on Monday and leave on Wednesday. Some would say spending the entire weekend with them was overkill. However, if the same circumstances had occurred again with a potential client, I would have done it all over again. Jan and I were empty-nesters, so the worst that could have happened was that we didn't like our guests or vice versa. Fortunately, the exact opposite was the case.

DOWN TO BUSINESS

On Monday morning, I took the guys to the IBM center in Portland to give them a demonstration of CLASS. They were all about business, and the mood of the group was friendly but serious. Jerry was accustomed to the bureaucratic way the state system worked for them and had difficulty understanding how our system would work for his operation. Several times, our discussion became contentious and uncomfortable; it was not until about an hour into the presentation that Jerry admitted he was intentionally being difficult because he wanted to see if, like my competitors, I would just say yes to all of his questions. After he made that statement, the remainder of our time was no longer awkward and much more upbeat. After lunch, we went to Myron Krause's materials-management (MM) department at Portland Adventist Medical Center for the site visit; as with other potential clients, it was almost unfair to take them there. Myron's department was so well run, and his staff's proficiency with using CLASS combined with their ability to adequately answer all questions regarding its capabilities was most impressive. After the visit was completed and we said our good-byes, Gary asked me if Myron and his staff were on our payroll and if not, why not? I laughed and admitted we were very fortunate to have his operation as our number-one site visit. They then changed the subject to talking about when and how they would install CLASS in their facility.

So our guests could make use of their fishing gear, I took them to Lost Lake on Tuesday, a remarkably beautiful spot located at the base of Mount Hood. Jan was unable to join us because *somebody* had to work for a living. Gary actually hiked around the entire lake, while the rest of us stayed in one place. Our time at the lake was a nice way to end our time together. When I returned them to the hotel and as we were saying our good-byes, they advised me they planned on purchasing CLASS, but warned me about the bureaucratic red tape involved, and that the acquisition process could be quite lengthy—something to be expected when selling to a government organization.

When I visited the folks at the University of Oklahoma Medical Center for the first time in late October, Gary and Jerry met me in the parking lot and joined me at the car so they could take me on a cook's tour of the campus. The MM operation was huge, comprised of several buildings spread throughout the campus, and included three different inventories. Their organization was definitely going to be our largest undertaking for a single institution and would put CLASS to the test like never before. I went back again just one month later to train the staff for the initial file build.

It was time for their online conversion in May '94, just one year after their visit to Portland. Jan took her team to train the staff in

Oklahoma. Because the MM department was spread throughout the university campus, she asked me to join them. I mentioned earlier how Jan was always introduced to our client with a different last name so that she would not be seen as someone who got her position because she was my wife. After she established a rapport with the new clients, she would tell the clients about our relationship. On our sixth day of training, our new MM staff was becoming comfortable with CLASS, and we decided to go to dinner with them and discuss their progress. There were ten people at the table that evening, and all of us were quite pleased with the way things were going.

In a matter-of-fact way Jan mentioned, to no one in particular, "You know, Tim and I are husband and wife."

A lady in the crowd said, "What a relief!" Others nodded their heads.

I immediately responded, "Have we been inappropriate in some way or too friendly with each other to make you want to say that?"

Gary chimed in, "Not at all, you two have been very professional when dealing with all of us, but if two people were ever meant for each other, it's you two."

"Jan, I guess that means we should stay together."

Despite the size of the MM operation at Oklahoma, it turned out to be one of the easier online conversions we encountered over the years. Gary was the project manager and driving force behind ensuring that success.

THE UNTHINKABLE

During the following year, Gary and his team became quite proficient with CLASS for managing their inventories. The next step was to put them online using the handheld devices for managing the supply processing and distribution center. After Lentz customized a rather elaborate interface with their patient charge system, he and Jan returned to Oklahoma once again on Saturday, April 15, 1995, for another training session. On Wednesday, the 19th, I was flying to Athens, Georgia, to give a presentation, and when I stopped in Denver to change planes for my final destination of Atlanta I saw the news report about the bombing of the federal building in Oklahoma City. When I arrived at my destination later that evening, I called Jan to find out how the training was going and was surprised when she told me the federal building was only one block away from the medical center where Jan was conducting the training session. She said all training came to a halt because all of them (including Jan and her staff) were busy recovering victims from the federal building. She asked me to join her when I was finished with my presentation, so I could assist her with making up for the lost training time. Instead of flying to Portland on Friday, I joined her in Oklahoma, but by the time I arrived, Jan had been able to make up for the lost time and did not need my help after all. Of course, I didn't mind having the opportunity to spend the weekend with her. At five o'clock that afternoon, Jan and I walked over to see the damage done to the federal building. There were about three hundred people in the middle of the street with us and you could have heard a pin drop; nobody said a word. The idea that a US citizen could intentionally levy such devastation on fellow Americans and feel justified in doing so was unimaginable.

OPENING NEW DOORS

Earlier, I shared the fact that I believed CLASS was a powerful-enough system to handle any size institution. Yet we had never taken on an organization that was spread out like the MM department at the University of Oklahoma Medical Center. During our earlier years, oftentimes new clients would expect us to retrofit our system to accommodate the way they were accustomed to doing things. As time progressed, we realized we had to hold our ground as best as possible and emphasize the need for them to change the way they operated; when we did so, the transition was usually much smoother. Fortunately for us, Gary and his staff were always positive and looked to us for answers on how to change their environment to work better with CLASS rather than the other way around. Without a doubt, it was because of their success that MM departments at the likes of Ohio

State University Medical Center (1,500 beds) and Washington Hospital Center (1,000 beds) soon expressed interest in what we had to offer. The positive attitudes of Gary, Jerry, and his staff were infectious; they knew just how small of a company we represented, yet treated us as if we were as big as our competitors. Their confidence in us boosted our confidence in knowing we could, indeed, work with the larger institutions.

16. THE USERS' MEETING

After surviving the toughest time of our existence, it was important to ensure we never reached that point again. As part of living up to the promise of keeping the clients better informed, it was time to form a users' group for our clients. Our competitors were hosting them, and as I began presenting to larger institutions, the question about a users' group always came up. All things considered, it just seemed like the right time to do something about it. The name CLASS had been well-received and had always given us good name recognition. Accordingly, I used it whenever possible when naming a new product. For example, I used the names CLASS-Acct for our accounts-payable package and CLASSic News as the name for our quarterly newsletter. In keeping with the theme, I named our users' meeting the CLASS Reunion. We scheduled our first meeting for September, just six months after our release went out to the field and put us back in good graces with our clients. It was important to keep the good vibes going, and this meeting was a means for showing how serious we were about moving forward. Jan, Lentz, and Patti took on the responsibility for preparing for the new event, while I went back on the road to close some more sales.

Two weeks later, I found myself at a health-care convention in Southern California with an opportunity to speak with a sales rep from one of our competitors. We exchanged war stories, and I mentioned we were planning our first users' meeting. He quipped with scorn, "Good luck." I asked about his disdain and he replied, "For us, it's just another opportunity for the clients to beat up on us." He said they spent a lot of money and time only to come away with the feeling they had just left a battle zone. He wasn't able to elaborate because we were interrupted by the speaker taking the podium. I felt bad for him, because I was looking forward to *our* meeting. When I returned home and shared my brief encounter with the others at the office, they assured me we would have a positive experience.

When it came to scheduling the meeting, we did not want to compete with summer vacations, nor did we want to compete with the holiday season in early fall. Instead we scheduled the event for the Sunday and Monday after Labor Day (of '92), to be held at the downtown Portland Marriott Hotel. Downtown Portland is a beautiful and clean waterfront city, and we always enjoyed showing the city to others.

PLANNING FOR THE BIG EVENT

When it came to dealing with anything pertaining to computers, hardware, and software, Lentz was a miracle worker. He managed the process where he and Patti moved all of our computer equipment (the IBM AS/400 and all of the terminals) from our office to the conference room located in the Portland Marriott Hotel. All was accomplished on the Friday before the meeting. In addition to the two-day seminar, we offered Saturday activities for those arriving early enough to participate. We leased a bus with a driver for the event. Twelve people signed up for the first excursion and Lentz, Faun, Jan, and I all went along with the group. For our first outing, we took in some of the sights along the Columbia Gorge, culminating with a luncheon at Multnomah Falls.

All had a great time and expressed their appreciation for seeing the sights and for the opportunity to meet other CLASS users at an informal gathering. When all of the users met for the formal gathering the next morning, the feedback from the Saturday group to those who did not attend was that the others missed out.

A BETTER-THAN-EXPECTED OUTCOME

At the time, we had sixty clients, of which fifteen were from the Adventist hospitals. There were twenty-five attendees at the first meeting. It would have been nice to have more, but it was plenty for our first attempt. There was a welcome synergy among everyone in the room from the very beginning. I'm not talking just about the clients—the chemistry among the users and the Health-Ware staff was magical. When I introduced the staff to everyone, many knew most of our employees but not all of them. When I introduced Patti Kelm, there was a huge outburst of applause by the group, as she was mostly a behind-the-scenes person; she often took customer-service calls on the phone, but had never met many of our clients in person. She provided much training, solved many issues over the phone, and was instrumental to implementing the software upgrades when disseminated to all of the clients. Seeing the smile on Patti's face after the users responded to her introduction was worth more than I could have ever imagined. Later at the next coffee break, many of the users made a point of going up and introducing themselves to Patti. It became obvious the meeting was not just for the benefit of our clients, because all of us at Health-Ware were rewarded by the event.

Admittedly, not all of our clients loved us from day one. In fact, many of our clients were intimidated when they first went live with CLASS. Our system provided results much faster than those of our competitors, and when one makes a mistake, the unwanted results also occur at a much faster rate than they were accustomed. So there was a lengthy honeymoon process that occurred with some of our clients, and it usually required an extra effort on our part to get them to the point of being satisfied. At the first CLASS Reunion, there were a few clients who did not have the best opinion of us as a vendor. Their body language said it all: they wanted some answers, and when we greeted them they were polite but curt. Of course, we could not expect *everyone* to be enamored with us; we expected to have some difficult times during the open meetings. However, the power of the group came to our rescue when someone posed questions of concern. There were users only too eager to answer the questions for us. When they did so, many in the crowd would voice their approval and even embellish on the answers.

The following year, we had our meeting as planned, and the group was even more positive than that of the year before. Sal Ramirez from St. Francis Hospital in Santa Barbara was first on the agenda; he shared his experience as a part-time employee for Health-Ware when he assisted us with the installation at Casa Grande Hospital in Arizona. He related his experience as a positive one that gave him a different perspective on what it was like to put a client through an online conversion, as well as getting a better appreciation for his own operation. After Greg Van Riper from Merritt Peralta in Oakland, California, and Bethany Krom from the Mayo Clinic in Scottsdale, Arizona, heard Sal's recap of his experience on the road, they approached Jan and expressed their interest in becoming members of the part-time staff. Later, these folks, along with Sal, traveled with Jan to train new clients at several institutions around the nation.

It was great to have Dave from Valley Medical Center, our first client, and Terri from Evergreen Medical Center, our second client, both in the audience. They were strong managers and outstanding clients, providing the best examples of how to use CLASS as a tool for having a successful operation. As time progressed throughout the event, the users were all positive and gave us the vibe we needed to let us know it was worth the effort. It was like meeting with a group of peers wanting only the best for their individual organizations. Together we were able to create a punch-list for our next release, and everyone had a sense of satisfaction in that they were able to contribute to what would be included. After everyone left Monday afternoon, we all had a true sense of satisfaction with what we had just accomplished. We were exhausted, but couldn't wait to share ideas about making improvements for the next CLASS Reunion.

USING THE MEETING TO WIN OVER A CLIENT'S NEW EMPLOYEE

Before our fourth annual meeting, I made a call to Don Thompson, who was the director of purchasing at the Mayo Clinic in Scottsdale, Arizona. He had been a client of ours for six years and his operation was growing rapidly; his staff was five times bigger than when he first acquired CLASS. One of his new buyers came from the retail environment, and when she called our office she was extremely negative.

She definitely was not the friendliest person to have on the other end of the line.

When I called Don in July, I asked, "Don, would you please send Renae to the users' meeting in September?"

"Tim, you know she is not one of Health-Ware's biggest fans."

"I know that, Don; that's why I would like her to come to the meeting. I think we can win her over."

Don agreed to do so, admitted he wasn't sure I would get the desired outcome, and ended by wishing me luck.

By the time of our next users' meeting, we had taken on as a new client the University of Oklahoma Medical Center. Fifty people had signed up for the meeting, and twenty-five of them also signed up for the Saturday event. Surprisingly, Renae also signed up for the Saturday excursion, which was a trip to the Oregon coast. We took them to various sites like Cannon Beach and Seaside, and finished with a late lunch at a restaurant that had a beautiful view of the coast. At the beginning of the trip, Renae was distant and standoffish. Fortunately, Gary from the University of Oklahoma was also part of the group and was not about to let Renae put a damper on the gathering. By our late afternoon lunch, it seemed his positive outlook on life and his obvious satisfaction with our company and product were starting to have a positive impact on Renae.

The first day of the official meeting was even more positive than those of previous years. Jan gave an incredible presentation about the upcoming features of our next release that created a great deal of excitement in the room. We then opened up the room for a question-and-answer session. The talk was lively and was a forum where the audience ultimately expressed its satisfaction with CLASS and our level of customer service.

When we took a coffee break two hours later, Renae came up to me and said, "Tim, I have been unfair to you and your staff. It's obvious you care a great deal about your clients and that you are willing to listen to us. I apologize for the way I treated your staff, and I want to thank you for this event."

Even though it was the outcome I had hoped for, I was sincerely moved by Renae's gesture. I thanked her and let her know I was looking forward to working with her in the future.

After Renae returned to work on Tuesday, I received a call from Don at Mayo. "Tim, what did you do to change Renae's attitude toward you and your staff? She is now a big fan of Health-Ware."

"I didn't do anything, Don; Renae finally had a chance to see what we were all about. She didn't have the opportunity to see us from the beginning; now she looks to us as a viable resource instead of the enemy."

The most rewarding outcome came on Thursday when Patti finished with a call and let us all know, "That was Renae from Mayo, and she was very pleasant on the phone and told me to say hi to everyone." The CLASS Reunions really did have unexpected benefits.

FACING A PROBLEM HEAD-ON

Rule Applied:

8. Be Consistent; Be Decisive

The idea of intentionally inviting Renae could have backfired on me, but I knew, as a whole, our clients were supportive of our company and were pleased with our level of customer service.

I believed if the meeting was going to be anything like the previous CLASS Reunions, the chances were high that she would have a good experience. The fact that it had such a positive impact on her was a welcome bonus.

One final anecdote: when we had our CLASS Reunion in 1995, the Saturday culminated with a dinner at Mount Hood Meadows. When I entered the restaurant, the manager came to greet me and thank us for having our class reunion at his facility. He then asked, "With the huge age disparities in the group, are there many child prodigies in the group?" We both had a good laugh after I explained the meaning of *our* CLASS Reunion.

17. CELEBRATING HEALTH-WARE'S TENTH ANNIVERSARY

It was a Thursday morning in late May '95 when Rosalind Parkinson from Ohio State University called to ask, "Are you going to be at the annual trade show next week being held in Las Vegas by the Healthcare Materials Management Society?" She was the third client to call asking the same question. I wanted to be there, but I couldn't justify the amount of money (between $10,000 and $20,000) it took to pull it off. The logistics of putting up a booth with computer displays, creating handouts, having people there to staff the booth, and all of the expenses related to travel and lodging would be significant. Some companies spend untold amounts to put on lavish displays, and our presence would pale in comparison with others. Yet I thought it would be good if we could just *show the flag,* so to speak.

AN IMPROMPTU CELEBRATION

Jan came into my office when she heard I was on the phone with Rosalind; she headed up the training team at Ohio State and wanted to ensure all was well. After I finished my call, I assured Jan everything was fine at Ohio State. However, I shared my concerns about how the folks from the larger institutions were wondering why I wasn't going to be in Vegas.

Jan suggested, "Maybe you should go anyway, without a booth."

I agreed. "Maybe I could throw a cocktail party or something of the sort. Of course, it's probably too late to whip something up at this late date."

Jan volunteered to find out if there was any way I could do something on such short notice, and immediately left for her office. She returned about thirty minutes later and told me to pack my bags. She had spoken with the catering manager at the Mirage and was told they had a ballroom that was in the center of the five conference rooms where the conferees were attending their last classes of the seminar on Tuesday. Jan arranged for an open bar and a wait staff to assist with what they described as heavy hors d'oeuvres, which they said could actually suffice as a meal for some. The minimum cost for the event would be $1,500 plus the cost of the soda, beer, wine and liquor served at the open bar. Jan arranged for a microphone, speaker system, and round tables (seating up to six people each) with chairs to be placed throughout the room with the food and bar nearby.

In early 1993, our son Geoffrey sublet some of our office space for his leasing company. During his slow periods, he worked part-time for Health-Ware as a trainer and made sales calls when he was not needed on the road. Lentz and Jan both suggested I have Geoffrey accompany me on the trip (it didn't take much to convince him).

With no time to advertise for the event, I made placards for placing in conspicuous places when we arrived. There was little doubt we were taking a gamble; it could turn out to be a flop where nobody showed up, one of those times where I again found myself throwing the dice (though it was certainly the right place to be doing so). On the flip side, conceivably I could have too many people attend and not be able to give adequate attention to our guests.

Geoffrey and I arrived early Tuesday afternoon with just enough time to scope out the place and make sure everything was going according to plan. The catering manager at the Mirage was most accommodating and professional; all of our needs were met. As for the placard in front of each of the classrooms, there was an easel displaying the subject matter for the next class. With the final classes in session, Geoffrey and I reversed the easels so they were facing the participants as they exited the classroom, and placed one of our placards on each of them, inviting the attendees to join us for hors d'oeuvres and an open bar to help us celebrate our tenth anniversary. I figured it would be difficult for box-kickers to turn us down for free food and drinks.

Just across the hall from where we were having our cocktail party was the entrance to the exhibition pavilion with the doors wide open. We saw the vendors busy disassembling their booths as the seminar participants were attending their last class. The only time I participated in a trade show was when I was invited by the Bergen group to join them in their booth in Phoenix for the meeting of the Arizona Medical Association. We had just signed our five-year marketing agreement, and going to the event seemed like the right thing to do at the time. I remember thinking while standing in Bergen's booth with our computer on display, *This must be what it's like to be a salesperson in an automobile showroom who approaches people only to hear, "I'm only looking."* It was their way of politely telling salespeople to back off. At best, of the hundreds of people I saw that day, only three were remotely interested in hearing what I had to say. I remembered not liking the experience, so my prior regrets about not having a booth quickly dissipated.

TAKING A TRUE GAMBLE

Admittedly, I was uncertain as to how our cocktail party was going to turn out. The rationale for going ahead with this venture was, *If twenty people came to our event and I met just one potential client, it would be worth the money and effort.* When we opened the doors at four o'clock, imagine our surprise when thirty people entered the room all at once. I was accustomed to greeting people one at a time when they entered—however, this event was not a presentation, nor was it practical. Besides, these folks were there for food and drink. Within the first fifteen minutes, all of the tables were occupied, and we were left with standing room only. During the two and a half hours, a total of 140 people joined us for our festivities. It was gratifying to see that five of our clients from different parts of the country joined us and all sat together at one table. I saw several people I had previously met from my travels around the country during the previous ten years. One man in particular was Scott Frost from Redding, California; I had given a presentation to him four years before but was unable to cinch the deal because he belonged to a group out of Sacramento that would not approve him going rogue with his own system. He was very gracious and told me he was happy to see that my company had become so successful. He had changed jobs and gone to a hospital using a mainframe system. He was unhappy with his MMIS but was unable to make a switch at the time. Nevertheless, he asked for my business card, saying, "One never knows what lies in the future." After everyone was seated, Geoffrey took the podium; he introduced himself, thanked everyone for attending our gathering, and then introduced me as the president of Health-Ware to the group. I then took the microphone and also thanked the folks in the group for joining us, and then I gave a brief background about our company, explaining how we initially established a presence on the west coast and ultimately moved eastward over the past five years. I pointed to the table with some of our clients around it and said that those who wanted more information about our system could perhaps talk with one of them. I then walked to each table, greeted each group, and asked where they were from. In total, the people in the group represented hospitals from twenty-three states around the country. Surprisingly, a sales rep from Enterprise Systems, Inc., came up to me after I made my rounds and introduced himself. He asked me how I was able to get the ballroom for the gathering. Rather than elaborate, I replied, "I guess I was just lucky."

He then said, "I have seen all of these people during the past two days, and they walked right by my booth without stopping. You have a captive audience here. Our cocktail party was at eight last night with only a third of what you have here today. Nice job."

Later that evening, two of our clients in the group joined us in our suite. It was a nice way to end the day.

Oh, and about needing to justify the $2,100 spent for the event— seven months later, I received a call from the COO at Global Software Company of Raleigh, North Carolina. He said he was given my business card by Scott Frost, a client of his from San Jose, California. He told me they were interested in our company and wondered if we would be willing to meet with his company chairman as well as the president. It was a call that never would have occurred had it not been for our impromptu cocktail party.

18. A COMPETITOR GETS CREATIVE

When we were invited by the larger institutions from around the nation, oftentimes I would bump into some of my competitors while waiting our turn to present. Some of them had several hundred clients, while we were just approaching *one* hundred. In fact, the top salesman for the number-one company (based on number of clients) in the health-care materials-management (MM) software business had gone up against us and lost the contract one too many times and decided to become creative with his presentations. One time, I had just given a presentation to Sal Ramirez, the director of MM at the University of Washington, located in Seattle. Of course, Sal was one of my first clients when he worked at St. Francis Hospital in Santa Barbara, California, and was our first client to work with us on the road as a part-time employee. He was a pro with CLASS and wanted to attempt to acquire it for his new hospital. After being in his new position in Washington for about a year, he initiated the lengthy process for acquiring a new software package for his department. I responded to the request for proposal (RFP) because it was obvious Sal wrote it based on the features of CLASS.

After responding to the RFP, we were one of the three companies invited to present our solution to the software selection committee. The presentation given to Sal and thirty other hospital staff members went well. It was very important I impress his staff, so it didn't appear Sal was showing favoritism to a friend, or that he was inflexible and had to have his way with bringing in a system he used at his *small* hospital (been there, done that) in Santa Barbara. When I was leaving at the end of the presentation, Sal expressed sincere appreciation for our efforts and said his staff was excited with what we had presented. He requested I give him a call in two days, as Enterprise Systems, Inc. (ESI), our main competitor, was giving its presentation the next day.

THE COMPETITION TELLS A BALD-FACED LIE

As requested, I called him two days later. Sal took my call, but it was obvious something was not right. I asked him how the presentation from the competition had gone and he told me it had gone as expected, and it wasn't the system he or his staff really wanted. Normally, I would have been elated at such a comment, but something wasn't right about Sal's tone of voice.

I asked, "Sal, what's wrong?"

He said, "Well, I'm just sorry to hear you have filed for bankruptcy under Chapter 11."

I was shocked by his reply, and immediately replied (rather loudly), "Sal, the only time I was ever involved with chapter 11 was when I finished reading chapter 10 of the last Clancy novel I read, *Cardinal of the Kremlin.*"

"You mean you are *not* going bankrupt?"

"Of course not, and who told you we are?"

"When I told the ESI sales rep you were his competition, he told us 'Health-Ware has a good product, but it's just too bad they filed Chapter 11.'"

"Sal, that was a lie. Nothing could be further from the truth. We have been in business for ten years with six attempts to buy us out. ESI was obviously desperate in that they had to divert attention away from the shortcomings of their software. If we had filed for *any* chapter, it would only take one call from your legal counsel to the state of Oregon to verify such an accusation."

He sounded relieved and said he would keep in touch. A day later, he called back and said my claim was indeed verified by the hospital's legal counsel.

Admittedly, I was shaken after Sal informed me of the Chapter 11 claim by ESI. I had just enough time to relay the conversation to some of my staff when I received a call from one of our clients. It was Gary from the University of Oklahoma Medical Center. Gary was one of my favorite people and it was great to hear his voice; at the time, his organization was one of my biggest clients.

IT HAPPENED AGAIN

He knew me well enough to hear something in my voice that was not quite right, so he asked me, "What's wrong, Tim?"

"I was just told by a potential client that when he told the ESI rep we were the competition, the rep responded by saying it's too bad we filed Chapter 11, which of course is a total lie."

"Oh, they're doing that again?"

"What do you mean, Gary?"

"When the ESI rep presented to us, he told us the same thing about you."

"You're kidding—and that was two years ago, and you never mentioned it to me?"

"Tim, we had already done the due diligence on Health-Ware, and you passed with flying colors. Besides, you gave us twenty references versus ESI's three. We knew we were dealing with an honest, straight-shooting company when it came to you, and we never gave it a second thought."

I wondered just how many other times this lie had been told. This incident was a real eye-opener, so I called our attorney and asked for his advice. I was told litigation would probably be more trouble than it was worth and wouldn't render much of a return, as it would be difficult to prove damages. Ultimately, he wrote a letter for me to the ESI corporate executives to let them know we were aware of their gutter-type sales tactics. We never received a response, as our attorney predicted. However, after our next head-to-head with ESI, the rep was told they were up against us again. This time, he responded by saying, "Oh, Health-Ware is a formidable competitor." That time we won the contract again, a one-thousand-bed hospital in the heart of Washington, DC.

By the way, by size comparison, Health-Ware was an ant on ESI's wall. They were the largest MMIS company in the country, with almost ten times as many clients as we had. It was kind of amusing to think they were threatened by us. To end this dissertation on a positive note, one year later ESI was bought out by a company that sold a complete hospital information system.

19. A FORMAL INVITATION

CLASS was an expensive acquisition; depending on the size of the institution, it could cost anywhere from $60,000 to $500,000, with hardware ranging up to another $500,000. With big capital expenditures, a formal justification for such a large purchase is almost always required. Part of the process for the one making the request is to create a request for proposal (RFP), a document that delineates all of the requirements for the desired product, and after it is completed it is sent to vendors that have a materials-management information system (MMIS) on the market. An RFP is always quite lengthy, with detail relating to every process required for automating materials management. Of course, to create such a document, expertise is required on the part of the one making the request. I know it seems as if I am stating the obvious, but oftentimes I found the materials manager (MM) really did not know how to ask the right questions. I understood the dilemma, because had I not spent the days with the coveralls, I would not have had the detailed knowledge to adequately write an RFP myself.

Responding to an RFP is a lengthy process as well, requiring several hours of the vendor's time. Answering RFPs was my responsibility at Health-Ware, and after responding to eight different requests over a five-month period, I discovered similarities among three of them that were too alike to be just a coincidence. Some of the detailed questions were worded exactly the same, yet they were sent from hospitals located in different parts of the country. Also, the described features had nomenclature so precise, it was obvious the RFP had been written with a specific system in mind. I realized the RFPs for the three hospitals had been written for them by our competitor, which had already given them a demonstration of their software. In other words, the hospital submitting the RFP for completion had already seen the system they wanted, and getting responses from other vendors was a means for justifying their choice of system. Many of the MMs had already been sold on the system they wanted to buy and were not going to have their minds changed because of answers submitted on an RFP. Once they created and disseminated the RFPs, it was almost impossible to try to break through their mind-set and convince them they should invite us to give a presentation. In fact, some of the RFPs stipulated calls from vendors regarding the RFP would not be taken, that we would be notified about their decision after they evaluated the submissions. Getting in front of a potential client was the most important aspect of the sales process, and it had to be done before any RFP was written. Once I came to that conclusion, I realized answering an RFP from someone I had never met was an exercise in futility. I decided not to respond to RFPs unless the MM had already seen CLASS.

I never knew if I ever lost a sale after making that decision. However, after responding to the first eight RFPs from MMs who had not seen CLASS and not getting an invitation from any of them, I was comfortable with my decision. That is, until October 1993. Jan and I were going on a Caribbean cruise to celebrate our twenty-fifth wedding anniversary. Things were rather quiet at the time, and Lentz assured us he and the staff could hold down the fort in our absence. Geoffrey was taking any sales calls and promised to take care of any administrative details that could not wait for our return.

THE SEASONED TRAVELER

Before I get back to the story about RFPs, allow me a brief digression. As Health-Ware's client base increased, so did the amount of my air travel, until I was flying about a hundred thousand miles per year. With all of my travels connected with the air force and Health-Ware, I ultimately stepped foot in forty-seven of the fifty states, with Kentucky, Vermont, and Alaska as the only exceptions. I was very comfortable with the routines associated with air travel and was accustomed to making changes to my travel arrangements on a moment's notice.

One week before our scheduled departure for Florida, Jerry, the purchasing director from the University of Oklahoma Medical Center, called me and told me if I wanted Health-Ware to be awarded the MMIS contract, someone from our company had to attend a meeting being convened on the following Thursday, the day before we were leaving for Florida. Unfortunately, I was the only person at Health-Ware qualified to attend the meeting, so when I told Jan about the dilemma, she was her normal agreeable self and said she would meet me in Florida on Friday. Everything went according to schedule: I arrived on the following Wednesday; met with Jerry, Gary, and his staff; and attended the mandatory meeting on Thursday where Health-Ware was awarded the contract for the purchase of their new MMIS.

I left for our anniversary cruise early Friday morning. While waiting to board my flight for Dallas, Texas, with a connection to Fort Lauderdale, I called to check in with Jan. It was six thirty in Portland, and she was preparing to leave for the airport in fifteen minutes. Since I was arriving in Florida three hours before her, I joked about her needing to look for me at the hotel bar. We said our good-byes and I left for Dallas, where I had a one-hour layover. I called Lentz at the office and gave him a report about my visit to Oklahoma City and before I knew it, I was airborne again. After taking off from Dallas, I settled into my seat and resumed reading my latest Tom Clancy novel (the only time I had time to read was while I was traveling). After we leveled off, the flight attendant announced that because of a tail wind, we would be arriving ahead of time when we reached Louisville. I froze ... I was supposed to be going to Fort Lauderdale. Seasoned traveler that I was, I found myself headed not just to the wrong city, but to the wrong state. I thought about the departure, and remembered that when we boarded, there were two flights leaving at the same time. Two flight attendants were standing side by side as they were checking passengers' boarding passes. I just happened to step into the wrong line and ultimately boarded the wrong plane. After I took my seat, another passenger said I was sitting in his seat, and I promptly showed him my seat assignment to verify I was in the right seat. He was very gracious and called for a flight attendant who looked at our tickets for verification. Like me, she verified the seat assignment, but not the destination. Unfortunately for me, the flight was not full, and the other passenger was able to be seated elsewhere on the plane. After getting my wits about me and realizing what had happened, I pressed my call button for a flight attendant. When she answered my call, the flight attendant was on her way to another passenger at the back of the plane, but asked me what I needed as she was walking past me.

I told her, "I am afraid you have a stowaway onboard."

"Oh, are you on the wrong plane?"

"Yes, I am supposed to be on a plane to Fort Lauderdale to go meet with my wife."

She patted me on the shoulder as she moved to the back of the plane and said, "There's no need to worry, we have many flights going there from Atlanta, and I will check the schedule for you." I thought to myself, *We are going to Louisville, so what does Atlanta have to do with it?*

When she passed by again, I asked her, "You said there are plenty of flights to Fort Lauderdale from Atlanta, but aren't we going to Louisville?"

"I'm sorry, this plane goes on to Atlanta after we stop in Louisville, so we should be able to accommodate you."

After hearing me speak with the flight attendant, the passenger sitting next to me said, "You must be furious at Delta."

"No, not really. In fact, I have two reasons to be quite happy."

He looked astonished and asked quite loudly, "What could you possibly be happy about?" At this point, everybody on the plane was looking at me waiting for my answer.

"First of all, at least we are not on our way to Hawaii. I would never meet up with my wife in Florida." Everyone laughed.

"What's the other reason?"

"I have been to forty-seven of the fifty states, and Kentucky is one of the three I have never visited, so now I can mark this one off my list." (I have since been to Alaska, leaving Vermont as the last state for me to visit.)

Again, everyone laughed and wished me luck.

When we landed, the Delta pilot went way beyond the call of duty by personally escorting me at the Atlanta airport to my next flight (anybody familiar with the terminal train system in Atlanta understands what I mean about *beyond the call of duty*). I thought it was because he didn't want me to make the same mistake; instead, it was because he knew the flight had been overbooked and had a huge standby list. By escorting me, he was able to push me ahead of the twenty passengers already waiting and even saw to it that I flew in first class.

I told him it was my fault for getting on the wrong flight. He stopped me and said, "No, Tim, by letting you onboard, we essentially kidnapped you."

I will never forget the outstanding service all those at Delta Air Lines gave me that day. Ultimately, I arrived at the hotel thirty minutes after Jan and had a lot of explaining to do.

AN UNWANTED INVITATION

We had a great cruise and enjoyed a much-needed vacation, but when I returned to the office on Monday, Geoffrey had quite a story for me to digest. On the Monday after we left, he received a phone call from Terry Rich at Washington Hospital Center, a one-thousand-bed facility located in Washington, DC. Terry asked for me but was told I was on vacation for a week, and Geoffrey took the call.

Terry was the VP over materials management and told Geoffrey, "We are looking for a new software system, and I would like to invite you to respond to our RFP."

"I'm sorry, but Mr. Koprowski [he was so formal] won't respond to an RFP unless you have already had a demonstration of CLASS."

Geoffrey said there was a long pause, and then Terry simply thanked him and hung up the phone.

Someone not understanding my reasoning would think it odd that I would turn down the possibility for acquiring new business. Well, Terry must have thought so too, because he called back the next day.

"Geoffrey, this is Terry Rich again, and after looking at our distribution list for the RFP, I see we sent an RFP to your company in August."

"Well, because of his policy, Mr. Koprowski probably discarded it."

Again, Terry seemed not to believe our policy regarding RFPs and ended the call.

Well, Terry called again on Wednesday with a proposal. He told Geoffrey, "If Mr. Koprowski responds to the RFP, I will invite him out for a presentation."

The bottom line was that Geoffrey agreed to Terry's request and presented me with a rather thick document requiring my attention. I was puzzled at Terry's insistence that I respond to his RFP; we had never met or spoken with each other before, yet he knew about our company. I figured he just saw an advertisement of ours in one of the health-care journals.

SHOOTING MYSELF IN THE FOOT

I wasn't very happy with the outcome, especially after I reviewed the RFP. It was obviously written with the ESI system in mind. Because their design was so different from that of CLASS, it took a great deal of work to properly answer their RFP. Unfortunately, I let my feelings about having to answer the document spill onto my cover letter; I stated I was responding under duress. Two days later, Terry called Geoffrey to let him know he would *not* be inviting us for a presentation. Geoffrey happened to be in my office when he received the call and was rather shocked by what he heard. Although I could not hear what Terry was saying, it was not necessary because of what Geoffrey said. "I'm sorry you feel that way, Terry. The results have not been very good when we responded to RFPs sent to us by those who have not seen a demonstration of CLASS beforehand. Terry, I'll bet you haven't even read the RFP, and if that's true, shame on you, because you are going to miss seeing a system that could revolutionize the way you run your department." After Geoffrey ended the call, he told me Terry wasn't happy with my cover letter and was not inviting me for a presentation.

I pulled up the letter on my computer and after rereading it, I could see how he might not have received it well. When it came to answering the RFP, I should have swallowed that pill and not complained about it. In other words, I should have shut up and colored. It was never too late to learn a lesson. I made a bad impression on somebody I had not even met. To be truthful, shame on *me*!

The next morning, I was in Geoffrey's office when he received a phone call. I was about to leave when I heard Geoffrey say, "Good morning, Terry"—rather surprising, since we never thought we would hear from him again. The end result was that Terry admitted he had not read the RFP when he last called, and after reading it, he wanted to extend an invitation for a presentation, saying, "It will be you giving the presentation, right, Geoffrey?" It was obvious he did not want me to be the presenter. Geoffrey agreed, knowing he would not be the one going to the District of Columbia, but also knowing I would deal with it. The bottom line was that Terry liked my response to the RFP and wanted to see a demonstration of CLASS.

After arrangements were made with the local IBM office and Terry, I found myself flying to Washington, DC, within one week of Terry's invitation. I admit I was a bit nervous about meeting Terry, but it was my own fault. When the time arrived, Terry was reserved yet professional. I told him I was filling in for Geoffrey because of a scheduling conflict. It turned out my concerns about meeting Terry were unwarranted; he was very attentive and just wanted the best solution for his department. It was one of those presentations where I knew in the first fifteen minutes I had a new client. Actually, because the audience was so attentive and showed a sincere interest in what I had to say, the introductory portion went much longer than normal because of the abnormal amount of good questions that required in-depth answers.

NEED TO BE CAREFUL

Rule Applied:

5. Be an Effective Communicator

There is no doubt I violated my own principles when I responded to the RFP in such an unprofessional manner. Being an effective communicator is not a good attribute if the message is not well thought out. I learned a valuable lesson and was thankful Terry Rich was gracious enough to not only invite me out for a presentation but to be so professional when I arrived.

When we broke for coffee, Terry came up to me, and I said, "I can't believe I just spent an hour with you and haven't even turned the computer on."

"That's all right, Tim, we are excited about what you have to say and can't wait to see more." The rest of the day could not have gone better. By the end of the day, I knew Terry was a quality MM, and I looked forward to working with him in the future. Terry shared with me that he had heard about us from his son, Terry Jr., who at the time was the sales rep for Owens and Minor (the company that purchased the Bergen Brunswig Medical Supply company), and Ohio State University Medical Center was one of his clients. He knew his father was looking for a new system and told him about the successes enjoyed there in Ohio.

With software and hardware, it was a million-dollar contract. As a result, it was eight months before the contracts were signed and the hardware was in place, and then another eight months to complete the file build.

Only then could Jan take her team for the online training, which comprised of Bethany from the Mayo Clinic in Scottsdale; Greg and his wife, Mary, from Merritt Peralta in Oakland; Sal when he was working at St. Francis in Santa Barbara; and Gordon in San Jose. Because of the size of the organization, Jan asked me to come so I could spend time with the hospital executives and keep them out of the way.

To think I could have lost this contract because of the way I worded a cover letter—for me, it was truly a lesson in humility.

20. END OF THE ROAD

When we started Health-Ware, there was a great deal of excitement, anxiety, and fear of the unknown; yet after the decision was made to make a go of it, we made some good decisions and had a great deal of luck fall in our favor. When I reflect on the relative success of our company, I take comfort in knowing we never lost sight of what was most important: making our clients our highest priority. Of course, not everyone was pleased with us, especially during the earlier years when we were suffering from growing pains. However, it is safe to say that the vast majority of our clients were pleased with our product as well as the quality of our service.

As I mentioned earlier, I loved my job and looked forward to going to work every day, even during the worst of times. Then why would I even consider giving it all up? Trust me when I say that selling Health-Ware was the last move I ever wanted to make. Had I recommended against the sale, I know the board would have supported me. So, why sell?

UNEXPECTED NEWS

In the same way I did my best to make this book more about our company than about our software, I've avoided talking about personal problems any of us may have endured during the life of our company. In order to explain how I could consider stopping our adventure, I am compelled to share a personal challenge that ultimately convinced me to throw in the towel.

I had just turned thirty-six when we incorporated Health-Ware Management Company (June '85), and I was in the best of health. I worked out on a daily basis with rigorous squash matches and was without any medical conditions; I did not even have a personal physician. It was two years later, in Klamath Falls, when I woke up with an unexplainable condition: I could draw a line right down the middle of my face, where the right side was tingly numb, and the left side felt normal, without numbness. The condition was not painful, nor did it impair me in any way, so I was more curious than alarmed. At the time I experienced the numbness, Jerry—my daily squash opponent—was, coincidentally, a neurologist. When we were getting ready in the locker room for our match, I asked him if he had any idea as to what could be the cause for the numbness. Jerry took a pen from his shirt pocket and gave me an exam right there on the spot. Afterward, he told me, "I wouldn't worry about it, Tim. It's a neurological aberration and it should be gone in two or three weeks."

Sure enough, two weeks later the numbness disappeared, so the next time we were at the gym I told Jerry I was back to normal and thanked him for curing me. We both laughed and went off to play our next match. The next few weeks were filled with the usual chaos as my traveling demands found me in California, Washington, and all over Oregon. At the end of the road trip, I was in a hotel and woke up to the numbness again, this time located in my groin area. Again, split in half, with one side numb and the other side normal. This time, although there still wasn't any pain associated with the numbness, it was definitely uncomfortable. I returned home that evening and saw Jerry again the next morning. This time I saw him at his office for an official visit.

At the end of the exam, he said, "Tim, I want you to go to Portland and get an MRI."

"No."

"What do you mean, no?"

"Jerry, I saw it in your eyes when you finished the exam, and I know you already have a diagnosis, so what do I have?"

"I cannot confirm it until you have an MRI."

"Since I am *not* going to Portland, what do you *think* I have, with*out* the MRI?" When he realized I was serious about not getting the MRI, he said, "I think you might have multiple sclerosis."

I thought for a few seconds. "Okay, if you are correct, how long do you think before I end up in a wheelchair?"

"If I am correct about the diagnosis, probably between ten and eleven years if it escalates enough. In the meantime, you need to avoid stress, and patients with MS don't do well with heat, so you should stay away from hot tubs and the like. Understand, Tim, it is only my initial diagnosis. You still need the MRI to confirm my findings. Why are you so set against the MRI?"

"Jerry, you know, many do not understand MS; as a result, many think MS is a death sentence. You and I know better, but until a cure for the disease is found, I don't think attitudes are going to change much. If getting an MRI would lead to better treatment, I would do it, but from all that I have read and from the two friends of mine that do have MS, such is not the case. As the president of a small company, I don't need my clients or even my employees to know about your findings. Until my symptoms worsen, I have a company to run, hopefully for at least for the next ten or eleven years."

Nine months after that appointment, we moved to the Portland area, and I never had a reason to see Jerry again.

Some might consider my attitude as irresponsible, that it could have been something much worse than MS. However, I did not have any more symptoms until fifteen months later, in October '88, when Jan and I were celebrating our wedding anniversary and were on a Caribbean cruise. While at dinner, I was rubbing my left eye. While looking at a packet of sweetener on the table, I commented, "Jan, look how that packet is faded."

"What are you talking about, Tim? It's not faded."

I uncovered my left eye and, sure enough, the writing on the packet was normal. I covered my left eye again and looked at the packet again and then I looked at Jan. *She* was fading, and I realized I was losing vision in my right eye. By the next morning, I was completely blind in that eye. To say the least, it was rather disturbing, especially since I was symptom-free for so many months.

When we returned home, I had to board another plane and head for Wichita, Kansas, the next day. I wore an eye patch, telling my audience I had been hit in the eye and had to wear the patch until the eye healed. I was able to function just fine and gave a presentation that resulted in a sale to the Wichita Clinic. Jan made an appointment for me to see an ophthalmologist when I returned, and the physician said I had optic neuritis, a condition associated only with MS. He told me the condition could last for another four to six weeks and then my eyesight should return; although, there were no guarantees it would come back 100 percent. He was correct; my vision did come back, and everything went back to normal, kind of. I had not played squash for about seven months, and when I finally got back into the court, my depth perception was so impaired that I was no longer the competitive player I had been just months earlier. In fact, I was not someone to contend with ever again. Two months after the vision came back in my right eye, I lost total vision in my *left* eye. Again, the loss of sight lasted for about two months and returned back to normal. One of the most bizarre conditions that affected my vision was when the sight in my right eye was normal while my left eye was at a forty-five-degree slant. I definitely had to wear a patch during that eight-week episode.

When it comes to diseases, I call MS the Heinz 57 Variety disease when referring to the vast array of symptoms. The interesting aspect of the disease is that during the beginning years, almost nobody other than me was aware of the fact I was having a problem. If I did not complain about my symptoms, people around me were none the wiser. Although I told Jan, Lentz, Pat, and the other members of our board of directors in late 1988 about my condition, I kept it quiet to others outside of our company. Other than that brief appointment I had with the ophthalmologist, I did not see a physician about MS until 1992. During the six years that followed, I was put on all sorts of drugs and even received chemotherapy treatments; I was responsible for copays that ranged between two hundred and three hundred dollars per month, for drugs that did not guarantee anything (a good thing, too, or lawsuits would have been plentiful). The crazy thing about the disease is the medical community knows what MS is doing; they just don't know how to stop it. Research physicians have claimed MS is a genetic condition, and now some are speculating it to be a virus. For the most part, MS does not affect all patients in the same way. Almost all MS patients have difficulty walking, and 30 percent of men end up in a wheelchair, according to my neurologist.

I did my best to treat MS as an inconvenience; it was the only attitude I could have and still enjoy my job as much as I did. Jerry was correct about the need to avoid heat, as I found just two years later. I was uncomfortable with temperatures above seventy-five degrees. As long as I was able to keep cool, no one was the wiser about my condition. Some may ask why I wanted to stay in the closet, so to speak, when it came to telling others I had MS. I did not want my medical condition to be the main topic for discussion when I had so many more important things going on with my life, especially when it came to my family and the company. My doctor and nurses suggested I meet with other MS patients in support groups, but I didn't have the time or the desire. Admittedly, there are victims of MS having a much tougher time of it than I who probably benefit from such activities; MS does screw up a person's life when the symptoms come on like gangbusters. As long as I kept myself busy and had much more important things to be concerned about, MS had to take a backseat.

By 1993, I began using a cane to assist with walking, while at the same time my travel demands increased at an unbelievably fast rate. It was an exciting time for our company; we were beginning to receive attention from the larger medical institutions, and levels of satisfaction by our current clients were at an all-time high. MS was an issue, but it didn't stop me from doing my job. I was having too good of a time for it to hold me back.

All of this activity associated with the growth of our company was taking its toll on my health. By late 1995, it was becoming quite painful for me to walk. I was having difficulty walking at home, especially since at the time, Jan and I lived in a two-story home with the master bedroom upstairs. Trying to ignore the symptoms of MS was no longer an easy task, and Jan kept asking me how much longer I thought I could keep up with the demands of the company. At the same time, my neurologist was encouraging me to stop working, suggesting the stress of the job was only exacerbating my symptoms.

In February 1996, I received a call from the chief operating officer at Global Software of Raleigh, North Carolina, who told me they were interested in our company. They were looking for a sound materials-management information system (MMIS) that operated on an IBM System AS/400. They heard about us from Scott Frazier, who was one of their mainframe clients in San Jose, California. I first met Scott when I presented to him five years earlier, when he was the materials manager at a hospital in Redding, California. I saw him again four years later when he joined us at our tenth anniversary celebration in Las Vegas. He asked for my business card and then gave it to the folks at Global when they mentioned they were in the hunt for a good MMIS.

In my heart, I did not want to entertain even the *idea* of selling Health-Ware. I was still having a great time with what we were doing, and with the university medical centers doing so well, our reputation was as solid as ever. However, I knew it was only a matter of a couple of years before I found myself in a wheelchair; traveling alone would be almost impossible. Our clients, our employees, and our investors were counting on me to ensure stability for the future. Because of my declining health, I was uncertain as to whether or not I could continue to meet those expectations. After six attempts by other companies to buy us out in eleven years, I was finally open to the idea of considering an offer. My biggest mistake with the entire process was not hiring a professional negotiator to assist me with the sale of the company. Nevertheless, my employees were taken care of, our clients were put in the hands of a reputable software company for support, and my investors were given a modest return on their investment.

I lasted two years with the transition of moving our software under the care of the new company. It was never the same for me, as I was no longer in control of outcomes. In 1998, almost eleven years after I was told it could happen, I found myself needing a wheelchair to get around, and I went into an early retirement. I could spend a great deal of time recapping the years since I left the business, but that would take away from the purpose of this book. I *will* say, for the first three years after I stopped working, I had a difficult time accepting the contrast from being a jet-setter to a permanent sitter.

DEALING WITH MS

The following describes how I have learned to deal with MS. If you are not interested, you may want to skip to the section entitled "Suggestions for Entrepreneurs."

Probably the best advice I can give for those caregivers and close family members of the MS victim is: *do not baby them.* If anything, see to it they are much busier than they want to be, that they have some sort of physical activity to occupy their time. You hear about senior citizens who go downhill when they are told they can no longer drive. Their independence and their inability to live life as they are accustomed is very depressing. Well, the same logic applies to many of those with MS, except it usually happens long before they become senior citizens. Help these victims remain as active as possible. Doing everything for them is *not* the answer. Take it from someone who has been there—it was more damaging to me both mentally and physically than I can adequately share with you.

I will skip twelve years of my life to the past three years, and tell you that I have received intense physical therapy from Karen Baltz-Gibbs, a doctor of physical therapy, who has changed my life. With her, everything is possible, even when she has been told it is impossible; for the first time in thirteen years, I am able to use a walker. I have a long way to go, and the idea of walking again seems an impossible goal to me, but if Karen has anything to do with it, I will walk again. In my opinion, physical therapists are the unsung heroes of medicine, as they often deal with patients who have been sent for physical therapy after the surgeons and medical doctors cannot do anything more for them. These patients have been given a raw deal in life and are having difficulty accepting the consequences of their condition. The physical and occupational therapists are given the unenviable task of having to deal with patients who are already feeling low and assist them with learning how to improve their situation and/or learn how to live with their condition for the remainder of their lives. To make it real, I find that if you ever feel like you have it rough, just take a look at the people around you. When I go to the gym at the physical-therapy department,

I work on being able to walk again on my own two legs, while I watch others next to me trying to walk on their artificial legs; what do *I* have to complain about? I will never forget when a fellow patient came to the clinic for his first appointment after he had his leg amputated just above the knee. He wouldn't say hi or crack a smile for three months. Nevertheless, after those three months, he was walking and saying hi to strangers. It never would have happened had it not been for the professional therapists that brought him to this point.

I became aware of the fact I had MS twenty-five years ago, and from the beginning, emphasis was on reducing stressful situations, doing my best to keep my body cool, and avoiding any kind of competition. In other words, changing my environment to the complete opposite from what I was accustomed. It is easy for me to second guess those who have given me advice and medical treatment over the years; however, I feel there must be a balance for the treatment of MS patients. Pulling the rug out from under their lives might cause more damage than having them live through the disease, instead of just living a subdued life during the remaining years of their lives. My point is, medicine has not cured anyone from MS, and there is still no magic solution for the future. Every time an advance for the treatment of MS (usually involving drugs) is announced, the projected efficacy is usually forecasted to apply to 25 percent of the patient population of MS victims. Maybe the 25 percent of patients reporting positive results from the new drug are just experiencing a psychological boost where they only *believe* they are doing better. I am not trying to put a damper on the hopes of my fellow victims of MS; rather, I caution them to not put too much hope into maybes. If I had a dollar for every poke by a syringe and/or IV over the years with MS drugs, I could buy a nice car—and if I did so, that would have been the benefit of the treatments. Until the medical community has found a way to treat MS with real results, doing something for oneself is probably the best treatment overall. I see my neurologist at the university MS clinic once a year; that fact by itself speaks volumes. I will wait for the cure, but I am not holding my breath. In other words, I will continue to shut up and color.

SUGGESTIONS FOR FUTURE ENTREPRENEURS

I'm not sure I am one to be making suggestions for those who want to take the entrepreneurial plunge, but when has that ever stopped me? If you find yourself considering the idea of starting a company, make sure you are doing it for the right reasons. Doing it just for making money may not be enough. I won't deny that in the beginning, the potential for making a good amount of money was part of our decision for starting the company. However, when I was able to see others reap benefits from what we had developed even before we ventured out on our own, I knew the future was going to be about more than just focusing on how much money we made. From our first sale, it was obvious we were growing a community of fellow materials managers who had something in common by virtue of them having our software; it was their acceptance and excitement that allowed us to look forward to going to work each day. We never knew what challenges were in store for us when we entered the office, but we had the satisfaction of knowing we were capable of dealing with them.

When one is passionate about a possible endeavor, there is a much better chance for success. When any of us from Health-Ware were working with our clients, nobody could accuse of us doing the job just to receive a paycheck, as we worked with little regard for the clock and always addressed issues on the spot. All of us were well aware of the fact that many of our clients were feeling overwhelmed with new procedures, and it was our job to make sure they were comfortable with all they were learning from us. I was proud of our employees (including those clients who worked part-time for us); they were well aware of how important it was that we ensured our new clients were adequately trained.

If you plan to start a venture that involves having employees, make sure you know how to manage people. They are your most valued commodity; never take them for granted, and make sure you treat them the same way you would want to be treated. I take comfort in the fact that I never wavered from the management principles defined in "Play by the Rules"; it proved to be a reliable foundation for the management challenges I encountered throughout the years.

If managing people is not your forte, don't make the mistake of trying to wing it. Get training, or hire someone else who *is* good with people and can manage them for you.

We could have made more money. Just ask the folks from Global Software (now Medi-Click); their biggest complaint was that we were not charging enough money for our products and services. They were correct. I was too involved with our clients and unable to objectively look at our pricing structure from our company's point of view. It was kind of like *not seeing the forest because of the trees.* Don't sell yourself short and don't be afraid to assess a fair price for all that you do.

Manage growth with caution. Small businesses seldom have the luxury of working with a huge pot of cash to cover their mistakes. Therefore the casualties usually relate to letting people go because of poor planning. When I fired someone, the blame belonged to the employee. Layoffs were *my* fault.

On a lighter note, the most sound piece of advice I can give to those flirting with the idea of being an entrepreneur is, make sure you have fun. Not every day will be a "whistle while you work" experience, but the majority of your time should make up for the lows you encounter. Otherwise, you will find yourself regretting the day you started your company in the first place. You will spend more waking hours on the job than you will at home. Life is too short, so don't squander it.

SO WHAT ABOUT THE FOG?

I do believe one does not need to know everything there is to know about running a business; sure, it doesn't hurt, but I don't believe even the most successful entrepreneurs knew everything they needed to know about running a company from the very beginning. Most ventures are on-the-job training experiences; it can even be invigorating when you learn as you go.

The overriding theme of this book has been that sound management is the key to making an entrepreneurial endeavor worthwhile. If one is struggling with managing people, I suggest adhering to the twenty-three concepts outlined in "Play by the Rules." This philosophy is the roadmap for attaining success. It doesn't happen overnight, but implementing them one day at a time can ultimately result in satisfaction by all. Remember that most employees willingly follow a competent manager. If you need to, it is never too late to change.

People have asked me if I had any regrets, and the answer is simple: "Absolutely not." All of us at Health-Ware can hold our heads high knowing that all of our activities were done so for the right reasons. If I had the opportunity, I would do it all over again, wheelchair and all. Perhaps the epigraph at the beginning of this book best describes my feelings: "If it hadn't been for the fog, we might not have taken the risk ... and we would have missed the experience of a lifetime." If you have a good idea and you are a competent individual (you know whether or not you are), take the plunge and never look back.

DIFFICULT TO BELIEVE IT'S ALL DONE

No, I'm not talking about the company. I'm referring to this book. This experience has been rather cathartic for me, and I am certain you can agree I enjoyed the entrepreneurial adventure I just wrote about. This, too, has been a great adventure.

Now, if you haven't already done so, go experience your own adventure, and remember: never look back, and by all means, have *fun*.

ACRONYMS

ADS	American Data Services, Chicago, Illinois
American or AHS	American Hospital Supply, Chicago, Illinois
CLASS	Computerized Logistics and Supplies System
CS/SPD	Central sterile supply/supply processing and distribution
EOQ	Economic order quantity
ESI	Enterprise Systems, Inc., Chicago, Illinois
Health-Ware	Health-Ware Management Company
HCMMS	Healthcare Materials Management Society
IS	Information systems
IT	Information technology
MM	Materials management (or manager)
MMIS	Materials-management information system